TALES FROM THE QUEEN
OF THE DESERT

TALES FROM THE QUEEN OF THE DESERT

GERTRUDE BELL

Published by Hesperus Press Limited
28 Mortimer Street, London W1W 7RD
www.hesperuspress.com

Persian Pictures first published in the UK in 1894
Syria: The Desert and the Sown first published in the UK in 1907
This selection first published by Hesperus Press Limited, 2015

Typeset by Roland Codd

ISBN: 978-1-84391-547-8

PERSIAN PICTURES

1

The modern capital of Persia lies in a plain ringed halfway round by mountains, which on the northern side touch with frozen summits the regions of eternal snow, and on the east sink into low ranges of hills, stretching their naked arms into the desert. It is the chief city of a land of dust and stones – waste and desolate, Persia unfolds her monotonous length, broken only by ridges of hills even more barren than the plain itself, southward from the gates of Tehran. There is a certain fine simplicity in a landscape from which the element of water, with all the varied life it brings in its murmuring train, is entirely absent. The empty world looks like a great room cleared for the reception of some splendid company; presently it will be filled by a vast pageant of men or angels: their lance-heads will flash back the dazzling rays of the sun, their banners will float out many-coloured against the sombre background, the peal of their trumpets will re-echo from mountain to mountain. But no! day after day rises upon the same silence, the same solitude, and at length the watcher turns away impatiently, with the conviction that he has been gazing with futile expectation upon the changeless features of the dead. The pageant has long since swept over the land – swept onward. Mother of human energies, strewn with the ruins of a Titanic past, Persia has slipped out of the vivid world, and the simplicity of her landscape is the fine simplicity of death. 'Alas, poor Yorick!' says Hamlet, yielding, in an exceptionally unpremeditated moment, the natural tribute of pity from the living to the dead. Persia in such an aspect may be pitiful enough, but it is not admirable.

To the north of Tehran, however, the lower slopes of the Shimran range are clothed with gardens and cornfields, as though the dense vegetation which, by a strange freak of nature, stretches its belt of green along the southern shore of the Caspian, between the shifting sands of the Oxus and the black, naphtha-saturated earth of Baku, had sent its roots through the very heart of the mountains and found a foothold for its irrepressible luxuriance even among dust and stones. The capital itself, as you approach it from the west, presents the appearance of a wood rather than of a city – nor minaret, nor tower, nor dome forms a landmark above it, the trees of its gardens conceal its stunted buildings, and it is not until the traveller finds himself under its very walls that he can say, 'Here is Tehran!' It owes its life to the snow mountains, from whence its water flows; the ground between them and the town is undermined by a network of passages, vaulted over with stone, and ventilated by air-holes at intervals of about fifty yards, each hole being protected by a mound of earth. Within, these arteries of the city are the width of a man's shoulders, and scarcely high enough to allow him to walk upright; he stumbles, knee-deep in water, along the uneven bed, bending himself double where the vault drops lower, squeezing past narrow corners cut out of the solid rock. On either side black apertures open into more passages, bringing in tributary streams from right and leftward, and at intervals the darkness is broken by the ray of sunlight which strikes through one of the air-holes, burying itself, like an ill-directed spear, deep into the earth. No other form of irrigation remains, no storage of water, in a country where these arts were probably familiar to the far larger population which dwelt in former ages at the foot of the mountains. The present system is clumsy and laborious. Constant watchfulness is needed to keep the Kanats from falling into disrepair and from becoming blocked by masses of roots, and if this were to be relaxed, Tehran would in a few years cease to exist.

To what merit it owes its position of capital remains a mystery. It is the seat of no native industry; arid deserts and narrow mountain-passes, traversed only by caravans of mules, cut it off from all convenient intercourse with the west. Isfahan is invested with the traditions of a former importance; about Shiraz linger the vestiges of a still mightier antiquity; Casvin lies a hundred miles nearer to the Ospian; Tehran is only a modern seat of government called to importance by the arbitrary will of the present race of sovereigns.

Many gates lead into the city, breaking the level of the mud walls, with their arches and turrets, which are decorated with tiles of faience set into patterns and pictures and inscriptions. The space enclosed by the walls is a large one, but it is not by any means filled with houses. Passing through one of the western gateways, you will find yourself at first in desolate tracts of sand, stretching between unfinished or ruined buildings; occasionally the open doorway in a long mud wall will reveal to you a luxuriant garden full of tanks and fountains and flowerbeds, under whose plane trees stands the house of some rich man who can afford himself a weekly sufficiency of water to turn the wilderness into fertile pleasure-grounds; further on you will come upon wide streets, very empty and silent, fringed by low, mud-built houses; gradually the streets narrow, the sloping counters of shops present their wares to the passers-by: fruit and vegetables, and the broad thin flaps of Persian bread; here and there a European shop-window, behind which the goods are more miscellaneous than tempting; here and there the frontage of some government building, with a doorway gaily patterned in coloured bricks. As the streets grow narrower, they become more crowded. A kaleidoscopic world of unfamiliar figures passes to and fro beneath the white mulberry trees which spring out between the cobblestones of the pavement: grave elders holding their cloaks discreetly round them, dervishes with a loincloth about their waists and a brilliant scarf bound over their ragged locks, women enveloped from head to foot in loose black garments, a linen veil hanging over their faces and making them look like the members of some strange religious order, negro slaves and white-robed Arabs, beggars and loiterers, and troops of children pressing in and out between the horsemen and the carriages. Sometimes a beggar will accost you – a woman, perhaps, drawing aside a corner of her veil and imploring alms in a sweet high voice. If you turn a deaf ear to her prayers she will invoke curses on your head, but a copper coin will purchase you every blessing known to man, including the disappearance of the lady in question, who would otherwise have followed you with unblushing persistence, shouting, 'Pul! pul! pul!' – Money! money! money! – in your ear.

At a street corner a group of soldiers are shaking the branches of a mulberry tree, and eagerly devouring the sickly fruit which falls into the dust at their feet. Judging from the appearance of the Persian army, a foreigner would be tempted to conclude that it subsisted entirely upon white mulberries, and was reduced to a state of starvation when the summer was over. The hands of paymasters are adhesive in the East; but a small proportion of his earnings reaches the common soldier, and mulberries, flavoured with dust, have at least the merit of furnishing him with an inexpensive meal. His outward man is not calculated to inspire much alarm in the breast of his enemies. His gait is slouching, his uniform torn and discoloured; not infrequently he wears his shirt outside his trousers, and the ragged flounce of brownish-grey linen hanging below his tunic lends him an air anything but martial. His temperament seems to be childlike and peaceable in the extreme. He amuses himself while he is on guard with foolish games, constructing, for instance, a water-mill of tiny wheels, which the stream in front of the palace will set a-turning, and whose movement will delight his eyes as he passes up and down. It is even related (and the tale is scarcely past credence) that on a certain occasion when a person of importance was visiting a southern fortress, he found one of the men who guarded the gateway engaged in knitting stockings, and the other turning an honest penny by the sale of apples. Nevertheless, the Shah is proud of his army. He spends happy hours devising new uniforms for his men – uniforms which are the strangest jumble of European reminiscences and an Oriental love of bright colour.

Bearing towards the north-eastern quarter of the city, you will enter a broad square which is looked upon as the *ne plus ultra* of municipal magnificence. It is here that the Shah causes his part in the annual Feast of Sacrifice to be performed, and here the inhabitants of Tehran assemble in great numbers to witness the slaughter of a camel by the mollahs in token that his Majesty has not forgotten, amid the cares of State, how Abraham bound Ishmael upon the altar (for the Mohammedans assert that it was the son of Hagar who was the hero of the legend) in obedience to the command of God.

Immediately after the camel has fallen he is cut up by the knives of the mollahs, and the nearest bystanders, pouncing upon some portion of the victim, make off with it at full speed to the palace, where the first comer receives a large reward.

It must be confessed that in spite of its size, the square makes no favourable impression upon the mind of the sophisticated European. The gates leading into it are adorned with ugly modern tiles, the buildings round it lack all trace of architectural merit. Their stucco face is questionably embellished by a fresco of lions, exceedingly ill drawn, each animal looking nervously round at the sun disc with its spiked circle of rays, which rises from behind its shoulders. Nor does it contain any press of human activity to atone for its lack of beauty. About the gate which leads into the Ark, where the palace is situated, there are indeed some signs of life – groups of soldiers are diversified by the figures of servants of the palace, clad in brilliant scarlet uniforms, and mounted on horses wearing bits and collars of solid silver, and by the fantastic liveries of the Shah's runners, whose dress closely resembles that which is depicted on a court-card, and whose headgear partakes equally of the nature of a beadle's and of a jester's; but for the rest this square is comparatively empty, and the wind sweeps the dust-clouds round the park of antiquated cannon which stands in its midst.

More narrow, squalid streets bring you to the bazaar, where, though little really beautiful or precious is to be found, the thronging Oriental life is in itself an endless source of delight. Ride through it on a summer morning, when its vaulted coolness will offer you a grateful shelter from the sun, and before its activity has been hushed by the heat of midday. In the shadow of the entrance there stands a small merchant, posted on the doorstep like an emblem of Oriental commerce – a solemn, long-robed child, so little that his mother's heart must have ached when she trusted the dear turbaned head out of her sight.

This morsel of humanity has brought some bunches of flowers to sell, and has spread them out on a large stone in front of him. In his improvised shop he stands, motionless and imperturbable, watching the comers and goers, and waiting in dignified patience till one of them shall pause and buy. Wish him good luck under your breath (for he would resent the blessings of unbelievers), and pass on beneath the dark arches of the bazaar.

Here, at any rate, is bustle enough; trains of laden mules and donkeys shoulder your horse into the gutter, paying small heed to your cries of 'Avardah!' – Make room! – skilful housewives block the narrow way, driving hard bargains under the protection of their veils; groups of hungry men cluster round the roasters of kabobs anxiously awaiting a breakfast. The shopkeepers alone are unmoved by the universal haste, but sit cross-legged among their wares, smoking the morning kalyan. On either side of the street arched doorways lead into caravanseries and high market-places. In one of them the sellers of cotton goods have established themselves, their counters laden with piles of cheap printed stuffs, bearing the Manchester stamp in one corner; next door is the booksellers' court, and a certain air of scholastic leisure pervades it; here are a row of fruit-shops, where the blue earthenware bowls of curds stand among heaped-up grapes and melons; there you may buy narrow-necked bottles of rose water; further on you find yourself in a street of metal-workers, where the bright mule-bells hang in festoons over the counters; round the next corner the fires of smithies gleam on half-naked figures, labouring with strained muscles at their anvils. The whole bazaar resounds with talk, with the cries of the mule-drivers, the tinkling bells of the caravans, and the blows of the smiths' hammers. The air is permeated with the curious smell, half musty, half aromatic, of fruits and frying meats, merchandise and crowded humanity.

The light comes from the top through a round hole in each of the countless tiny domes of the roof; through each hole falls a shaft of brilliant sunshine, cutting the surrounding darkness like a sword, and striking the hurrying multitude in successive flashes, white turban and bright-coloured robe gleaming – fading, gleaming – fading, in an endless sequence of sun and shadow, as their wearers pass to and fro.

So you may ride through street after narrow crooked street till your ears are full of sound, and your eyes of colour, and your mind of restless life, and before you have had time to recover your composure, you will find yourself in the sunny square, filled with stacks of hay and tenanted by disbanded armies of mules, which lies within the Meshed Gate. Here, too, the town is afoot. Like a swarm of bees the people jostle one another through the archway. Peasants are driving in their donkeys laden with roped bundles of grass from the meadows of Shah Abdul Azim, strings of camels file through the gate, bringing in the produce of the great cities of the south and east, busy officials are hurrying Tehranwards in the early morning about their affairs, sellers of salted nuts have established themselves under the trees, beggars are lying by the roadside, pilgrims returning from Meshed hasten their step as the homeward goal comes into sight.

With the impression of the deserted western roads still fresh in your memory, the appearance of the bazaars and of this eastern gate will fill you with surprise. Tehran, which from the west looked almost like a city of the dead, cut from all intercourse with the outer world, is alive after all and in eager relationship with a world of its own. Here in the dust and the sunshine is an epitome of the living East, and, standing unnoticed in such a doorway, you will admit that you have not travelled in vain. But as the wonderful procession of people files past you, too intent upon their own affairs to give you more than a contemptuous glance, you will realise what a gulf lies between you. The East looks to itself; it knows nothing of the greater world of which you are a citizen, asks nothing of you and of your civilisation.

2

Hundreds of years ago, when the Persian race first issued from unknown Bactria and the grim Hyrcanian forests, passing through the Caspian Gates, they came upon a fertile land lying to the north-east of the country, which was subsequently named Media. There on the edge of the province known today as Khorasan they founded a city, which with the rolling centuries gathered greatness and riches and power; the Greeks (for her fame had penetrated to the limits of the civilised world) called her Rages. Key to Hyrcania and Parthia, the geographical position of the Median city lent her considerable importance. The Jews knew her well: in Rages dwelt that Gabelus to whom the pious Tobit entrusted his ten talents of silver in the days of the Captivity; there Tobias was journeying when the angel Raphael met him and instructed him in the healing properties of fishes; there, relates the author of the Book of Judith, reigned Phraortes whom Nebuchadnezzar smote through with his darts and utterly destroyed.

Rages, the Ancient of Days, passed through many vicissitudes of fortune in the course of her long-drawn life. Under her walls fled the last Darius when Alexander's army chased him, vanquished at Arbela, over the wide plains of Khorasan – fled to the mountains of the Caspian to seek a luckless fate at the hands of the cruel Bactrian satrap. At Rages, perhaps, the generous

Alexander mourned the untimely death of his rival, from her palaces hurled his vengeance against Bessus, and saw the satrap dragged a captive to execution. Twice the city was destroyed, by earthquake and by Parthian invaders, twice to rise up afresh under new names. At length, in the twelfth century, an enemy more devastating than the Parthian hordes, more vindictive than the earthquake, swept over pleasant Khorasan and turned the fertile province into the Wilderness it is to this day. Tartars from the uttermost ends of the earth left no stone of Rages standing, and the great Median city vanished from the history of men. A few miles to the north-east Tehran has sprung up to be the capital of modern Persia – a Persia to whom the glorious traditions of the past are as forgotten as the strength of Phraortes' walls. 'The Lion and the Lizard keep the courts where Jemshyd gloried and drank deep,' but the foundations of Rages, the mother of Persian cities, can be traced only by conjecture.

Through waste and solitary places we rode one morning to the city and the citadel of the dead. It was still so early that the sun had not overtopped the range of eastern mountains. We rode out of sleeping Tehran, and took our way along the deserted track that skirts its walls; to our left lay the wilderness, wrapped in transparent shadow, and sloping gradually upwards to the barren foothills over which winds the road to Meshed. Before we had gone far, with a flash and a sudden glitter, the sun leapt up above the snow-peaks, and day rushed across the plain – day, crude and garish, revealing not the bounteous plenty of the cornfields and pastures which encircled Rages, but dust and stones and desert scrub, and the naked, forbidding mountains, wrinkled by many winters.

To us, with the headlong flight of Darius and the triumph of the conqueror surging before our eyes, the broken ground

round the site of the ancient stronghold piled itself into ruined turret and rampart, sank into half-obliterated fosse and ditch. Where we imagined the walls to have been, we discovered a solid piece of masonry, and our minds reeled at the thought that it was wildly possible Alexander's eyes might have rested on this even brickwork. Time has made gates in the battlements, but the desert has not even yet established unquestioned rule within them. At the foot of the wall we came upon a living pool lying under the shadow of a plane tree. Round such a pool the sick men of Bethsaida gathered and waited for the stirring of the waters, but in Rages all was solitude, 'and the desired angel came no more'.

Towards the east two parallel lines of hills rear themselves out of the desert, dividing it from the wider stretch of desert that reaches southward to Isfahan. Between the hills lies a stony valley, up which we turned our steps, and which led us to the heart of desolation and the end of all things. Halfway up the hillside stands a tower, whose whitewashed wall is a landmark to all the country round. Even from the far distant peaks of the opposite mountains the Tower of Silence is visible, a mocking gleam reminding the living of the vanity of their eager days. For the tower is the first stage in the weary journey of the dead; here they come to throw off the mantle of the flesh before their bones may rest in the earth without fear of defiling the holy element, before their souls, passing through the seven gates of the planets, may reach the sacred fire of the sun.

The tower is roofless; within, ten or twelve feet below the upper surface of its wall, is a chalky platform on which the dead bodies lie till sun and vultures have devoured them. This grim turret-room was untenanted. Zoroaster's religion has faded from that Media where once it reigned, and few and humble now are the worshippers who raise prayers to Ormuzd under the open heaven, and whose bodies are borne up the stony valley and cast into the Tower of Silence.

We dismounted from our horses and sat down on the hillside. The plain stretched below us like a monotonous ocean which had billowed up against the mountain flanks and had been fixed there for ever; we could see the feet of the mountains themselves planted firmly in the waves of dust, and their glistening peaks towering into the cloudless sky; the very bones of the naked earth were exposed before us, and the fashion of its making was revealed.

With the silence of an extinct world still heavy upon us, we made our way to the upper end of the valley, but at the gates of the plain Life came surging to meet us. A wild hollyhock stood sentinel among the stones; it had spread some of its yellow petals for banner and on its uplifted spears the buds were fat and creamy with coming bloom. Rain had fallen in the night, and had called the wilderness itself to life, clothing its thorns with a purple garment of tiny flowers; the delicious sun struck upon our shoulders; a joyful little wind blew the damp, sweet smell of the reviving earth in gusts towards us; our horses sniffed the air and, catching the infection of the moment, tugged at the bit and set off at racing speed across the rain-softened ground. And we, too, passed out of the silence and remembered that we lived. Life seized us and inspired us with a mad sense of revelry. The humming wind and the teeming earth shouted 'Life! Life!' as we rode. Life! life! the bountiful, the magnificent! Age was far from us – death far; we had left him enthroned in his barren mountains, with ghostly cities and outworn faiths to bear him company. For us the wide plain and the limitless world, for us the beauty and the freshness of the morning, for us youth and the joy of living!

3

There is a couplet in an Elizabethan book of airs which might serve as a motto for Eastern life:

'Thy love is not thy love,' says the author of the songs in the 'Muses' Garden of Delights' (and the pretty stilted title suits the somewhat antiquated ring of the lines):

> *Thy love is not thy love if not thine own,*
> *And so it is not, if it once be known.*

If it once be known! Ah yes! the whole charm of possession vanishes before the gaze of curious eyes, and for them, too, charm is driven away by familiarity. It takes the mystery of a Sphinx to keep the world gazing for thirty centuries. The East is full of secrets – no one understands their value better than the Oriental; and because she is full of secrets she is full of entrancing surprises. Many fine things there are upon the surface: brilliance of colour, splendour of light, solemn loneliness, clamorous activity; these are only the patterns upon the curtain which floats for ever before the recesses of Eastern life: its essential charm is of more subtle quality. As it listeth, it comes and goes; it flashes upon you through the open doorway of some blank, windowless house you pass in the street, from under the lifted veil of the beggar woman who lays her hand on your bridle, from the dark, contemptuous eyes of a child; then the East sweeps aside her curtains, flashes a facet of her jewels into your dazzled eyes, and disappears again with a mocking little laugh at your bewilderment; then for a moment it seems to you that you are looking her in the face, but while you are wondering whether she be angel or devil, she is gone.

She will not stay – she prefers the unexpected; she will keep her secrets and her tantalizing charm with them, and when you think you have caught at last some of her illusive grace, she will send you back to shrouded figures and blank house-fronts.

You must be content to wait, and perhaps some day, when you find her walking in her gardens in the cool of the evening, she will take a whim to stop and speak to you and you will go away fascinated by her courteous words and her exquisite hospitality.

For it is in her gardens that she is most herself – they share her charm, they are as unexpected as she. Conceive on every side such a landscape as the dead world will exhibit when it whirls naked and deserted through the starry interspace – a grey and featureless plain, over which the dust-clouds rise and fall, build themselves into mighty columns, and sink back again among the stones at the bidding of hot and fitful winds; prickly low-growing plants for all vegetation, leafless, with a foliage of thorns; white patches of salt, on which the sunlight glitters; a fringe of barren mountains on the horizon… Yet in this desolation lurks the mocking beauty of the East. A little water and the desert breaks into flower, bowers of cool shade spring up in the midst of dust and glare, radiant stretches of soft colour gleam in that grey expanse. Your heart leaps as you pass through the gateway in the mud wall; so sharp is the contrast, that you may stand with one foot in an arid wilderness and the other in a shadowy, flowery paradise. Under the broad thick leaves of the plane trees tiny streams murmur, fountains splash with a sweet fresh sound, white-rose bushes drop their fragrant petals into tanks, lying deep and still like patches of concentrated shadow. The indescribable charm of a Persian garden is keenly present to the Persians themselves – the 'strip of herbage strown, which just divides the desert from the sown', an endlessly beautiful parable. Their poets sing the praise of gardens in exquisite verses, and call their books by their names. I fear the Muses have wandered more often in Sa'di's Garden of Roses than in the somewhat pretentious pleasure-ground which our Elizabethan writer prepared for them.

The desert about Tehran is renowned for the beauty of its gardens. The Shah possesses several, others belong to his sons, others to powerful ministers and wealthy merchants. Sometimes across the gateways a chain is drawn, denoting that the garden is Bast – sanctuary – and into these the European may not go; but places of refuge for the hunted criminal are, fortunately, few, and generally the garden is open to all comers. Perhaps the most beautiful of all is one which belongs to the Shah, and which lies under a rocky hillock crowned with the walls and towers of a palace. We found ourselves at its gate one evening, after an aimless canter across the desert, and determined to enter. The loiterers in the gateway let us pass through unchallenged. We crossed the little entrance-court and came into a long dark avenue, fountains down the middle of it, and flowerbeds, in which the plants were pale and meagre for want of light; roses, the pink flowers which scent the rose water, and briars, a froth of white and yellow bloom, growing along its edges in spite of the deep shade of the plane trees. Every tiny rill of water was fringed with violet leaves – you can imagine how in the spring the scent of the violets greets you out in the desert when you are still far away, like a hospitable friend coming open-armed down his steps to welcome you. We wandered along intersecting avenues, until we came to one broader than the rest, at the end of which stood a little house. Tiny streams flowed round and about it, flowed under its walls, and into its rooms; fountains splashed ceaselessly in front of it, a soft light wind swayed the heavy folds of the patterned curtains hanging halfway down across its deep balconies. The little dwelling looked like a fairy palace, jewelled with coloured tiles, unreal and fantastic, built half out of the ripple of water, and half out of the shadowy floating of its great curtains. Two or three steps and a narrow passage, and we were in the central room – such a room to lie and dream in through the hot summer days! – tiled with blue, in the middle an overflowing fountain, windows on either side opening down to the ground, the vaulted ceiling and the alcoved walls set with a mosaic of looking-glass, in whose diamonds and crescents the blue of the tiles and the spray of the tossing waters were reflected.

As we sat on the deep step of the windowsill, a door opened softly, and a long-robed Persian entered. He carried in his hand a twanging stringed instrument, with which he established himself at the further side of the fountain, and began to play weird, tuneless melodies on its feeble strings – an endless, wailing minor. Evening fell, and the dusk gathered in the glittering room, the fountain bubbled lower and sank into silence, the wind blew the sweet smell of roses into us where we sat – and still the Persian played, while in the garden the nightingales called to one another with soft thrilling notes.

A week or two later we came back to Doshan Tepe. This time we found it peopled by a party of Persians. They were sitting round the edge of one of the tanks at the end of the avenue, men and little children, and in their green and yellow robes, they looked to us as we entered like a patch of brilliant water-plants, whose vivid colours were not to be dimmed by the shade of the plane leaves. But the musician did not reappear; he was too wise a magician to weave his spells 'save to the span of heaven and few ears'.

There was a deserted garden at the foot of the mountains which had a curious history. It belonged to the Zil es Sultan, the Shah's eldest son, who had inherited it from his mother, that Schöne Müllerin whose beauty captivated the King of Kings in the days of his youth. The Zil (his title, being interpreted, signifies 'The shadow of the King') has fallen into disgrace. The Shah casts his shadow far, and in order that it may never grow less, the Zil is not allowed to move from Isfahan; his Shimran garden therefore is empty, and his house is falling into disrepair. It stands on the edge of a rushing mountain torrent, which, we will hope, turned the mill-wheels in old days (though some men assert that the girl was not a miller's daughter, after all), and it boasts some magnificent plane trees, under which we picnicked one evening, hanging Persian lanterns from the boughs. The night had brought tall yellow evening primroses into flower, and their delicious smell mingled with that of the jessamine, which covered the decaying walls. The light of our lanterns shone on the smooth tree trunks, between the leaves glimmered a waning moon, and behind us the mountainsides lay in sheets of light. We did not envy the Zil his palaces in Isfahan.

Once in another garden we found the owner at home. It was early in the morning; he was standing on his doorstep, judging between the differences of two people of his village, a man and a veiled woman, who had come to seek his arbitration. They were both talking loudly, she with shrill exclamations and calls upon God to witness, in her eagerness forgetting the laws of modesty, and throwing aside her thick linen veil, that she might plead with eyes and expression, as well as voice – or perhaps it was policy, for she had a beautiful face, dark-eyed and pale, round which the folds of black cloak and white linen fell like the drapery round the head of a Madonna. When our unknown host saw us, he dismissed his clamorous petitioners, and greeted us with the courtesy which is the heirloom of the Persian race. Seats were brought for us, tea and coffee served to us, a blue cotton-clothed multitude of gardeners offered us baskets of unripe plums, dishes of lettuce, and bunches of stiffly-arranged flowers. We sat and conversed, with no undue animation, here and there an occasional remark, but the intervals were rendered sociable by the bubbling of kalyans. At length we rose to go, and as we walked down the garden-paths many compliments passed between us and our host. At the gate he assured us that our slave had been honoured by our acceptance of his hospitality, and with low bows we mounted our horses and rode away.

We had not in reality trenched upon his privacy. There was, indeed, a part of his domains where even his hospitality would not have bidden us enter. Behind the house in which we were received lay the women's dwelling, a long, low, verandaed building standing round a deep tank, on whose edge solemn children carry on their dignified games, and veiled women flit backwards and forwards. Shaded by trees, somewhat desolate and uncared-for in appearance, washed up at the further end of the garden beyond the reach of flowers, the sight of the andarun and of its inhabitants knocks at the heart with a weary sense of discontent, of purposeless, vapid lives – a wailing, endless minor.

So in the wilderness, between high walls, the secret, mysterious life of the East flows on – a life into which no European can penetrate, whose standards, whose canons, are so different from his own that the whole existence they rule seems to him misty and unreal, incomprehensible, at any rate unfathomable; a life so monotonous, so unvaried from age to age that it does not present any feature marked enough to create an impression other than that of vague picturesqueness, of dullness inexpressible, of repose which has turned to lethargy, and tranquillity carried beyond the point of virtue.

And these gardens, also with their tall trees and peaceful tanks, are subject to the unexpected vicissitudes of Eastern fortune. The minister falls into disgrace, the rich merchant is ruined by the exactions of his sovereign; the stream is turned off, the water ceases to flow into the tanks and to leap in the fountains, the trees die, the flowers wither, the walls crumble into unheeded decay, and in a few years the tiny paradise has been swept forgotten from the face of the earth, and the conquering desert spreads its dust and ashes once more over it all.

4

Towards the middle of July the month of Muharram began – the month of mourning for the Imam Hussein. Such heat must have weighed upon the Plain of Kerbela when the grandson of the Prophet, with his sixty or seventy followers, dug the trenches of their camp not far from the Euphrates stream. The armies of Yezid enclosed them, cutting them off from the river and from all retreat; hope of succour there was none; on all sides nothing but the pitiless vengeance of the Khalif – the light of the watch-fires flickered upon the tents of his armies, and day revealed only the barren plain of Kerbela behind them – the Plain of Sorrow and Vexation.

In memory of the sufferings and death of that forlorn band and of their sainted leader, all Persia broke into lamentation. He, the holy one, hungered and thirsted; the intercessor with God could gain no mercy from men; he saw his children fall under the spears of his enemies, and when he died his body was trampled into the dust, and his head borne in triumph to the Khalif. The pitiful story has taken hold of the imagination of half the Mohammedan world. Many centuries, bringing with them their own dole of tragedy and sorrow, have not dimmed it, nor lessened the feeling which its recital creates, partly, no doubt, because of the fresh breeze of religious controversy which has swept the dust of time perpetually from off it, but partly, too, because of its own poignant simplicity. The splendid courage which shines through it justifies its long existence. Even Hussein's enemies were moved to pity by his patient endurance, by the devotion of his followers, and by the passionate affection of the women who were with him. The recorded episodes of that terrible tenth of Muharram are full of the pure human pathos which moves and which touches generation after generation. It is not necessary to share the religious convictions of the Shiahs to take a side in the hopeless battle under the burning sun, or realise that tragic picture of the Imam sitting before his tent-door with the dead child in his arms, or lifting the tiny measure of water to lips pierced through by an arrow-shot – a draught almost as bitter as the sponge of vinegar and hyssop. 'Men travel by night,' says Hussein in the miracle play, 'and their destinies travel towards them.' It was a destiny of immortal memory that he was journeying to meet on that march by night through the wilderness, side by side with El Hurr and the Khalif's army.

Shortly after we landed in Persia we came unexpectedly upon the story of the martyrdom. In the main street of Kasvin, up which we were strolling while our horses were being changed (for we were on our way to Tehran), we found a crowd assembled under the plane trees. We craned over the shoulders of Persian peasants, and saw in the centre of the circle a group of players, some in armour, some robed in long black garments, who were acting a passion play, of which Hussein was the hero. One was mounted on a horse which, at his entries and exits, he was obliged to force through the lines of people which were the only wings of his theatre; but except for the occasional scuffle he caused among the audience, there was little action in the piece – or, at least, in the part of it which we witnessed – for the players confined themselves to passing silently in and out, pausing for a moment in the empty space which represented the stage, while a mollah, mounted in a sort of pulpit, read aloud the incidents they were supposed to be enacting.

But with the beginning of Muharram the latent religious excitement of the East broke loose. Every evening at dusk the wailing cries of the mourners filled the stillness, rising and falling with melancholy persistence all through the night, until dawn sent sorrow-stricken believers to bed, and caused sleepless unbelievers to turn with a sigh of relief upon their pillows. At last the tenth day of Muharram came – a day of deep significance to all Mohammedans, since it witnessed the creation of Adam and Eve, of heaven and hell, of life and death; but to the Shiahs of tenfold deeper moment, for on it Hussein's martyrdom was accomplished.

Early in the afternoon sounds of mourning rose from the village. The inhabitants formed themselves into procession, and passed up the shady outlying avenues, and along the strip of desert which led back into the principal street – a wild and savage band whose grief was a strange tribute to the chivalrous hero whose bones have been resting for twelve centuries in the Plain of Kerbela. But tribute of a kind it was. Many brave men have probably suffered greater tortures than Hussein's, and borne them with as admirable a fortitude; but he stands among the few to whom that earthly immortality has been awarded which is acknowledged to be the best gift the capricious world holds in her hands. If he shared in the passionate desire to be remembered which assails every man on the threshold of forgetfulness, it was not in vain that he died pierced with a hundred spears; and though his funeral obsequies were brief twelve hundred years ago, the sound of them has echoed down the centuries with eternal reverberation until today.

First in the procession came a troop of little boys, naked to the waist, leaping round a green- robed mollah, who was reciting the woes of the Imam as he moved forward in the midst of his disordered crew. The boys jumped and leapt round him, beating their breasts – there was no trace of sorrow on their faces. They might have been performing some savage dance as they came onwards, a compact mass of bobbing heads and naked shoulders – a dance in which they themselves took no kind of interest, but in which they recognised that it was the duty of a Persian boy to take his part. They were followed by men bearing the standards of the village – long poles surmounted by trophies of beads and coloured silks, streamers and curious ornaments; and in the rear came another reciter and another body of men, beating their breasts, from which the garments were torn back, striking their foreheads and repeating the name of the Imam in a monotonous chorus, interspersed with cries and groans.

But it was in the evening that the real ceremony took place. The bazaar in the centre of the village was roofed over with canvas and draped with cheap carpets and gaudy cotton hangings; a low platform was erected at one end, and the little shops were converted into what looked very like the boxes of a theatre. They were hung with bright-coloured stuffs and furnished with chairs, on which the notabilities sat and witnessed the performance, drinking sherbet and smoking kalyans the while. We arrived at about nine o'clock and found the proceedings in full swing. The tent was crowded with peasants, some standing, some sitting on the raised edge of a fountain in the centre. Round this fountain grew a mass of oleander trees, their delicate leaves and exquisite pink flowers standing out against the coarse blue cotton of the men's clothing, and clustering round the wrinkled toil-worn peasant faces. On the platform was a mollah, long-robed and white-turbaned, who was reading exhortations and descriptions of the martyrdom with a drawling, chanting intonation. At his feet the ground was covered with women, their black cloaks tucked neatly round them, sitting with shrouded heads and with the long strip of white linen veil hanging over their faces and down into their laps. They looked for all the world like shapeless black and white parcels set in rows across the floor. The mollah read on, detailing the sufferings of the Imam: 'He thirsted, he was an hungered!' The women rocked themselves to and fro in an agony of grief, the men beat their bare breasts, tears streamed over their cheeks, and from time to time they took up the mollah's words in weary, mournful chorus, or broke into his story with a murmured wail which gathered strength and volume until it had reached the furthest corners of the tent: 'Hussein! Hussein! Hussein!'

It was intensely hot. Cheap European lamps flared and smoked against the canvas walls, casting an uncertain light upon the pink oleander flowers, the black-robed women, and the upturned faces of the men, streaming with sweat and tears, and all stricken and furrowed with cruel poverty and hunger – their sufferings would have made a longer catalogue than those of the Imam. The mollah tore his turban from his head and cast it upon the ground, and still he chanted on, and the people took up the throbbing cry: 'Hussein! Hussein! Hussein!'

Presently a dervish shouldered his way through the throng. A scanty garment was knotted round his loins, his ragged hair hung over his shoulders, and about his head was bound a brilliant scarf, whose stripes of scarlet and yellow fell down his naked back. He had come from far; he held a long staff in his hands, and the dust of the wilderness was on the shoes which he laid by the edge of the platform. He stood there, reciting, praying, exhorting – a wild figure, with eyes in which flashed the madness of religious fanaticism, straining forward with passionate gestures through the smoky light which shone on his brilliant headgear and on his glistening face, distorted by suffering and excitement. When he had finished speaking he stepped off the platform, picked up his shoes and staff, and hurried out into the night to bear his eloquence to other villages...

There is nothing more difficult to measure than the value of visible emotion. To the Englishman tears are a serious matter; they denote only the deepest and the most ungovernable feelings, they are reserved for great occasions. Commonplace sensations are, in his opinion, scarcely worth bringing on to the surface. The facile expression of emotion in a foreigner is surprising to him – he can scarcely understand the gestures of a nation so little removed from him as the French, and he is apt to be led astray by what seems to him the visible sign of great excitement, but which to them is only a natural emphasis of speech. In the East these difficulties are ten times greater. The gesture itself has often a totally different significance; the Turk nods his head when he says 'No' and shakes it when he wishes to imply assent; and even when this is not the case, the feeling which underlies it is probably quite incomprehensible – quite apart from the range of Western emotion – and its depth and duration are ruled by laws of which we have no knowledge.

The first thing which strikes us in the Oriental is his dignified and impassive tranquillity. When we suddenly come upon the other side of him, and find him giving way, for no apparent reason, to uncontrolled excitement, we are ready to believe that only the most violent feelings could have moved him so far from his habitual calm. So it was that evening. At first it seemed to us that we were looking upon people plunged into the blackest depths of grief, but presently it dawned upon us that we were grossly exaggerating the value of their tears and groans. The Oriental spectators in the boxes were scarcely moved by an emotion which they were supposed to be sharing; they sat listening with calm faces, partook of a regular meal of sweetmeats, ices, and sherbets, and handed round kalyans with polite phrases and affable smiles. Our Persian servants were equally unmoved; they conformed so far to the general attitude as to tap their well-clad chests with inattentive fingers, but they kept the corners of their eyes fixed upon us, and no religious frenzy prevented them from supplying our every want. And on the edges of the crowd below us the people were paying no heed to what was going forward; we watched men whose faces were all wet with tears, whose breasts were red and sore with blows, stepping aside and entering into brisk conversation with their neighbours, sharing an amicable cup of tea, or bargaining for a handful of salted nuts, as though the very name of Hussein were unknown to them. Seeing this, we were tempted to swing back to the opposite extreme, and to conclude that this show of grief was a mere formality, signifying nothing – a view which was probably as erroneous as the other.

But whatever it meant, it meant something which we could not understand, and the whole ceremony excited in our minds feelings not far removed from disgust and weariness. It was forced, it was sordid, and it was ugly. The hangings of the tent looked suspiciously as though they had come from a Manchester loom, and if they had, they did not redound to the credit of Manchester taste; the lamps smelt abominably of oil, the stifling air was loaded with dust, and the grating chant of the mollahs was as tedious as the noise of machinery. How long it lasted I do not know; we were glad enough to escape from it after about an hour, and as we walked home through the cool village street, we shook a sense of chaotic confusion from our minds, and heard with satisfaction the hoarse sounds fading gradually away into the night air...

After such fashion the Shiahs mourn the death of the Imam Hussein, the Rose in the Garden of Glory; and whether he and his descendants are indeed the only rightful successors of the Prophet is a question which will never be definitely settled until the coming of the twelfth and last Imam, who, they say, has already lived on earth, and who will come again and resume the authority which his deputy, the Shah, holds in his name. 'When you see black ensigns' – so tradition reports Mohammed's words – 'black ensigns coming out of Khorasan, then go forth and join them, for the Imam of God will be with those standards, whose name is El Mahdi. He will fill the world with equity and justice.'

5

Slowly, slowly through the early summer the cholera crept nearer. Out of the far East came rumours of death... the cholera was raging in Samarkand... it had crossed the Persian frontier... it is in Meshed! said the telegrams. A perfunctory quarantine was established between Tehran and the infected district and the streams of pilgrims that flock ceaselessly to Meshed were forbidden to enter the holy city. Then came the daily bulletins of death, the number of the victims increasing with terrible rapidity. Meshed was almost deserted, for all whom the plague had spared had fled to the mountains, and when a week or two later its violence began to abate, flashed the ominous news: 'It is spreading among the villages to the westward.' From day to day it drew ever closer, leaping the quarantine bulwark, hurrying over a strip of desert, showing its sudden face in a distant village, sweeping northwards, and causing sanguine men to shake their heads and murmur: 'Tehran will be spared; it never comes to Tehran' – in a moment seizing upon the road to the Caspian and ringing the city round like a cunning strategist. Then men held their breath and waited and almost wished that the suspense were over and the ineluctable day were come. Yet with the cholera knocking at their doors they made no preparations for defence, they organized no hospitals, they planned no system of relief; cartloads of over-ripe fruit were still permitted to be brought daily into the town, and the air was still poisoned by the refuse which was left to rot in the streets. It was the month of Muharram; every evening the people fell into mad transports of religious excitement, crowding together in the Shah's theatre to witness the holy plays and to mourn with tears the death of Hussein. Perhaps a deeper fervour was thrown into the long prayers and a greater intensity into the wailing lamentations, for at the door the grim shadow was standing, and which of the mourners could answer for it that not on his own shoulder the clutching hand would fall as he passed out into the night? The cloud of dust that hung for ever over the desert and the city assumed a more baleful aspect; it hung now like an omen of the deeper cloud which was settling down upon Tehran. And still above it the sun shone pitilessly, and under the whole blue heaven there was no refuge from the hand of God. So the days passed, and the people drank bad water and gorged themselves on rotten fruit, and on a sudden the blow fell – the cholera was in Tehran.

Woe to them that were with child in those days and to them that were sick! One blind impulse seized alike upon rich and poor – flight! flight! All who possessed a field or two in the outlying villages, and all who could shelter themselves under a thin canvas roof in the desert, gathered together their scanty possessions, and, with bare necessaries of life in their hands, crowded out of the northern gateways. The roads leading to the mountains were blocked by a stream of fugitives, like an endless procession of Holy Families fleeing before a wrath more terrible than that of Herod: the women mounted on donkeys and holding their babes in front of them wrapped in the folds of their cloaks, the men hurrying on foot by their side. For the Vengeance of the Lord is swift; in the East he is still the great and terrible God of the Old

Testament; his hand falls upon the just and upon the unjust, and punishes folly as severely as it punishes crime. In vain the desert was dotted over with the little white tents of the fugitives, in vain they sought refuge in the cool mountain villages. Wherever they went they bore the plague in the midst of them; they dropped dead by the roadside, they died in the sand of the wilderness, they spread the fatal infection among the country people.

Oriental fatalism, which sounds fine enough in theory, breaks down woefully in practice. It is mainly based upon the helplessness of a people to whom it has never occurred to take hold of life with vigorous hands. A wise philosophy bids men bear the inevitable evil without complaint, but we of the West are not content until we have discovered how far the coil is inevitable, and how far it may be modified by forethought and by a more complete knowledge of its antecedents. It may be that we turn the channel of immediate fate but little, but with every effort we help forward the future safety of the world. But fatalism can seldom be carried through to its logical conclusions – the attitude of mind which prevented the Persians from laying in medical stores did not save them a fortnight later from head-long flight.

The most degrading of human passions is the fear of death. It tears away the restraints and the conventions which alone make social life possible to man; it reveals the brute in him which underlies them all. In the desperate hand-to-hand struggle for life there is no element of nobility. He who is engaged upon it throws aside honour, he throws aside self-respect, he throws aside all that would make victory worth having – he asks for nothing but bare life. The impalpable danger into whose arms he may at any moment be precipitating himself unawares tells more upon his nerves and upon his imagination than a meeting with the most redoubtable enemy in the open; his courage breaks under the strain.

Such fear laid hold of the people of Tehran.

The Persian doctors, whose duty it was to distribute medicines among the sufferers, shut up their stores, and were among the first to leave the stricken city; masters turned their servants into the streets and the open fields, if they showed symptoms of the disease, and left them to die for want of timely help; women and little children were cast out of the andaruns; the living scarcely dared to bury the bodies of the dead.

One little group of Europeans preserved a bold front in the midst of the universal terror. The American missionaries left their homes in the villages and went down into the town to give what help they could to the sick, and to hearten with the sight of their own courage those whom the cholera had not yet touched. They visited the poorer quarters, they distributed medicines, they started a tiny hospital, in which they nursed those whom they found lying in the streets, giving them if they recovered, clean and disinfected clothes, and if they died a decent burial. They tried to teach a people who received both their help and their wisdom at the point of the sword, the elementary laws of common sense to prevent them from eating masses of fruit, and to put a stop to a fertile cause of fresh infection by persuading them to burn the clothes of the dead instead of selling them for a few pence to the first comer. Sometimes we would meet one of these men riding up from the town in the cool of the evening, when ceaseless labour and much watching had rendered it imperative that he should take at least one night's rest. His face had grown thin and white with the terrible strain of the work, and in his eyes was the expression which the sight of helpless suffering puts into the eyes of a brave man.

'One morning,' related the doctor months afterwards, 'as I was going out early to make my rounds, I found a woman lying on the doorstep. She was half naked, and she had been dead some hours, for her body was quite cold. A child crept round her, moaning for food, and on her breast was a little living baby fast asleep. It was the most terrible thing I ever saw in my life,' he added after a moment. The missionaries were aided by one or two European volunteers and native pupils from their own schools, who stood shoulder to shoulder with them, and helped them to bear the heat and burden of the day. Their courage and their splendid endurance will remain graven on the minds of those who knew of it long after shameful memories of cowardice have been forgotten.

For it was not only the Persians who were terror-stricken; among the Europeans also there were instances of cowardice. There were men who, in spite of former protestations of indifference, turned sick and white with fear when the moment of trial came; there were those who fled hastily, leaving their servants and their companions to die in their deserted gardens; and there were those who took to their beds and who even went to the length of giving up the ghost, victims of no other malady than sheer terror. The English doctor had his hands full both in the town and in the country; by many a sickbed he brought comfort where his skill could not avail to save, and courage to many who were battling manfully with the disease.

Religious fervour grew apace under the influence of fear. Men to whom travel and intercourse with foreigners had given a semblance of Western civilisation, exchanged their acquired garb for a pilgrim's cloak, and set forth on the long journey to Mecca. The air was full of rumours. It was whispered that the mollahs were working upon native fanaticism, and pointing to the presence of

Europeans as a primary cause of evil which must be straightway removed. Today an incredible number of deaths were reported to have taken place in Tehran during the last twenty-four hours, tomorrow the news would run from lip to lip that the Shah himself had succumbed. At the time when the cholera broke out in Tehran, his Majesty was making his summer journey through the country. He at once despatched an order to the effect that the disease was on no account to be permitted to come near his camp, but it was not within his conception of the duties of kingship to take precautions for the safety of any dweller in his realms but himself. He appeared to be considerably alarmed by the approach of an enemy who is no respecter of persons. He dismissed the greater part of his followers, and, making a few nights' halt in a palace in the neighbourhood of his capital, he hurried on into the mountains. Even in those nights forty or fifty people died in his camp, but he was kept in ignorance of this untoward occurrence. Fortunate indeed were those ladies of his andarun who accompanied him on his travels, or who had enough influence to succeed in having themselves transported to one of the numerous country palaces; the others were obliged to continue in the town, no one having time to spare them any attention, and it was not till the fury of the cholera was spent that the poor women were allowed to move into a less dangerous neighbourhood.

The cholera was not of very long duration. A slight fall of rain reduced the daily number of deaths by several hundreds; before six weeks were past the people were returning to the streets they had quitted in precipitate haste; a fortnight later the surrounding villages also were free of sickness, and had resumed their accustomed aspect, except for an air of emptiness in the tiny bazaars, from which in some cases a third of the population had been reft, and a corresponding number of fresh graves in the burial-grounds. But another disease follows on the heels of cholera; typhoid fever is the inevitable result of an absolute disregard of all sanitary laws. The system of burial among the Persians is beyond expression evil. They think nothing of washing the bodies of the dead in a stream which subsequently runs through the length of the village, thereby poisoning water which is to be used for numberless household purposes, and in their selection of the graveyard they will not hesitate to choose the ground lying immediately above a kanat which is carrying water to many gardens and drinking-fountains. Even when they are buried, the bodies are not allowed to rest in peace. The richer families hold it a point of honour to lay the bones of their relations in some holy place – Kerbela, where Hussein was slain, or the sacred shrine of Meshed. They therefore commit them only temporarily to the earth, laying them in shallow graves, and covering them with an arched roof of brickwork, which practice accounts for the horrible smell round the graveyards after an outbreak of cholera. A few months later, and long before time has killed the germs of disease, these bodies are taken up, wrapped in sackcloth, and carried, slung across the backs of mules, to their distant resting-place, sowing not improbably the seeds of a fresh outbreak as they go. The wonder is, not that the cholera should prove fatal to so many, but that so large a proportion of the population should survive in a land where Ignorance is for ever preparing a smooth highway for the feet of Death.

6

When the Shah takes a girl into his andarun it is said to be a matter of universal rejoicing among her family, not so much because of the honour he has done her, as because her relatives look to using her influence as a means of gaining for themselves many an envied favour. For aught I know to the contrary, the girl, too, may think herself a fortunate creature, and the important position of the one man she may possibly govern may console her for the monotony of her kingdom; but however delightful as a place of abode the royal andarun may be, in one respect it must fall short of the delights of the kingdom of heaven – there cannot fail to be endless talk of marrying and giving in marriage within its walls. The number of Shah's wives is great, and he is blessed with a proportionately large family; it must therefore be difficult to find a sufficiency of high-born suitors with whom to match his daughters. Moreover, there may be a trace of reluctance in the attitude of the suitors themselves, for the privilege of being the Shah's son-in-law is not without its disadvantages. If the nobleman selected happen to be wealthy, the Shah will make their close relationship an excuse for demanding from him large gifts; if at any subsequent period he should have a mind to take another wife, the etiquette of the Court will stand in his way; and still worse, if he be already married, he will find himself obliged to seek a divorce from his wife that he may obey the Shah's command. The negotiations preceding the match must be complicated in the extreme, and great must be the excitement in the andarun before they are concluded.

With one such household we were acquainted. The husband, whose title may be translated as the Assayer of Provinces, was a charming person, who had spent much of his youth (much also of his fortune) in Paris. He was a cultivated man and an enthusiast for sports; a lover of dogs, which for most Persians are unclean animals, and a devotee to the art of fishing. He had suffered not a little at the hands of his royal father-in-law, and had withdrawn in indignation from all public life, spending his days in hunting and shooting, in improving his breed of horses, and in looking after his estates. His residence abroad had made him more liberal-minded than most of his countrymen. He paid special attention to the education of his daughters, refused to allow them to be married before they had reached a reasonable age, and gave them such freedom as was consistent with their rank. They were two in number; we made their acquaintance, and that of the Princess their mother, one afternoon in Tehran.

Now, an afternoon call in Persia is not to be lightly regarded; it is a matter of much ceremony and it lasts two hours. When we arrived at the house where the three ladies lived, we were conducted through a couple of courts and a long passage, and shown into a room whose windows opened into a vine-wreathed veranda. There was nothing Oriental in its aspect: a modern French carpet, with a pattern of big red roses on a white ground, covered the floor; photographs and looking-glasses hung upon the walls; the mantelpiece was adorned with elaborate vases under glass shades, and on some brackets stood plaster casts of statues. We might have imagined ourselves in a French château, but for the appearance of the châtelaine.

The Princess was a woman of middle age, very fat and very dark; her black eyebrows met together across her forehead; on her lips there was more than the suspicion of a moustache; the lower part of her face was heavy, and its outline lost itself in her neck. The indoor costume of a Persian lady is not becoming. She wears very full skirts, reaching barely to the knee, and standing out round her like those of a ballet-dancer; her legs are clothed in white cotton stockings, and on her feet are satin slippers. These details are partly concealed by an outer robe, unfastened in front, which the wearer clutches awkwardly over her bulging skirts, and which opens as she walks, revealing a length of white cotton ankles. In the case of the Princess this garment was of pale blue brocade. She wore her hair loose, and a white muslin veil was bound low upon her forehead, falling down over the hair behind. She was too civilised a woman to have recourse to the cosmetics which are customary in the East; the orange-stain of henna was absent from her fingernails, and in the course of conversation she expressed much disapproval of the habit of painting the eyes, and great astonishment when we informed her that such barbarism was not unknown even in England.

It must not be imagined that the conversation was of an animated nature. In spite of all our efforts and of those of the French lady who acted as interpreter, it languished woefully from time to time. Our hostess could speak some French, but she was too shy to exhibit this accomplishment, and not all the persuasions of her companion could induce her to venture upon more than an occasional word. She received our remarks with a nervous giggle, turning aside her head and burying her face in her pocket-handkerchief, while the Frenchwoman replied for her, 'Her Royal Highness thinks so and so.' When the interview had lasted for about half an hour, cups of tea were brought in and set on a round table in the midst of us; shortly afterwards the two daughters entered, sweeping over the floor towards us in green and pink satin garments, and taking their places at the table. The younger girl was about sixteen, an attractive and demure little person, whose muslin veil encircled a very round and childish face; the other was two years older, dark, like her mother, though her complexion was of a more transparent olive, and in her curly hair there were lights which were almost brown. Her lips were, perhaps, a little too thick, though they were charmingly curved, and her eyes were big and brown and almond-shaped, with long lashes and a limpid, pathetic expression as you see in the trustful eyes of a dog when he pushes his nose into your hand in token of friendship. Nor did her confiding air belie her: she took our hands in her little brown ones and told us shyly about her studies, her Arabic, and her music, and the French newspapers over which she puzzled her pretty head, speaking in a very low, sweet voice, casting down her black eyelashes when we questioned her, and answering in her soft guttural speech: 'Baleh Khanum' – 'Yes, madam,' or with a little laugh and a slow, surprised 'Naghai-ai-r!' when she wished to negative some proposition which was out of the range of her small experience.

During the course of the next hour we were regaled on lemon ices, and after we had eaten them it was proposed that we should be taken into the garden. So we wandered out hand-in-hand, stopping to speak to an unfriendly monkey who was chained under the oleanders, and who turned a deaf ear to all our blandishments. In the garden there was a large pond, on the banks of which lay a canoe – an inconvenient vessel, one would imagine, for ladies attired in stiff and voluminous petticoats! Tents were pitched on the lawn, for our hostesses were on the eve of departure for their summer camp in the mountains, and had been examining the condition of their future lodgings. The garden, with its tents and its water, was like some fantastic opera stage, and the women, in their strange bright garments, the masqueraders, who would begin to dance a *pas de trois* before us as soon as the orchestra should strike up. But the play was unaccountably delayed, and while we sat under the trees servants appeared bringing coffee, a signal that the appointed time of our visit had come to an end, and that we might be permitted to take our leave. The girls accompanied us into the outer court, and watched us through the half-open doors till we drove away, wishing, perhaps, that they too might drive out into the world with such unfettered liberty, or perhaps wondering at our unveiled shamelessness.

We went to see the three ladies again when we were in the mountains. Their camp was pitched about a mile lower down the river than ours, on a grassy plateau, from which they had a magnificent view down the long bare valley and across mountains crowned by the white peak of Demavend. No sooner had we forded the river in front of our tents than a storm of wind and rain and hail broke upon us, but we continued dauntlessly on our way, for the day of our visit had been fixed some time before, and it was almost pleasant after the summer's drought to feel the rain beating on our faces. When we reached the Persian camp we dismounted before a canvas wall which surrounded the women's tents, a curtain was drawn aside for us by a negro slave, and we were taken into a large tent, where the Princess was sitting on a rolled-up bed for sofa. We greeted her with chattering teeth and sat down on some wooden chairs round her, carrying on a laboured conversation in the French tongue, while our wet clothes grew ever colder upon us. We remembered the steaming cups of tea of our former visit, and prayed that they

49

might speedily make their appearance, but alas! on this occasion they were omitted, and lemon ices alone were offered to us. It is not to be denied that lemon ices have their merit on a hot summer afternoon, but the Persian's one idea of hospitality is to give you lemon ices – lemon ices in hailstorms, lemon ices when you are drenched with rain, lemon ices when a biting wind is blowing through the tent door – it was more than the best regulated constitution could stand. We politely refused them.

An important event had taken place in the household during the last two months: a marriage had been arranged between the eldest daughter and a young Persian nobleman, whose wealth and influence matched themselves satisfactorily with her rank. He, too, was spending the summer in the mountains; his camp lay a little beyond ours, and we were therefore able to observe the daily visits which took place between him and his future father-in-law, when they rode, attended by troops of mounted servants, backwards and forwards along the stony bridle-path on the opposite bank. Doubtless great discussions of the approaching marriage and of the art of fly-fishing took place in those August days. We stood in the centre of this Oriental romance, and felt as though we were lending a friendly hand to the negotiations. Certainly if good wishes could help them, we did much for the young couple.

The Assayer of Provinces spent most of his time trout-fishing. He used to make us presents of gaudy flies manufactured by his negro slave (himself a most successful fisherman), and we found that these attracted the trout of the Lar considerably more than our March browns and palmers. The eldest daughter shared her father's taste. When she and her sister joined us in her mother's tent that thundery afternoon, we fell into a lively discussion of the joys and the disappointments of the sport, comparing the number of fish we had killed and the size of our largest victims. The Persian girls had never gone far afield – they contented themselves with the pools and streams near their tents – but that they should fish at all spoke volumes for their energy. To throw a well-considered fly is a difficult art at best, but to throw it when you are enveloped from head to foot in sweeping robes must be well-nigh impossible.

This second visit passed more cheerfully than the first. The fresh mountain wind had blown away the mists of ceremony, there was no interpreter between us, and we had a common interest on which to exchange our opinions. That is the secret of agreeable conversation. It is not originality which charms; even wit ceases in the end to provoke a smile. The true pleasure is to recount your own doings to your fellow-man, and if by a lucky chance you find that he has been doing precisely the same thing, and is therefore able to listen and reply with understanding, no further bond is needed for perfect friendship. Unfortunately, this tie was lacking between us and the monkey, who was also in villeggiatura by the banks of the Lar, and in consequence we got no further forward with him than before. Our presence seemed, indeed, to exasperate him more than ever. He spent the time of our visit making spiteful dashes at us, in the vain hope that the gods might in the end reward his perseverance and lengthen his chain sufficiently to allow him to bite us but once before we left.

But the gods have eternity in their hand, and we must hasten, for our time is short; long ere the monkey's prayer was answered we had risen and taken leave of the three ladies. We left them gazing after us from behind their canvas walls. Their prisoned existence seemed to us a poor mockery of life as we cantered homewards up the damp valley, the mountain air sending a cheerful warmth through our veins. The thunderstorm was past, the sun dropped in clear splendour behind the mountains, leaving a red glory to linger on the slopes of Demavend, and bearing the fullness of his light to the Western world – to our own world.

7

Cholera had swept through Tehran since last we set foot in its streets, and they seemed to us more than usually empty and deserted in the vacant sunshine that autumn morning. But the Ark, the centre and heart of the city, was crowded still. Though many of the tiny shops had been closed by owners whose own account had been closed summarily and for ever, the people who remained went about their business as cheerfully as before, gesticulated over their bargains, drew their long robes round them in dignified disgust as we passed, and sipped their glasses of tea with unimpaired enjoyment. The motley crowd was yet further diversified by the scarlet coats of the Shah's farrashes, the many-coloured garments and fantastic headgear of the servants of the palace, and the ragged uniforms of the soldiers who hung about the street corners – an army scarcely more efficient, I should imagine, than its rudely-painted counterpart upon the walls. These rough drawings satisfy the eye and tickle the artistic taste of the King of Kings. He is not difficult to please. Take a wooden soldier for model (carefully omitting his little green stand), magnify him to the size of life, put the brightest colours into his uniform and his cheeks, and you will be furnished with a design which is considered worthy of decorating not only the principal gateways of Tehran, but all the streets leading to the palace.

In Eastern life there are no modulations. As the day leaps suddenly into night with no warning time of twilight, so, to adapt the words of Omar the Tent-Maker, between the house of riches and of penury there is but a breath. We were accustomed to strange contrasts, yet it scarcely seemed possible that this gaudy squalor could be the setting of the priceless Treasure of the King. The stories we had heard of its magnificence must be due to the fecundity of the Oriental imagination. The East is the birthplace of wonders; there the oft-repeated tale gains a semblance of veracity which ends by deceiving not only credulous listeners, but him also who invented it. We should have received it like other fairy stories, sedulously nursing the happy faith which flies all opportunity of proving itself a superstition.

We stopped before an unregal gateway, and were conducted with much ceremony into the palace. The palace was unexpectedly beautiful, after all. Crossing a narrow strip of garden, we found ourselves in its first court – a court of Government offices, we were told, though the word *office* conveys no impression of the graceful buildings, from the upper galleries of which curtains floated, fanning the air within to coolness. Our guides led us beneath more archways, through high, dark passages, and out into the sunlight of the central garden. It was built round with an irregular architecture. Here the walls were radiant with faience, there a row of arches stood back from the sun-beaten pavement – delicate arches which might have graced some quiet Italian cloister – beyond them stood the much-decorated building where the Shah sits in state on the day of the New Year, and which was separated from the garden in front only by the folds of an immense curtain, which, when it is drawn back, discloses the carved throne set in a grove of columns. Still further on we reached the palace itself, two-storied and many-windowed, from whose steps stretched the dainty pleasure-grounds, with their paved paths and smooth, fresh grass, their trees and gay flowerbeds, between which fountains leapt joyfully, and streams meandered over their blue-tiled beds. They were bounded by the impenetrable and forbidding walls of the andarun.

Mounting the marble staircase, we found ourselves before a big wooden doorway, the seal on whose lock had to be broken ere it could be thrown open to us. We stood expectantly while the Minister, our guide, fumbled at the lock. Perhaps he was really some powerful efreet whom, after long captivity, our presence had released from the bottle in which Solomon had prisoned him. We were half prepared for the fairy treasures he had come forth to reveal to us.

Prepared? Ah, no, indeed! For what sober mortal could be prepared for the sight that burst upon us?

A great vaulted room with polished floor and painted walls, with deep alcoves through whose long narrow windows splashes of sunlight fell and everywhere jewels! Jewels on all the shelves of the alcoves, thick-sewn jewels on the carpets which hung against the walls, jewels coruscating from the throne at the top of the room, jewels in glass cases down the middle, flashing and sparkling in the sunlight, gleaming through dark corners, irradiating the whole hall with their scintillant brightness. With dazzled eyes we turned to one of the alcoves, and fell to examining the contents of the shelves. Here were swords sheathed in rubies; here were wands and sceptres set from end to end with spirals of turquoise and sapphire; diamond crowns, worthy to throw a halo of light round the head of an emperor; breastplates and epaulets, from whose encrusted emeralds the spear of the enemy would glance aside, shields whose bewildering splendour would blind his eyes. Here were rings and bracelets and marvellous necklaces, stars and orders and undreamt-of ornaments, and, as though the ingenuity of the goldsmiths had been exhausted before they had reached the end of their task, rows and rows of tiny glasses filled with unset stones – diamonds, sapphires, topazes, amethysts – the nectar of an Olympian god frozen in the cup. Under glass cases lay the diadems of former kings, high, closed helmets ablaze with precious stones; masses of unstrung pearls; costly and hideous toys, remarkable only for their extraordinary value – a globe, for instance, supported by an unbroken column of diamonds, whose seas were made of great flat emeralds, and whose continents of rubies and sapphires; and scattered with lavish profusion among the cases, festoons of turquoise rings and broad gold pieces which have long passed out of use, but in which regal currency, it is related, an immense subsidy was once paid to the Czar. On the other side of the room the treasures were scarcely less valuable and even more beautiful, for cupboard after cupboard was filled with delicate enamel, bowls and flagons, and the stems of kalyans all decorated with exquisite patterns in the soft blended colours whose freshness is immortal. These lay far beyond the criticism of captious connoisseurs, who would not have failed to point out to us that the jewels were tinsel-backed, after all, and that most of the enormous rose diamonds were flawed and discoloured.

Taking an honoured place among the jewels and the enamel there were some objects which raised a ripple of laughter in the midst of our admiration. The royal owner of the treasure-house, doubtless anxious to show that he considered no less the well-being of the inward than the adornment of the outward man, had filled some of his upper shelves with little bottles of – what could those silvery globules be? we wondered, gazing curiously upwards. Not white enough – or pearls, and yet they could not be, though they looked suspiciously like – yes, they were! – they were pills! Yes, indeed they were pills – quack remedies which the Shah had collected on his Western travels, had brought home and placed among his treasures. After this discovery we were not surprised to find bottles of cheap scents and tooth-powder among the diamonds, nor to observe that some of the priceless cloisonné bowls were filled with toothbrushes; nor was it even a disillusion when we were solemnly told that the wooden cases placed at intervals down the room, each on its small table, were only musical boxes, which it is the delight of the Protector of the Universe to set a-playing all at once when he comes to inspect his treasures. Heaven knows by what fortunate combination of circumstances he finds those treasures still intact, for they seemed to us very insufficiently guarded, unless the tutelary efreet watches over them. There is, indeed, a locked door, of which the King and the Prime Minister alone possess a key; but a thief is not usually deterred by the necessity of forcing a lock, and if a scrupulous sense of honour prevented him from breaking the royal seal, with a little ingenuity he might contrive an entrance through one of the many windows, or even through the roof, were he of an enterprising disposition; and once within, nothing but the glass cupboard doors would separate him from riches so vast that he might carry away a fortune without fear of detection.

We were next taken to see the world-famous Peacock Throne, which is reported to have been brought from Delhi by a conquering Shah. A scarlet carpet sewn with pearls covered its floor, on which the King sits cross-legged in Eastern fashion, surrounded by a blaze of enamel and precious stones. A year ago this throne had been the centre of a hideous story of cupidity and palace intrigue – who can tell what forgotten crimes have invested its jewels with their cruel, tempting glitter? We passed on into a long succession of charming rooms with low, painted ceilings, walls covered with a mosaic of looking-glass, and windows facing the smiling garden. Execrable copies of the very worst European pictures adorned them; one was hung with framed photographs – groups taken on the Shah's travels, in which his shabby figure occupied a prominent place, and all wearing that inane vacuity of expression which is characteristic of photographic groups, whether they be of royal personages or of charity school children. Here and there a wonderful carpet lent its soft glow to the rooms, but for the most part the floors were covered with coarse productions of European looms – those flaming roses, and vulgar, staring patterns, which exercise an unfortunate attraction over the debased Oriental taste of today.

With a feeling of hopeless bewilderment, we at length quitted the palace where we had been dazzled by inconceivable wealth and moved to ridicule by childish folly. Wealth and childishness seemed to us equally absurd as we rode home in silence along the dusty roads.

Before our garden gates there dwelt a holy dervish. He, too, was a king – in the realms of poverty – and over the narrow strip of wilderness he bore undisputed sway. He levied pious alms for taxes, his palace was a roof of boughs, four bare poles were the columns of his throne, and the stones of the desert his crown jewels. His days were spent in a manner which differed little from that of his neighbour and brother sovereign. The whole long summer through he had collected the surrounding stones and piled them into regular heaps. His futile religious exercise was almost completed, he was putting the finishing touches to a work which winter winds and snows would as surely destroy as the winter of ill-fortune will scatter the other's wealth. But the dervish was untroubled by thoughts of the future; he laboured to the glory of God in his own strange fashion, and though his jewels needed neither locks nor seals nor men-at-arms to guard them, their human interest lent them a value unattained by the Treasure of the King.

8

I used to watch him coming round the curve of the avenue, his quick step somewhat impeded by the long robes he wore, holding his cloak round him with one hand, his head bent down, and his eyes fixed on the ground. As he drew near he would glance up, wrinkling his eyebrows in the effort to pierce the darkness of the great tent under which I was sitting. The plane trees grew straight and tall on each side of the road; overhead their branches touched one another, arching together and roofing it with leaves fresh and green, as only plane-leaves can be all through the hot summer. Between the broad leaves fell tiny circles of sunshine, which flickered on his white turban and on the linen vest about his throat as he came. He looked like a very part of his surroundings, for his woollen cloak was of a faded grey, the colour of Persian dust, and his under-robe was as green as the plane-leaves, and his turban gleamed like the sunshine; but his face was his own, brown and keen, with dark eyes, deep set under the well-marked brows, and his thin brown hands were his own too, and instinct with character. If you had only seen the hands, you might fairly have hazarded a guess at the sort of man he was, for they were thoughtful hands, delicate and nervous, with thin wrists, on which the veins stood out, and long fingers, rather blunt at the tips; and the skin, which was a shade darker than the sun can tan, would have told you he was an Oriental. I believe he came up from Tehran on a mule on the days appointed for our lesson, and reached our village at some incredibly early hour in order to avoid the morning heat; but the six-mile journey must have been disagreeable at best, for the roads were ankle-deep in dust, and the sun blazed fiercely almost as soon as it was above the horizon. The cool shaded garden and the dark tent, with an overflowing tank in the midst of it, and a stream of fresh water running over the blue tiles in front, was a welcome refuge after the close heat of the town and the dusty ride.

'Peace be with you!' he would say with a low bow. 'Is the health of your Excellency good?' 'Thanks be to God, it is very good,' I would answer. 'Thanks be to God!' he would return piously, with another bow. Then he would draw up a chair and sit down in front of me, folding his hands under his wide sleeves, crossing his white-stockinged feet, and gazing round him with his bright quick eyes. He made use of no gestures while he talked, his hands remained folded and his feet crossed, and only his keen, restless glances and the sudden movements round the corners of his lips told when he was interested. He never laughed, though he smiled often, and his smile was enigmatical, and betokened not so much amusement as indulgent surprise at the curious views of Europeans. I often wondered what thoughts there were, lurking in his brain, that brought that odd curl round the corners of his mouth, but I never arrived at any certainty as to what was passing through his mind, except that sometimes he was indubitably bored, and was longing that the lesson were over, and that he might be permitted to go and sleep through the hot hours. On these occasions he expressed his feelings by yawns, very long and very frequent – it certainly was hot! I was often sleepy too, for I had been up and out riding quite as early as he.

Our intercourse was somewhat restricted by the fact that we had no satisfactory medium through which to convey our thoughts to each other. He spoke French – such French as is to be acquired at Tehran! and I – ah well! I fear my Persian never carried me very far. Nevertheless, we were accustomed to embark recklessly on the widest discussions. He was a bit of a reformer was Sheikh Hassan; indeed, he had got himself into trouble with the Government on more occasions than one by a too open expression of his opinions, and the modern equivalent for the bow-string had perhaps flicked nearer his shoulders than he quite liked; a free-thinker too, and a sceptic to the tips of his brown fingers. A quatrain of Omar Khayyam's would plunge us into the deepest waters of philosophic uncertainty, with not even the poor raft of a common tongue to float us over, from whence we would emerge, gasping and coughing, with a mutual respect for each other's linguistic efforts, but small knowledge of what they were intended to convey. Pity that such a gulf lay between us, though I dare say it came to much the same in the end, for, as Hafiz has remarked in another metaphor, 'To no man's wisdom those grim gates stand open, or will ever stand!'

The Sheikh had an unlimited contempt for Persian politics. 'It is all rotten!' he would say –'rotten! rotten! What would you have?' (with a lifting of the eyebrows). 'We are all corrupt, and the Shah is our lord. You would have to begin by sweeping away everything that exists.' But his disbelief in the efficacy of European civilisation was equally profound, and his pessimism struck me as being further sighted than the careless optimism of those who seek to pile one edifice upon another, a Western upon an Eastern world, and never pause to consider whether, if it stands at all, the newer will only stand by crushing the older out of all existence. Sheikh Hassan, at all events, was not very hopeful. 'Triste pays!' he would say at the end of such a conversation. 'Ah, triste pays!' and though I knew he had his own views as to the possible future of his country, he was far too discreet a man to confide them to frivolous ears.

Concerning his private life I never liked to question him, though I would have given much to know what his own household was like. He had a wife and children down in Tehran. The good lady looked with unmitigated disapproval upon infidel foreigners, and her husband was obliged to conceal from her how many hours of the day he spent with them. Judging by an anecdote I heard of her during the cholera time, she must have ruled the establishment with a hand of iron. The Sheikh, being much concerned over the risk his family was running in the plague-stricken town, had taken the precaution of having in six bottles of brandy, the most convenient medicine he could obtain, and hearing at the same time that a good bargain offered itself in the matter of olive oil, he, as a prudent man, had also purchased six bottles of oil and stored them too in his cellar. But on one luckless morning, when his wife happened to enter there, she espied the brandy lurking in a dark corner. Being a lady of marked religious convictions, she at once called to mind the words which the Prophet has pronounced against alcoholic liquors, and without more ado opened the bottles and poured out their contents upon the floor. On further search her eldest daughter discovered the oil in another corner. Having observed the conduct of her mother, she concluded that she could not do better than imitate it, and accordingly the innocent liquid also streamed out over the cellar floor, libation to an unheeding god. The unfortunate Sheikh found on his return that his foresight and his skill in bargaining had alike been brought to nought by the misguided fervour of the female members of his family.

To none of them did the cholera prove fatal, though the wife suffered from a slight attack; but Sheikh Hassan spent anxious weeks until the danger was over. 'For thirty-seven nights,' he told me pathetically, 'I lay awake and considered what could be done for my children's safety.' With true Oriental fatalism, he did not seem to have taken any active steps in the matter, and at the end of his thirty-seven nights of thought he was as far from any conclusion as ever. Happily the extreme fury of the cholera had by that time abated.

The mysteries of Eastern education were no less unfathomable to me. Though he was a man of middle age, Sheikh Hassan had only recently quitted the Madrasseh, a sort of religious college, of which he had been a student. There he had been taught Arabic, geography and astronomy; he had read some philosophy too, for he was acquainted, in a translation, with the works of Aristotle, and he had learnt much concerning the doctrines of religion, which study had profited him little, since he heartily disbelieved in them all. He wrote a beautiful hand, and was very proud of the accomplishment. He would sharpen a reed pen and sit for half an hour writing out quatrains with elaborate care and the most exquisite flourishes, and he evinced such delight over the performance that I could not find it in my heart to interrupt him. He was very anxious that I, too, should acquire this art. I asked him how much time I should have to devote to it. 'Well,' he replied reflectively, 'if for five or six years you were to spend three hours of every day in writing, you might at the end be tolerably proficient.' He did not appear to consider that the achievement was in any way incommensurate with the labour he proposed that I should undergo, and I abstained from all criticism that might hurt his feelings. I wrote him long letters in Persian characters. 'Duste azize man,' they began – 'Dear friend of mine.' He would read them during the lesson, and answer them in terms of the most elaborate politeness – 'My slave was honoured by my commands,' and so forth; and my crude and uncertain lines became abhorrent to me when I saw him covering his paper with a lovely decorative design of courteous phrases. He was not without dreams of literary fame. One day he laid before me a vast scheme of collaboration: we were to compile a Persian grammar together; it would be such a grammar as the world had never seen (in which statement I fancy he came nearer the truth than he well knew!); he would write the Persian, and I should translate it into French. I agreed to all, being well assured that we should never bring our courage to the sticking point. We never did – the grammar of the Persian language is still to be written. The one really useful piece of knowledge he possessed had not been taught him at the Madrasseh – he had picked up French by himself, he told me. I could have wished that he had picked it up in a somewhat less fragmentary condition, for his translations did but little to define the meaning of the original Persian. We read some of Hafiz together, but the Sheikh had only one gender at his disposal, and the poet's impassioned descriptions of his mistresses were always conveyed to me in the masculine. 'Boucles de cheveux' seemed at first a strange beauty in a lady, but custom, the leveller of sensations, brought me to accept without question even this Gorgon-like adornment. The Sheikh took a particular pleasure in the more philosophical verses. Over these I would puzzle for long hours, and in all innocence arrive at the conclusion that some anecdote of angels, or what not, appertaining, doubtless, to the Mohammedan religion, was related in them. The Sheikh would then proceed to annotate them in halting French, pointing out that a pun was contained in every rhyme, that half the words bore at the smallest computation two or three different meanings, and that therefore the lines might be done into several English versions, each with an entirely different significance, and with an equally truthful rendering of the Persian. At this my brain would begin to whirl. I was unable to deal with the confusion of difficulties among which the Sheikh Hassan was delightfully battling; it was enough for me if I could seize some of the beauty which lay like a sheath about the poems, the delicate, exquisite rhythm of the love-songs, the recurrent music of the rhyme, and the noble swing of the refrains. I received and admired their proud stoicism as it stood written: women were women and wine red wine for me, the cup-bearer was the person whose advent was most eagerly to be greeted; roses and nightingales, soft winds and blooming gardens, were all part of a beautiful imaginative world, and fit setting for a poet's dreams.

But this was wilful stupidity. If I had listened to the wisdom of Sheikh Hassan, I should have realised that we were in the midst of sublime abstractions, and that the most rigid morality and the strictest abstinence were inculcated by those glowing lines. In practice, however, I had the poets themselves on my side; the days of Hafiz sped merrily, if tradition has not belied him, and the last prayer of the Tent-Maker was that he might be buried in a rose-garden, where the scented petals would fall softly upon his head and remind him after his death of the joys he had loved on earth.

Were these things also abstractions?

For lighter reading we had the Shah's Diary, a work whose childlike simplicity admitted of but one interpretation. I never got through very much of it, but I read far enough to see that the royal author did not consider himself bound by the ordinary rules of literary production. He was accustomed in particular to pass from one subject to another with a rapidity which was almost breathless. The book began somewhat after this fashion: 'In the month of Sha'ban, God looked with extraordinary clemency upon the world; the crops stood high in the fields, and plenty was showered upon his fortunate people by the hand of Allah. I mounted my horse and proceeded to the review…'

At last the day of parting came; with much regret I told the Sheikh I was about to leave Persia. 'Ah, well,' he replied, 'I'm very glad you are going. Healthy people should not stay here; it's not the place for healthy people.' We fell to making many plans for a meeting in England, a country he had often expressed a desire to visit, I as often assuring him that an enthusiastic reception should be his. I fear these also will never be brought to fulfilment, but if he should ever come, it would be interesting to find what peculiarities in us and in our ways would attract the notice of his bright, observant eyes. I confess it would give me no small pleasure to meet him walking along Piccadilly in his white turban and flowing robes, and to hear once more the familiar salutation: 'The health of your Excellency is good? Thanks be to God!'

9

We were riding. We had left Tehran the previous evening in a storm of rain and hail, which had covered the mountaintops with their first sheet of winter snow. We had slept at a tiny post-house, sixteen miles from the city gates – an unquiet lodging it had proved, for travellers came clattering in all through the early hours of the night, and towards morning the post dashed past, changing horses and speeding forward on its way to Tabriz. The beauty of the night compensated in a measure for wakeful hours; the moon – our last Persian moon – shone out of a clear heaven, its beams glittered on the fields of freshly-fallen snow far away on the mountains, and touched with mysterious light the sleeping forms of Persian travellers stretched in rows on the ground in the veranda of the post-house. We were up before the autumn dawn, and started on our road just as the sun shot over the mountains. Ali Akbar led the way – Ali Akbar, the swiftest rider on the road to Resht, he with the surest judgment as to the merits of a post-horse, the richest store of curses for delinquent post-boys, the deftest hand in the confection of a pillau, the brightest twinkle of humour darting from under shaggy brows – friend, counsellor, protector, and incidentally our servant. He had wound a scarlet turban round his head, he made it a practice not to wash on a journey, and his usually shaven beard had begun to assume alarming proportions before we reached the Caspian. His saddle-bags and his huge pockets bulged with miscellaneous objects – a cake, a pot of marmalade, a crossed Foreign Office bag, a saucepan, a pair of embroidered slippers which he had produced in the rain and presented to us a mile or two from Tehran, with a view, I imagine, to establishing the friendliest relations between us. We followed; in the rear came two baggage-horses carrying our scanty luggage, and driven by a mounted post-boy, generally deficient. These three, the baggage-horses and the post-boy, were our weak point – a veritable heel of Achilles; they represented to us 'black Care', which is said to follow behind every horseman. What a genius those horses had for tumbling over stones! What a limitless capacity for sleep was possessed by those post-boys! How easily could the Gordian knot have been unloosed if its ropes had shared in the smallest measure that feeling for simplicity which animated those which bound our baggage!

The first stage that morning was pleasant enough; then came the heat and the dust with it. Sunshine – sunshine! tedious, changeless, monotonous! Not that discreet English sunshine which varies its charm with clouds, with rainbows, with golden mist, as an attractive woman varies her dress and the fashion of her hair – 'ever afresh and ever anew' as the Persian poet has it – here the sun has long ceased trying to please so venerable a world. The long straight road lay ahead; the desolate plain stretched southwards, mile after uninterrupted mile; the bare mountain barrier shut out the north; and for sound, the thud of our horses' feet as we rode, the heavy, tired thud of cantering feet, and the gasp of the indrawn breath, for as the stage drew to its close the weary beasts cantered on more and more sullenly through dust and heat.

At last far away, where the road dipped and turned, stood the longed-for clump of trees, clustered round the great caravanserai and the glittering blue-tiled dome of the little mosque. This was not an ordinary post-house, but a stately pile, four-square, built by some pious person in the reign of Shah Abbas, and the mosque was the shrine and tomb of a saint, a descendant of the Prophet. Behind it lay a huge mound of earth, a solid watch-tower heaped up in turbulent times. From its summit the anxious inhabitants of the caravanserai could see far and wide over the plain, and shut their gates betimes before an oncoming foe…War has passed away round the shrine of the Yengi Imam, yet it is not security, but indifference, that is high-priest under the blue dome, and though the shadows of the old watchers gazing from the earth-heap would see no sturdy band of Persian robbers rushing down on them from the mountains, they may tremble some day before a white-capped Russian army, marching resistless along the dusty road.

The clatter of the post-horses over the stones broke the noonday silence. Yengi Imam looked very desolate and uncared-for as we rode through the mud-heaps before its hospitable doors. Half the blue tiles had fallen from the dome, unnoticed and unreplaced, meagre poplars shivered in the sun, stunted pomegranate bushes carpeted the ground with yellow autumn leaves, their heavy dark-red fruit a poor exchange for the spring glory of crimson flower. Persians love pomegranates, and on a journey prize them above all other fruits, and even to the foreigner their pink fleshy pips, thick set like jewels, are not without charm. But it is mainly the charm of the imagination and of memories of Arabian Night stories in which disguised princes ate preserved pomegranate seeds, and found them delicious. Do not attempt to follow their example, for when you have tasted the essence of steel knife with which a pomegranate is flavoured, you will lose all confidence in the judgment of princes, even in disguise. And it is a pity to destroy illusions. But for beauty give me pomegranate bushes in the spring, with dark, dark green leaves and glowing flowers, thick and pulpy like a fruit, and winged with delicate petals, red as flame.

Through the low door of the caravanserai we entered the cool vault of the stable which ran all round the garden court. A lordly stable it was, lighted by shafts of sunshine falling from the glass balls with which each tiny dome was studded – vault beyond vault, dusty light and shadowy darkness following each other in endless succession till the eye lost itself in the flickering sunshine of a corner dome. Here stood weary post-horses, sore-backed and broken-kneed; here lay piles of sweet-smelling hay and heaped-up store of grain. At one corner was a minute bazaar, where we could buy thin flaps of bread if we had a mind to eat flour mixed in equal parts with sand and fashioned into the semblance of brown paper; raisins also, and dried figs, bunches of black grapes, sweet and good, and tiny glasses of weak hot tea, much sugared, which pale amber-coloured beverage is more comforting to the traveller on burning Persian roads than the choicest of the forbidden juices of the grape. The great stable enclosed a square plot of garden – orchard, rather, for it was all planted with fruit trees – which, after the manner of Eastern gardens, was elaborately watered by a network of rivulets flowing into a large central tank, roofed over to protect it from the sun. He did his work well, the pious founder of the caravanserai, but he thought more of the comfort of beasts than of men. One or two bare rooms opening into the garden, a few windowless, airless holes in the inner wall, a row of dark niches above the mangers – that was what he judged to be good enough for such as he; the high, cool domes were for weary horses and tinkling caravans of mules.

We were well content to stretch ourselves in the mules' palace with a heap of their hay for bed. Thirty-two miles of road lay behind us, thirty-two miles in front – an hour's rest at midday did not come amiss.

As we lay we saw in the garden a Persian, dressed in the pleated frock-coat and the tall brimless astrakhan hat which are the customary clothes of a gentleman. Round his hat was wrapped a red scarf to protect it from the dust of travelling; the rest of his attire was as spotless as though dust were an unknown quantity to him. He watched us attentively for some minutes, and then beckoned us to his room opposite. We rose, still stiff from the saddle, and walked slowly round the court. He greeted us with the calm dignity of bearing that sits as easily on the Oriental as his flowing robes. Manner and robe would be alike impossible in the busy breathless life of the West, where, if you pause for a moment even to gird your loins, half your competitors have passed you before you look up. The Oriental holds aloof, nor are the folds of his garments disturbed by any unseemly activity. He stands and waits the end; his day is past. There is much virtue in immobility if you take the attitude like a philosopher, yet to fade away gracefully is a difficult task for men or nations – the mortal coil is apt to entangle departing feet and compromise the dignity of the exit.

'Salaam uleikum!' said our new friend – 'Peace be with you!' and, taking us by the hand, he led us into his room, which was furnished with a mat and a couple of wooden bedsteads. On one of these he made us sit, and set out before us on a sheet of bread a roast chicken, an onion, some salt, a round ball of cheese, and some bunches of grapes; then, seeing that we hesitated as to the proper mode of attacking the chicken, he took it in his fingers, delicately pulled apart wings, legs and breast, and motioned us again to eat. He himself was provided with another, to which he at once turned his attention, and thus encouraged, we also fell to. Never did roast chicken taste so delicious! I judge from other experiences that he was probably tough; he was, alas! small, but, for all that, we look back to him with gratitude as having furnished the most excellent luncheon we ever ate. In ten minutes his bones, the onion, and a pile of grape skins were the only traces left of our repast, and we got up feeling that two more stages on tired post-horses were as nothing in the length of a September afternoon.

We said farewell to our unknown host, stammering broken phrases of polite Persian. 'Out of his great kindness we had eaten an excellent breakfast; the clemency of his nobility was excessive; we hoped that he might carry himself safely to Tehran, and that God would be with him.' But though our Persian was poor, gratitude shone from our faces. He bowed and smiled, and assured us that our servant was honoured by our having partaken of his chicken, but he would not shake hands with us because he had not yet washed his fingers, which, as he had used them as knives and forks both for himself and for us, were somewhat sticky.

So we mounted our horses, and rode away towards our crude Western world, and he mounted his and passed eastward into his own cities. Who he is, and what his calling, we shall never know – nor would we. He remains to us a type, a charming memory, of the hospitality, the courtesy, of the East. Whether he be prince or soldier or simple traveller, God be with him! Khuda hafez – God be his Protector!

10

Many, many years have passed since the ingenious Shahrazad beguiled the sleepless hours of the Sultan Shahriyar with her deftly woven stories, and still for us they are as entrancing, as delightful, as they were for him when they first flowed from her lips. Still those exciting volumes keep generations of English children on wakeful pillows, still they throw the first glamour of mystery and wonder over the unknown East. By the light of our earliest readings we look upon that other world as upon a fairy region full of wild and magical possibilities; imprisoned efreets and obedient djinns, luckless princesses and fortunate fish-ermen, fall into their appointed places as naturally as policemen and engine-drivers, female orators and members of the Stock Exchange with us; flying carpets await them instead of railway trains, and the one-eyed Kalender seeks a night's shelter as readily in the palace of the three beautiful ladies as he would hie him to the Crown Hotel at home. Yet though one may be prepared in theory for the unexpected, some feeling of bewilderment is excusable when one finds one's self actually in the midst of it, for even in these soberer days the East remembers enough of her former arts as to know that surprise lies at the root of all witchcraft. The supply of bottled magicians seems, indeed, to be exhausted, and the carpets have, for the most part, lost their migratory qualities – travellers must look nowadays to more commonplace modes of progression, but they will be hard put to it from time to time if they do not consent to resign themselves so far to the traditions of their childhood as to seek refuge under a palace roof. It may be that the modern dispensation is as yet incompletely understood, or perhaps civilisation marches slowly along Persian roads – at any rate, you will search in vain for the welcoming sign which hangs in English cottage windows, and if the village of mud huts be but a little removed from the track beaten by the feet of post-horses, not even the most comfortless lodging will offer itself to you. Fortunately palaces are many in this land where inns are few, and if the hospitality of a king will satisfy you, you may still be tolerably at ease. But luxury will not be yours. The palaces, too, have changed since the fairy-tale days; they are empty now, unfurnished, neglected, the rose-gardens have run wild, the plaster is dropping from the walls, and the Shah himself, when he visits them, is obliged to carry the necessaries of life with him. Take, therefore, your own chicken if you would dine, and your own bed if you have a mind to sleep, and send your servants before you to sweep out the dusty rooms.

It was to the palace of Afcheh, twenty miles to the north-east of Tehran, that we were riding one hot evening. Our road led us across a sun-scorched plain and over a pass, at the top of which we found ourselves looking down on to a long upland valley. A river ran through it, giving life to a belt of trees and corn-fields, and on each side rose the bare mountains which are the Shah's favourite hunting grounds. Down on the river bank stood a tea-house with an inviting veranda, roofed over with green boughs, under which a group of Persians were sitting, listening with inattentive ears to an excited story-teller while he wove some tale of adventure in the sleepy warmth of the twilight. The veranda was screened from the road by clumps of oleanders, whose pink flowers made an exquisite Japanese setting to the cluster of blue-robed peasants. Beyond the tea-house the river was spanned by a bridge, the arches of which were so skilfully fitted into the opposite hill that a carriage – if ever carriage comes – driving down the steep and crooked path must almost inevitably fall headlong into the water below. Night fell as we made our way along the valley; the moon rose, turning the mountainsides into gleaming sheets of light, filling the gorges with deepest, most mysterious shadow, and after an hour or two of foot-pace riding, we reached the village of Afcheh, our destination.

In the courtyard of the palace preparations for the night were already afoot. In one corner glowed a charcoal brazier, over which the cook was busily concocting a dinner, a table was spread in the middle, and at the further end, protected from the brilliant moonlight by the shadow of a wall, stood a row of camp-beds, for though numberless empty rooms were at our disposal, we had been warned that they were infested by insects, and had chosen the more prudent course of sleeping in the open air. Fortunately, the night was hot and fine, and the court was amply large enough to serve as kitchen, dining-room, and bedroom.

We retired, therefore, to rest, but an Eastern night is not meant for sleep. The animals of the village shared this conviction to the full. The horses, our near neighbours, moved to and fro, and tugged impatiently against their tethering ropes; a traveller riding down the stony streets was saluted by a mad outcry of dogs, who felt it incumbent upon them to keep up a fitful barking long after the sound of his footsteps had died away; and stealthy cats crept round our beds, and considered (not without envy) the softness of our blankets. It was too light for sleep. The moon flooded high heaven, and where the shadow of the wall ended, the intense brightness beat even through closed eyelids. The world was too lovely for sleep. It summoned you forth to watch and to wonder, to listen to the soft rush of mountain streams and the whispering of poplar leaves, to loiter through the vacant palace rooms where the moonbeams fell in patches from the latticed windows, to gaze down the terraced gardens bathed in the deceptive light which seemed to lay everything bare, and yet hid neglect and decay; to strain your eyes towards the shimmering mud roofs on which the villagers snatched a broken rest, turning over with a sigh and a muttered prayer or rising to seek a smoother bed; and yet away towards the dim ranges of mountains that stretched southwards. All the witchery of an Eastern night lay upon Afcheh – surely, if Shahrazad had but once conducted her lord to his open window, she might have spared her fertile imagination many an effort.

In the early hours of the morning the moon set and darkness fell upon the world, for though the sky was alive with newly revealed stars, their rays were lost in the depth of heaven, and left night to reign on the earth. A little wind shivered through the poplars in the garden, warning us it was time to continue on our way if we would reach the top of the next pass before the heat of day fell upon us, and we drank an early cup of tea in the dark, and waited under the clump of trees that served for stables while the mules were loaded and the horses saddled.

As we waited, suddenly the daystar flashed up over the mountains, a brilliant herald summoning the world to wake. The people on the house-tops lifted their heads, and saw that the night was past. As we rode down the village street they were rising and rolling up their beds, and by the time we reached the valley they were breakfasting on their doorsteps, and the glory of the star had faded in the white dawn. In some meadows watered by the mountain streams a family of nomads had already struck camp, and were starting out on their day's journey; the narrow path over the hills – at best little more than a steep staircase of rock – was blocked by trains of mules laden with coal (black stone, explained our servants); the air rang with the cries of the mule-drivers, and as we rode upwards in cold shadow, the sun struck the mountaintops, and turned them into solid gold. Day is swift-footed in the East, and man early abroad. Halfway up the pass we paused to look back at our last night's resting-place, but a shoulder of rock hid the palace, and we carried away with us only an impression of the mysterious beauty of its moonlit courts and gardens.

Autumn had come and had almost passed before we found ourselves a second time the guests of the Shah, and under his roof we spent our last two nights in Persia – the one willingly, the other unwillingly.

This other palace stood in the midst of a grove of orange trees; the waters of the Caspian lapped round its walls, and before its balconies stretched the densely wooded hills of Ghilan. The Russian steamer which was to take us to Baku (for no Persian flag may float on the inland sea) touched at Enzeli early in the morning to pick up passengers, and we had been advised to pass the night there, so that we might be ready betimes. Accordingly, we had driven through the damp flat country, a tangled mass of vegetation, that lies between Resht and the sea; we had been rowed by half-naked sailors up the long canal and across the lagoons, and in the evening we had reached the peninsula on which the village stands. We were conducted at once to the palace, and, passing down moss-grown garden paths, bordered by zinnias and some belated China roses, we came upon a two-storied house, with deep verandas, and a red-tiled roof rising above the orange trees. At the top of the staircase we found ourselves in an endless succession of rooms, most of them quite tiny, with windows opening on to the veranda – all unpeopled, all desolate. We chose our suite of apartments, and proceeded to establish ourselves by setting up our beds and dragging a wooden table into our dining-room. Next door to us Ali Akbar had organised his kitchen, and we sat hungrily waiting while he roasted a chicken and heated some boiled rice for our supper. Presently a shadow darkened our doorway, and from the veranda there entered a Persian general dressed in shabby uniform, with some inferior order on his breast, and the badge of the Lion and the Sun fastened into his kolah. He bowed, and politely claimed acquaintance with us, and after a moment of hesitation we recognised in him a fasting official who had come to meet us on our arrival in Persia. The month of Ramazan was then just over, and, in instant expectation of the appearance of the new moon, he had neglected to make a good meal just before dawn. For some reason unknown to us the moon had not been seen that night, and midday had found him still compelled to fast. He had sat for full two hours in suffering silence while we crossed the lagoons, but as we paused by the banks of the canal someone had shouted to him that the moon had, in fact, been signalled, and in jubilant haste he had jumped out of our boat, and had rushed away to enjoy his long-deferred breakfast, from which he returned to us smiling, contented, and, I trust, replete. This gentleman it was who now stood upon our palatial threshold; we brought some wooden chairs from one of the numberless untenanted rooms, and invited him and the friend he had with him to enter. They sat down opposite to us and folded their hands, and we sat down, too, and looked at them, and wondered how they expected to be entertained. After an interval of silence we ventured upon a few remarks touching the weather and similar topics, to which they replied with a polite assent that did not seem to contain the promise of many conversational possibilities. We questioned them as to the condition of Enzeli – what the people did there, how they lived, and, finally, how many inhabitants the peninsula contained. At this our military friend fell into deep thought, so prolonged that we argued from it that he was about to give us the most recent and accurate statistics. At length he looked up with a satisfied air, as though he had succeeded in recalling the exact figures to mind, and replied, 'Kheli!' – 'A great many!' No wonder the question had puzzled him. The matter-of-fact European mode of arriving at the size of a village had never before been presented to his Persian brain. How many people? Why, enough to catch fish for him, to make caviare, to sell in the bazaars and tend the orange-gardens – Kheli, therefore, a great many. The interview came to a close when our servant appeared with steaming dishes. Our two guests rose, and, saying they would leave us to the rest and refreshment we must surely need, bowed themselves out.

A curious savour of mingled East and West hung about the little palace. We slept in bare Persian rooms, the loaded orange boughs touched our verandas, and the soft air of the Eastern night rustled through the reed curtains that hung over them; but the brisk, fresh smell of the sea mixed itself with the heavy Oriental atmosphere; beyond the garden walls the moon shone on the broad Caspian, highway to many lands, and the silence of the night was broken by the whistling of steamers, as though Enzeli itself were one of those greater ports on busier seas to which we were speeding.

Speeding? Alas! we had forgotten that we were still in Persia. Next morning the steamer had not come in; we went down to the quay and questioned the officials as to the possible time of its arrival. They, however, shrugged their shoulders in mute surprise at our impatience. How could they know when it might please Allah to send the steamer? We strolled idly through the orange-grove and into a larger pleasure-ground, laid out with turf and empty flowerbeds, as though some Elizabethan gardener had designed it – and had left it to be completed by Orientals. The pleasant melancholy of autumn lay upon it all, but of an autumn unlike those to which we were accustomed, for it had brought renewed freshness to the grass, scorched by the summer sun, and a second lease of life to the roses. It was almost with surprise that we noticed the masses of fruit hanging on the green orange boughs which 'never lose their leaves nor ever bid the spring adieu'. In the inner garden stood a tower into whose looking-glass rooms we climbed, and from its balconies searched the Caspian for some sign of our ship. But none was to be seen. In despair we sallied forth into the bazaar, and purchased fish and fowls, honey and dried figs, on which we made an excellent breakfast.

All day long we waited, and how the 'many' inhabitants of Enzeli contrive to pass the time remains a mystery to us. As a watering-place, it is not to be recommended, for the tideless sea leaves all the refuse of the village to rot in the sand; sleep may prove a resource to them, as it did to us, for the greater part of the afternoon and evening; but their lot in the narrow peninsula did not seem to us an enviable one as we hurried through the orange-grove in the dawn, summoned by the whistling of the long-expected boat.

So we steamed away across the Caspian, and the sleepy little place vanished behind the mists that hung over its lagoons and enveloped its guardian mountains – faded and faded from our eyes till the Shah's palace was no longer visible; faded and faded from our minds, and sank back into the mist of vague memories and fugitive sensations.

11

Of the powers which come by prayer and fasting, every Mohammedan should have a large share. It is impossible, of course, for the uninitiated to judge how far the inward grace tallies with the outward form, but he can at least bear witness that the forms of the Mohammedan religion are stricter, and that they appear to be more accurately obeyed, than those of the Christian. Religious observances call upon a man with a rougher and a louder voice, and at the same time they are more intimately connected with his everyday life – before the remembrance of the things which are not of this world can have faded from his mind, the muezzin summons him again to turn the eye of faith towards Mecca. The mosques of Constantinople wear a friendly and a homelike air which is absent from Western churches; even those frequented shrines in some small chapel of one of our cathedrals, hung about with pictures and votive offerings, and lighted with wax tapers by pious fingers, do not suggest a more constant devotion than is to be found in the stern and beautiful simplicity of Mohammedan places of worship. At every hour of the day you may see grave men lifting the heavy curtain which hangs across the doorway, and, with their shoes in their hand, treading softly over the carpeted floor, establishing themselves against one of the pillars which support a dome bright with coloured tiles, reading under their breath from the open Koran before them, meditating, perhaps, or praying, if they be of the poorer sort which meditates little, but, however poor they may be, their rags unabashed by glowing carpets and bright-hued tiles. As you pass, slipping over the floor in your large shoes, they will look up for a moment, and immediately return to devotions which are too serious to be disturbed by the presence of unbelievers.

To the stranger, religious ceremonies are often enough the one visible expression of a nation's life. In his churches you meet a man on familiar ground, for, prince or beggar, Western or Oriental, all have this in common – that they must pray. We had seen the beggars, we were also to see the Sultan on his way to mosque in Stamboul. He crosses the Golden Horn for this purpose only twice in the year, and even when these appointed times come round, he is so fearful of assassination that he does his best to back out of the disagreeable duty – small wonder, when you think of the example he has behind him! When he finally decides to venture forth, no one knows until the last moment what route he will take; all the streets and bridges are lined with rows of soldiers, through which, when he comes, his carriage drives swiftly, followed by innumerable carriage-loads of the women of his harem, dressed in pink and blue and green satin, their faces very incompletely concealed by muslin veils – wrappings which are extremely becoming to dark-eyed beauties.

Every Friday Abdul Hamed goes to midday prayers in a small mosque near his palace of Yildiz Kiosk. We stood one sunny morning on the balconies of a house opposite the mosque waiting for his coming; the roads were again lined with soldiers – those tall lean Turks whose grim faces danger and hardship are powerless to disturb – bands played waltz tunes, the muezzin appeared upon the platform of the minaret, and the Sultan's horses came prancing through the crowds of spectators. Just as he turned into the enclosure of the mosque, a man broke through the crowd and rushed, shouting and waving a roll of paper above his head, towards the carriage window. He pushed his way through two lines of soldiers, with such impetuous force he came, but the third turned him back, still struggling and waving the petition above his head. The waltz tunes drowned his cries, the Sultan disappeared into the mosque, and the petitioner, having been shoved and buffeted from hand to hand, having lost his paper and the better part of his garments in the scuffle, was sent homeward sadly and in rags. When the Sultan came out half an hour later and drove his white horses back through the serried lines of people, the soldiers were again standing with imperturbable faces, and peace had been restored to the Ottoman Empire.

In Constantinople religious observances go far to paralyse the conduct of mundane affairs. Three days of the week are *dies non*: on Friday the Turks are making holiday, Saturday is the Jewish Sabbath, and on Sunday the Christians do no work. Moreover, as far as the Mohammedans are concerned, there is one month of the year when all business is at a standstill. During the twenty-eight days of Ramazan they are ordered by the Prophet to fast from an hour before sunrise until sunset. The Prophet is not always obeyed; the richer classes rarely keep the fast; those whose position does not lift them entirely beyond the pressure of public opinion, soften the harshness of his command by sleeping during the day and carousing during the night – a part of the bazaars, for instance, is not opened until midday in Ramazan, at which hour sleepy merchants may be seen spreading out their wares upon the counters with a tribute of many yawns to last night's wakefulness; but the common people still keep to the letter of the law, and to all Ramazan is a good excuse for postponing any disagreeable business.

Such a fast as that enjoined by Mohammed would fill the most ascetic Christian of today with indignant horror. Not only is every true believer forbidden to eat during the prescribed hours, but nothing of any kind may pass his lips: he may drink nothing, he may not smoke. These rules, which are to be kept by all except travellers and the sick, fall heavily upon the poorer classes, who alone preserve them faithfully. Porters carrying immense loads up and down the steep streets of Pera and Galata, caïquejis rowing backwards and forwards under the hot sun across the Golden Horn and the swift current of the Bosphorus, owners of small shops standing in narrow, stuffy streets and surrounded by smells which would take the heart out of any man – all these not one drop of water, not one whiff of tobacco, refreshes or comforts during the weary hours of daylight. As the sun sinks lower behind the hill of Stamboul, the tables in front of the coffee-shops are set out with bottles of lemon-water and of syrups, and with rows and rows of water-pipes, and round them cluster groups of men, thirstily awaiting the end of the fast. The moments pass slowly, slowly – even the European grows athirst as he watches the faces about him – the sun still lingers on the edge of the horizon. On a sudden the watchman sees him take his plunge into another hemisphere, and the sunset-gun booms out over the town, shaking minarets and towers as the sound rushes from hill to hill, shaking the patient, silent people into life. At once the smoke of tobacco rises an incense into the evening air, the narghilehs begin to gurgle merrily, the smoke of cigarettes floats over every group at the street corners, the very hamal pauses under his load as he passes down the hills and lights the little roll of tobacco which he carries all ready in the rags about his waist. Iced water and syrups come later; still later tongues will be loosened over the convivial evening meal; but for the moment what more can a man want than the elusive joy of tobacco-smoke?

From that hour until dawn time passes gaily in Constantinople, and especially in Stamboul, the Turkish quarter. The inhabitants are afoot, the mosques are crowded with worshippers, the coffee-shops are full of men eating, drinking, smoking, and listening to songs and to the tales of story-tellers. The whole city is bright with twinkling lamps; the carved platforms round the minarets, which are like the capitals of pillars supporting the great dome of the sky, are hung about with lights, and, slung on wires between them, sentences from the Koran blaze out in tiny lamps against the blackness of the night. As you look across the Golden Horn the slender towers of the minarets are lost in the darkness, rings of fire hang in mid-air over Stamboul, the word of God flames forth in high heaven, and is reflected back from the waters beneath. Towards morning the lamps fade and burn out, but at dusk the city again decks herself in her jewels, and casts a glittering reflection into her many waters.

On the twenty-fourth night the holy month reaches its culminating point. It is the Night of Predestination; God in heaven lays down His decrees for the coming year, and gives them to His angels to carry to the earth in due season. No good Mohammedan thinks of sleep; the streets are as bright as day, and from every mosque rise the prayers of thousands of worshippers. The great ceremony takes place in the mosque of St. Sophia. Under that vast dome, which the most ancient temples have been ransacked to adorn, until from Heliopolis, from Ephesus, from Athens, and from Baalbec, the dead gods have rendered up their treasures of porphyry and marble – under

89

the dome which was the glory of Christendom is celebrated the festival of the Mohammedan faith. By daylight St. Sophia is still the Christian church, the place of memories. The splendours of Justinian linger in it; the marbles glow with soft colour as though they had caught and held the shadow of that angel's wings who was its architect; the doves which flit through the space of the dome are not less emblems of Christianity than the carved dove of stone over the doorway; the four great painted angels lift their mutilated faces in silent protest against the desecration of the church they guard. Only the bareness, the vast emptiness, which keeps the beauty of St. Sophia unspoilt by flaring altars and tawdry decorations, reminds you that it is a mosque in which you are standing, and the shields hung high up above the capitals, whose twisted golden letters proclaim the names of the Prophet and his companions. Long shafts of dusty sunlight counterchange the darkness, weaving peaceful patterns on the carpeted pavement which was once washed with the blood of fugitives from Turkish scimitars.

But on the Night of Power Christian memories are swept aside, and the stern God of Mohammed fills with His presence the noblest mosque in all the world. As you look down between the pillars of the vast gallery your eyes are blinded by a mist of light – thousands of lamps form a solid roof of brightness between you and the praying people on the floor of the mosque. Gradually the light breaks and disparts, and between the lamps you see the long lines of worshippers below – long even lines, set all awry across the pavement that the people may turn their eyes not to the East, but further south, where the Ka'bah stands in holy Mecca. From the pulpit the words of the preacher echo round the mosque, and every time that he pronounces the name of God the people fall upon their faces with a great sound, which is like the sound of all nations falling prostrate before their Creator. For a moment the silence of adoration weighs upon the air, then they rise to their feet, and the preacher's voice rolls out again through arches and galleries and domes. 'God is the Light of Heaven and Earth!' say the golden letters overhead. 'He is the Light!' answer the thousands of lamps beneath. 'God is the Light!' reads the preacher. 'God is the Light!' repeats a praying nation, and falls with a sound like thunder, prostrate before His name.

With the Night of Predestination Ramazan is drawing to a close. On the fifth succeeding evening all the Mohammedan world will be agog to catch the first glimpse of the crescent moon, whose rays announce the end of the fast. Woe to true believers if clouds hang over the horizon! The heaven-sent sign alone may set a term to the penance imposed by heavenly decree, and not until the pale herald has ushered in the month of Shawwal may men return to the common comforts of every day.

12

'We lived together for the space of a month,' related the second of the three ladies of Baghdad to Haroun al Rashid, Ja'far the Wezir, and Mesroor the Executioner, 'after which I begged my husband that he would allow me to go to the bazaar to purchase some stuffs for dress.' She went, accompanied by the inevitable old woman, to the house of a young merchant whose father had recently died leaving him great wealth. 'He produced all we wanted, and we handed him the money, but he refused to take it, saying: "It is an offer of hospitality for your visit." I said: "If he will not take the money, I will return to him the stuffs." But he would not receive it again, and exclaimed: "By Allah! I will take nothing from you; all this is a present from me for a single kiss, which I will value more than the contents of my whole shop."' The Khalifeh, when the story was concluded – it went on through many and surprising adventures – expressed no astonishment at the young man's generosity. Such an exaggerated view of hospitality seemed to him quite natural on the part of a shopkeeper, nor did he pause to inquire whether the inflammable young man found that the wealth which his father had left him increased with any rapidity through his transactions with pretty ladies.

So reckless a disposition is no longer to be found among Eastern merchants; shopping is now conducted purely on business principles, though it is not without a charm which is absent from Western counters. Instead of the sleek young man, indistinguishable from his fellows, you have the turbaned Turk, bundled up in multitudinous baggy garments, which he holds round him with one hand, while he takes down his goods with the other; or the keen-featured Persian, from whom you need hope to make no large profit, wrapped in closely-hanging robes, his white linen shirt buttoned neatly across his brown chest; or the specious Armenian in his red fez, cunning and voluble, an easy liar, asking impossible prices for worthless objects, and hoping to ingratiate you by murmuring with a leer that he remembers seeing your face in Spitalfields last time he was there. Shopping with these merchants is not merely the going through of certain forms for the acquisition of necessary commodities – it is an end in itself, an art which combines many social arts, an amusement which will not pall, though many hours be devoted to it, a study in character and national characteristics.

It was in Brusa that we went out to purchase some 'stuffs for dress' – not that we contemplated making for ourselves ten robes each to the value of a thousand golden pieces, like the lady of Baghdad, but that we had heard rumours of certain of the Brusa silks which were suited to less extravagant requirements. It was a hot, streaming afternoon; we hired diminutive donkeys and rode down Brusa streets and under the many domes of the bazaar. The quick, short steps of the donkeys clicked over the cobblestones; we looked round us as they went at the rows and rows of shop-counters, the high vaults which arched away to right and leftward, the courtyards open to the sky, set round with shops, grown over with vines, gleaming with sunshine at the end of some dark narrow passage, the people standing about in leisurely attitudes, and the donkeys, which walked

94

diligently up and down, carrying now a veiled woman sitting astride on her padded saddle, now a turbaned Turk, and now a bale of merchandise. At length we came to the street of the silk merchants, and dismounted before the shop of an old Turk who was sitting cross-legged within.

He rose, and with many polite salaams begged us to enter, and set chairs for us round the low enamelled table. We might have been paying a morning call: we talked – those of us who could speak Turkish – of Sa'di and the musical glasses, we sipped our cups of delicious coffee, we puffed our narghilehs – those of us who could derive any other pleasure from a narghileh than that of a strong taste of charcoal flavoured with painted wood. Presently the subject of silks was broached and set aside again as unworthy of discussion; after a few more minutes our – host, shall I say? – laid before us a bundle of embroideries, which we examined politely, complimenting him upon his possessions. At length, as if the idea had just struck him, though he knew perfectly well the object of our visit, he pulled a roll of silk from a corner of the shop and laid it before us. We asked tentatively whether he would not permit us to see more, and the business of the afternoon began. The stuffs were certainly charming. There were the usual stripes of silk and cotton, there were muslins woven with tinsel lines, coarse Syrian cottons, and the brocades for which Brusa is famous, mixtures of cotton and silk woven in small patterns something like a Persian pattern, yellow on white, gold on blue, orange on yellow. No doubt we paid more for our purchases than they were worth, but not more than the pleasure of a delightful afternoon spent in the old Turk's company was worth to us.

On our way home we stopped before a confectioner's shop and invited him to let us taste of his preserves. He did not, like the confectioner in the *Arabian Nights*, prepare for us a delicious dish of pomegranate seeds, but he gave us Rabat Lakoum, and slices of sugared oranges, and a jelly of rose-leaves (for which cold cream is a good European substitute), and many other delicacies, ending with some round white objects, which I take to have been sugared onions, floating in syrup – after we had tasted them we had small desire to continue our experimental repast.

The bazaars in Constantinople are not so attractive: the crowds jostle you, the shopkeepers, throwing aside Oriental dignity, run after you and catch you by the sleeve, offering to show you Manchester cottons and coarse embroidered muslins. A fragrant savour, indeed, of fried meats and garlic hangs about the eating-shops, on whose counters appetizing mixtures of meat and rice are displayed, and bowls of a white substance like curds, into which a convenient spoon is sticking for the common use of all hungry passers-by, and under the high vaults of the carpet bazaar solemn merchants sit in state among their woven treasures, their silver, and their jewels.

We spent a morning among Persian and Circassian shopmen in Tiflis. There the better part of the bazaar is roofed over, and the shops open on to a street inches deep in dust or in mud, according to the weather, as is the manner of the streets of Tiflis. They were full of lovely silver ornaments, and especially we noted the heavy silver belts which were hanging in every window and round the waist of every Circassian merchant. We fixed upon one which was being thus informally exhibited round a waist, and, in spite of the many protestations of its wearer, we succeeded in buying it from him. It had belonged to his father, he said, and I think that it was with some reluctance that he pocketed our gold pieces and saw us carrying off his family heirloom.

In Persia the usual order of shopping is reversed: you buy not when you stand in need, but when the merchants choose to come to you. Moreover, the process is very deliberative, and a single bargain may stretch out over months. The counters are the backs of mules, which animals are driven into your garden whenever their owners happen to be passing by. As you sit under the shadow of your plane trees you become conscious of bowing figures before you, leading laden mules by the bridle; you signify to them that they may spread out their goods, and presently your garden-paths are covered with crisp Persian silks and pieces of minute stitching, with Turkoman tent-hangings, embroideries from Bokhara, and carpets from Yezd and Kerman, and the sunlight flickers down through the plane-leaves into the extempory shop. There is a personal note about these charming materials which lends them an interest other than that which could be claimed by bright colours and soft textures alone. They speak of individual labour and individual taste. Those tiny squares of Persian work have formed part of a woman's dress – in some andarun, years of a woman's life were spent stitching the close intricate pattern in blended colours from corner to corner; those strips of linen on which the design of red flowers and green leaves is not quite completed, come from the fingers of a girl of Bokhara, who, when she married, threw aside her embroidery-needle and left her fancy work thus unfinished.

The bargaining begins; you turn over the stuff with careless fingers – this one is very dirty, that very coarse; you lift a corner of the carpets, and, examining the wrong side with what air of knowledge you can summon to your aid, you mutter that they are only partially silken, after all. Finally you make your offer, which is received with indignant horror on the part of the mer-chant. He sweeps his wares aside, and draws from the folds of his garments a box of turquoises, which he displays to you with many expressions of admiration, and which you return to him with contemptuous politeness: 'Mal-e shuma!' – 'They are your possession!' He packs up his bundles and retires. In a week or two he will return with reduced demands; you will raise your offer a toman or two, and after a few months of coming and going and of mutual concessions, the disputed carpet will be handed over to you at perhaps half the price that the owner originally asked; or perhaps the merchant will return in triumph and inform you that he has sold it to someone less grasping than you.

Urbane Persian phrases are confusing at first to the brusque European; it was not until we had made several mistakes that we grew accustomed to them.

As we were coming through the garden in the dusk one evening a somewhat ragged stranger accosted us and handed us a long-haired kitten. 'Mal-e shuma!' he said. We were surprised, but since we had been making inquiries for long-haired kittens we thought that some kind acquaintance had heard of our wants and taken this opportunity of making us a present – presents from casual acquaintances being not uncommon in the East. We thanked the man and passed on with our mewing acquisition. But the Persian did not seem satisfied; he followed us with dogged persistence, and at length the thought struck us that it might not be a gift after all. We turned and asked:

'What is the cost?'

'Out of your great kindness,' he replied, 'the cost of the cat is three tomans' (about thirty shillings).

'By Allah!' we said, 'in that case it is your possession still;' and we gave the kitten back to him.

When you buy, you might think from the words that pass that you had gained, together with your purchase, a friend for life; and even when you refuse to buy, you veil the terms of your refusal in such a manner that the uninitiated would conclude that you were making a handsome present to your vagrant shopkeeper.

13

All the earth is seamed with roads, and all the sea is furrowed with the tracks of ships, and over all the roads and all the waters a continuous stream of people passes up and down – travelling, as they say, for their pleasure. What is it, I wonder, that they go out for to see? Some, it is very certain, are hunting the whole world over for the best hotels; they will mention with enthusiasm their recent journey through Russia, but when you come to question them, you will find that they have nothing to tell except that in Moscow they were really as comfortable as if they had been at home, and even more luxurious, for they had three varieties of game at the table of their host. Some have an eye fixed on the peculiarities of foreign modes of life, that they may gratify their patriotic hearts by condemning them when they differ (as they not infrequently do) from the English customs which they have left, and to which their thoughts turn regretfully; as I have heard the whole French nation summarily dismissed from the pale of civilization because they failed to perceive that boiled potatoes were an essential complement to the roast. To some travelling is merely the traversing of so many hundred miles; no matter whether not an inch of country, not an object of interest, remains in the eye of the mind – they have crossed a continent, they are travellers. These bring back with them only the names of the places they have visited, but are much concerned that the list should be a long one. They will cross over to Scutari that they may conscientiously say they have been in Asia, and traverse India from end to end that they may announce that they have visited all the tombs. They are full of expedients to lighten the hardships of a road whose varied pleasures have no charm for them. They will exhibit with pride their bulky luncheon-baskets, and cast withering glances at that humble flask of yours which has seen so many adventures over the edge of your coat-pocket. 'Ah,' they will say, 'when you have travelled a little you will begin to learn how to make yourself comfortable.' And you will hold your peace, and hug your flask and your adventures closer to your heart.

All these, and more also, are not travellers in the true sense of the word; they might as well have stayed at home and read a geography book, or turned over a volume of photographs, and engaged a succession of cooks of different nationalities; but the real travellers, what pleasures are they seeking in fresh lands and strange cities? Reeds shaken in the wind are a picturesque foreground, but scarcely worth a day's journey into the wilderness; men clothed in soft raiment are not often to be met with in hotel or caravanserai, and as for prophets, there are as many at home, maybe, as in other places.

Well, every man carries a different pair of eyes with him, and no two people would answer the question in the same fashion. For myself, I am sometimes tempted to believe that the true pleasure of travel is to be derived from travelling companions. Such curious beings as you fall in with, and in such unexpected places! Although your acquaintance may be short in hours, it is long in experience; and when you part you feel as intimate as if you had shared the same slice of bread-and-butter in your nursery, and the same bottle of claret in your college hall. The vicissitudes of the road have a wonderful talent for bringing out the fine flavour of character. One day may show a man in as many different aspects as it would take ten years of the customary life to exhibit. Moreover, time goes slowly on a ship or in a railway train, and a man is apt to better its pace by relating the incidents of his career to a sympathetic listener. In this manner the doors of palaces and of secret chambers in remote corners of the world fly open to you, and though you may have crossed no more unfamiliar waters than those of the North Sea, you pass through Petersburg and Bokhara, Poland and Algeria, on your way to Antwerp. English people are not so communicative, even abroad, and what they have to tell is of less interest if you are athirst for unknown conditions; their tales lack the charm of those which fall from the lips of men coming, as it were, out of a dream-world, crossing but once the glow of solid reality which lights your own path, and vanishing as suddenly as they came into space. Like packmen, we unfasten our wares, open our little bundle of experiences, spread them out and finger them over: the ship touches at the port, and silks and tinsel are gathered up and strapped upon our backs and carried – God knows where!

The man who carried the most amusing wares we ever examined was a Russian officer, and he spread them out for our inspection as we steamed round the eastern and northern coasts of the Black Sea. He was a magnificent creature, fair-haired, blue-eyed, broad-shouldered, and tall; he must have stood six feet four in those shining top boots of his. His beard was cut into a point, and his face was like that of some handsome, courteous seventeenth-century nobleman smiling out of a canvas of Vandyke's. He was a mighty hunter, so he told us; he lived with his wife and daughters out in Transcaspia, where he governed a province and hunted the lions and the wolves (and perhaps the Turkomans also) with packs of dogs and regiments of mounted huntsmen. He was writing a book about Transcaspia; there would be much, he said, of hunt in its pages. He spoke English, and hastened to inform us that every Russian of good family learnt English from his youth up. I trust that the number of his quarterings was in direct proportion to the number of grammatical errors he perpetrated in our tongue, for if so our friend must have been as well connected as he said he was. He told wonderful stories of the wealth and splendour of his family; all the great Slav houses and all their most ancient names seemed to be united in his person. His mother was Princess This, his wife was Princess That, his father had been a governor of such and such a province; he himself, until a few years back, was the most brilliant of the officers in the Czar's guards – indeed, he had only left Petersburg because, with a growing family, he could no longer afford to spend 40,000 a year (or some such sum – I remember it seemed to us enormous). 'And you know,' he added, 'under 40,000 a year you cannot live in Petersburg – not as I am accustomed to live.' So he had retired to economise among the lions and the Turkomans until his fortunes should retrieve themselves, which there was every prospect of their doing, since his wife was to inherit one of the largest properties in Russia and he himself would come into the second largest on the death of his mother. Of that lady he spoke with a gentle sorrow: 'She is very miser,' he would say whenever he alluded to her. 'She send her blessing, but no pence!' We murmured words of sympathy, but he was not to be comforted – her avarice rankled. 'Ah, yes,' he sighed, when her name came up again in the course of conversation, 'she is very miser!'

It may be that our agreeable companion did not consider himself to be bound by those strict rules of accuracy which tied in a measure our own tongues; his velvets may have been cotton-backed, and his diamonds paste, for all their glitter. We had the opportunity of testing only one of his statements, and I must confess that we were lamentably disappointed. One evening at dinner he was telling us of the prodigies of strength he had accomplished, how he had lifted men with one finger, thrown stupendous weights, and grappled with wild beasts of monstrous size. He even descended into further details. 'In the house of my mother,' he said, 'I took a napkin and bent him twenty times and tore him across!' We were interested, and, to beguile the monotony of the evening, we begged him to perform the same feat on the captain's linen; he acceded, and after dinner we assembled on deck full of expectation. The napkin was produced and folded three or four times; he tore and tore – not a thread gave way! Again he pulled and wrenched until he was red in the face with pulling (and we with shame), and still the napkin was as united as ever. At length we offered some effete excuses – in the house of his mother, even though she was so very miser, the linen was probably of finer quality; no one could be expected to tear one of the ship's napkins, which was as coarse as sackcloth. He accepted the explanation, but nothing is so disconcerting as to be convicted of exaggeration, and though we were heartily sorry for our indiscretion, our acquaintance never again touched those planes of intimacy which it had reached before. Next morning we arrived at Odessa, and parted company with distant bows, nor will he ever, I fear me, send us the promised volume containing some description of Transcaspia and much of hunt.

There is a curious reservation in the communicativeness of a Russian. He will tell you all you wish to know (and more) of himself and of his family, but once touch upon his country or his Government and he is dumb. We noticed this trait in another casual travelling acquaintance, who talked so freely of his own doings, and even of more general topics, such as the novels of Tolstoi, that we were encouraged to question him concerning the condition of the peasantry. 'What of the famine?' we asked. 'Famine!' he said and a blank expression came over his face. 'I have heard of no famine – there is no famine in Russia!' And yet credible witnesses had informed us that the people were dying by thousands in the southern provinces, not so far removed from Batoum, where our friend occupied a high official position. Doubtless, if we had asked of the Jews, he would have replied with the same imperturbable face – 'Jews! I have heard of no Jews in Russia!'

The charm of such friendships lies in their transient character. Before you have time to tire of the new acquaintances they are gone, and in all probability the discussion, which was beginning to grow a little tedious, will never be renewed. You meet them as you meet strangers at a dinner-table, but with less likelihood that the chances of fortune will throw you again together, and less within the trammels of social conventions. Ah, but for those conventions how often might one not sit beside the human being instead of beside the suit of evening clothes! People put on their indistinctive company manners with their indistinctive white shirt-fronts, and only once can I remember to have seen the man pierce through the dress. The transgressor was a Turkish secretary of legation. He was standing gloomily before a supper-table, eyeing the dishes with a hungry glance, when someone came up and asked him why he would not sup. 'Ah,' he sighed, 'ma ceinture! Elle est tellement serrée que je ne puis rien manger!' There was a touch of human nature for you! The suffering Turk said nothing memorable for the rest of the evening, but his own remark brands itself upon the mind, and will not be easily forgotten. I have often wondered at what compromise he and his waistband have arrived during the elapsing years, which must, in spite of all his care, have added certain inches to his circumference.

Not with such fugitive acquaintanceships alone may your fellow-travellers beguile the way: there are many whom you never come to know, and who yet afford a delightful field for observation. In the East a man may travel with his whole family, and yet scarcely interrupt the common flow of everyday life, and by watching them you will learn much concerning Oriental habits which would never otherwise have penetrated through the harem walls. A Turk will arrive on board a ship with half a dozen of his womenkind and as many misshapen bundles, scarcely to be distinguished in form from the beveiled and becloaked ladies themselves. In the course of the next half-hour you will discover that these bundles contain the beds of the family, their food, and all the necessaries of life for the three or four days of the voyage. They will proceed presently to camp out on some portion of the deck roped off for their protection, spreading out their mattresses and their blankets under the open sky, performing what summary toilet they may under their feridgis, eating, sleeping, praying, conversing together, or playing with the pet birds they have brought with them, all in full view of the other passengers, but with as little heed to them as if the rope barrier were really the harem wall it simulates. Meantime, the grave lord of this troop of women paces the deck with dignified tread, and from time to time stops beside his wife and daughters and throws them a word of encouragement.

These family parties may prove of no small inconvenience to other passengers, as once when we were crossing the Sea of Marmora we found the whole of the upper deck cut off from us by an awning and canvas walls, and occupied by chattering women. We remonstrated, and were told that it was unavoidable; the women were great ladies, the family of the Governor of Brousa, with their attendants; they were going to Constantinople, there to celebrate the marriage of one of his daughters with the son of a wealthy pasha. Hence all the laughter and the subdued clatter of tongues, and the air of festive expectation which penetrated through cloaks and veils and canvas walls. But we, who had not the good fortune to be related to pashas, were obliged to content ourselves with the stairs which led on to the deck, on which we seated ourselves with the bad grace of Europeans who feel that they have been cheated of their rights.

Such comparative comfort is enjoyed only by the richer sort; for the poor a sea-voyage is a matter of considerable hardship. They, too, sleep on deck; down on the lower deck they spread their ragged mattresses among ropes and casks and all the miscellaneous detritus of a ship, with the smell and the rattle of the engines in the midst of them, and their rest disturbed by the coming and going of sailors and the bustle of lading and unlading. They cook their own food, for they will not touch that which is prepared by Christian hands, and on chilly nights they seek what shelter they may under the warm funnels. We used to watch these fellow-travellers of ours upon the Caspian boat, setting forth their evening meal as the dusk closed in – it needed little preparation, but they devoured their onions and cheese and coarse sandy cakes of bread with no less relish, and scooped out the pink flesh of their watermelons until nothing but the thinnest paring of rind remained. And as we watched the strange dinner-party of rags and tatters, we fancied that we realised what the feelings of that hasty personage in the Bible must have been after he had gathered in the people from the highways and the byways to partake of his feast, and we congratulated ourselves that we were not called upon to sit as host among them.

Pilgrims from Mecca form a large proportion of the Oriental travellers on the Black Sea. There were two such men on our boat. They were Persians; they wore long Persian robes of dark hues, and on their heads the Persian hat of astrakhan; but you might have guessed their nationality by their faces – the pale, clear-cut Persian faces, with high, narrow foreheads, deep-set eyes and arching brows. They were always together, and held little or no converse with the other passengers, than whom they were clearly of a much higher social status. They stood in the ship's bow gazing eastward, as though they were already looking for the walls of their own Meshed on the far horizon, and perhaps they pondered over the accomplishment of the holy journey, and over the aspect of the sacred places which they. too, had seen at last, but I think their minds were occupied with the prospect of rejoining wife and children and Heimat out there in Meshed, and that was why their silent gaze was turned persistently eastward.

We tried to picture what miseries these people must undergo when storms sweep the crowded deck, and the wind blows through the tattered blankets, and the snow is bed-fellow on the hard mattresses; but for us the pleasant summer weather lies for ever on those inland seas, sun and clear starlight bathe coasts beautiful and desolate sloping down to green water, the playing-ground of porpoises, the evening meals are eaten under the clear skies we knew, and morning breaks fresh and cool through the soft mists to light mysterious lands and wonderful.

SYRIA: THE DESERT
AND THE SOWN

1

To those bred under an elaborate social order few such moments of exhilaration can come as that which stands at the threshold of wild travel. The gates of the enclosed garden are thrown open, the chain at the entrance of the sanctuary is lowered; with a wary glance to right and left you step forth, and, behold! the immeasurable world. The world of adventure and of enterprise, dark with hurrying storms, glittering in raw sunlight, an unanswered question and an unanswerable doubt hidden in the fold of every hill. Into it you must go alone, separated from the troops of friends that walk the rose alleys, stripped of the purple and fine linen that impede the fighting arm, roofless, defenceless, without possessions. The voice of the wind shall be heard instead of the persuasive voices of counsellors, the touch of the rain and the prick of the frost shall be spurs sharper than praise or blame, and necessity shall speak with an authority unknown to that borrowed wisdom which men obey or discard at will. So you leave the sheltered close, and, like the man in the fairy story, you feel the bands break that were riveted about your heart as you enter the path that stretches across the rounded shoulder of the earth.

It was a stormy morning, the 5th of February. The west wind swept up from the Mediterranean, hurried across the plain where the Canaanites waged war with the stubborn hill dwellers of Judaea, and leapt the barrier of mountains to which the kings of Assyria and of Egypt had laid vain siege. It shouted the news of rain to Jerusalem and raced onwards down the barren eastern slopes, cleared the deep bed of Jordan with a bound, and vanished across the hills of Moab into the desert. And all the hounds of the storm followed behind, a yelping pack, coursing eastward and rejoicing as they went. No one with life in his body could stay in on such a day, but for me there was little question of choice. In the grey winter dawn the mules had gone forward carrying all my worldly goods – two tents, a canteen, and a month's provision of such slender luxuries as the austerest traveller can ill spare, two small mule trunks, filled mainly with photographic materials, a few books and a goodly sheaf of maps. The mules and the three muleteers I had brought with me from Beyrout, and liked well enough to take on into the further journey. The men were all from the Lebanon. A father and son, Christians both, came from a village above Beyrout: the father an old and toothless individual who mumbled, as he rode astride the mule trunks, blessings and pious ejaculations mingled with protestations of devotion to his most clement employer, but saw no need to make other contribution to the welfare of the party – Ibrahīm was the name of this ancient; the son, Habīb, a young man of twenty-two or twenty-three, dark, upright and broad-shouldered, with a profile that a Greek might have envied and a bold glance under black brows. The third was a Druze, a big shambling man, incurably lazy, a rogue in his modest way, though he could always disarm my just indignation in the matter of stolen sugar or missing piastres with an appealing, lustrous eye that looked forth unblinking like the eye of a dog. He was greedy and rather stupid, defects that must be difficult to avoid on a diet of dry bread, rice and rancid butter; but when I took him into the midst of his blood enemies he slouched about his work and tramped after his mule and his donkey with the same air of passive detachment that he showed in the streets of Beyrout. His name was Muhammad. The last member of the caravan was the cook. Mikhāil, a native of Jerusalem and a Christian whose religion did not sit heavy on his soul. He had travelled with Mr. Mark Sykes, and received from him the following character: 'He doesn't know much about cooking, unless he has learnt since he was with me, but he never seems to care twopence whether he lives or whether he is killed.' When I repeated these words to Mikhāil he relapsed into fits of suppressed laughter, and I engaged him on the spot. It was an insufficient reason, and as good as many another. He served me well according to his lights; but he was a touchy, fiery little man, always ready to meet a possible offence halfway, with an imagination to the limits of which I never attained during three months' acquaintance, and unfortunately he had learned other things besides cooking during the years that had elapsed since he and Mr. Sykes had been ship-wrecked together on Lake Van. It was typical of him that he never troubled to tell me the story of that adventure, though once when I alluded to it he nodded his head and remarked: 'We were as near death as a beggar to poverty, but your Excellency knows a man can die but once,' whereas he bombarded my ears with tales of tourists who had declared they could not and would not travel in Syria unsustained by his culinary arts. The arak bottle was his fatal drawback; and after trying all prophylactic methods, from blandishment to the hunting-crop, I parted with him abruptly on the Cilician coast, not without regrets other than a natural longing for his tough ragouts and cold pancakes.

I had a great desire to ride alone down the desolate road to Jericho, as I had done before when my face was turned towards the desert, but Mikhāil was of opinion that it would be inconsistent with my dignity, and I knew that even his chattering companionship could not rob that road of solitude. At nine we were in the saddle, riding soberly round the walls of Jerusalem, down into the valley of Gethsemane, past the garden of the Agony and up on to the Mount of Olives. Here I paused to recapture the impression, which no familiarity can blunt, of the walled city on the hill, grey in a grey and stony landscape under the heavy sky, but illumined by the hope and the unquenchable longing of generations of pilgrims. Human aspiration, the blind reaching out of the fettered spirit towards a goal where all desire shall be satisfied and the soul find peace, these things surround the city like a halo, half glorious, half pitiful, shining with tears and blurred by many a disillusion. The west wind turned my horse and set him galloping over the brow of the hill and down the road that winds through the Wilderness of Judaea.

At the foot of the first descent there is a spring, 'Ain esh Shems, the Arabs call it, the Fountain of the Sun, but the Christian pilgrims have named it the Apostles' Well. In the winter you will seldom pass there without seeing some Russian peasants resting on their laborious way up from Jordan. Ten thousand of them pour yearly into the Holy Land, old men and women, for the most part, who have pinched and saved all their life long to lay together the £30 or so which carry them to Jerusalem. From the furthest ends of the Russian empire they come on foot to the Black Sea, where they take ship as deck passengers on board a dirty little Russian boat. I have travelled with 300 of them from Smyrna to Jaffa, myself the only passenger lodged in a cabin. It was mid-winter, stormy and cold for those who sleep on deck, even if they be clothed in sheepskin coats and wadded top-boots. My shipmates had brought their own provisions with them for economy's sake – a hunch of bread, a few olives, a raw onion, of such was their daily meal. Morning and evening they gathered in prayer before an icon hanging on the cook's galley, and the sound of their litanies went to Heaven mingled with the throb of the screw and the splash of the spray. The pilgrims reach Jerusalem before Christmas and stay till after Easter that they may light their tapers at the sacred fire that breaks out from the Sepulchre on the morning of the Resurrection. They wander on foot through all the holy places, lodging in big hostels built for them by the Russian Government. Many die from exposure and fatigue and the unaccustomed climate; but to die in Palestine is the best of favours that the Divine hand can bestow, for their bones rest softly in the Promised Land and their souls fly straight to Paradise. You will meet these most unsophisticated travellers on every high road, trudging patiently under the hot sun or through the winter rains, clothed always in the furs of their own country, and bearing in their hands a staff cut from the reed beds of Jordan. They add a sharp note of pathos to a landscape that touches so many of the themes of mournful poetry. I heard in Jerusalem a story which is a better illustration of their temper than pages of description. It was of a man who had been a housebreaker and had been caught in the act and sent to Siberia, where he did many years of penal servitude. But when his time was up he came home to his old mother with a changed heart, and they two set out together for the Holy Land that he might make expiation for his sins. Now at the season when the pilgrims are in Jerusalem, the riff-raff of Syria congregates there to cheat their simplicity and pester them for alms, and one of these vagabonds came and begged of the Russian penitent at a time when he had nothing to give. The Syrian, enraged at his refusal, struck the other to the earth and injured him so severely that he was in hospital for three months. When he recovered his consul came to him and said, 'We have got the man who nearly killed you; before you leave you must give evidence against him.' But the pilgrim answered, 'No, let him go. I too am a criminal.'

Beyond the fountain the road was empty, and though I knew it well I was struck again by the incredible desolation of it. No life, no flowers, the bare stalks of last year's thistles, the bare hills and the stony road. And yet the Wilderness of Judaea has been nurse to the fiery spirit of man. Out of it strode grim prophets, menacing with doom a world of which they had neither part nor understanding; the valleys are full of the caves that held them, nay, some are peopled to this day by a race of starved and gaunt ascetics, clinging to a tradition of piety that common sense has found it hard to discredit. Before noon we reached the khan halfway to Jericho, the place where legend has it that the Good Samaritan met the man fallen by the roadside, and I went in to lunch beyond reach of the boisterous wind. Three Germans of the commercial traveller class were writing on picture-post-cards in the room of the inn, and bargaining with the khānji for imitation Bedouin knives. I sat and listened to their vulgar futile talk – it was the last I was to hear of European tongues for several weeks, but I found no cause to regret the civilisation I was leaving. The road dips east of the khān, and crosses a dry water-course which has been the scene of many tragedies. Under the banks the Bedouin used to lie in wait to rob and murder the pilgrims as they passed. Fifteen years ago the Jericho road was as lawless a track as is the country now that lies beyond Jordan: security has travelled a few miles eastward during the past decade. At length we came to the top of the last hill and saw the Jordan valley and the Dead Sea, backed by the misty steeps of Moab, the frontier of the desert. Jericho lay at our feet, an unromantic village of ramshackle hotels and huts wherein live the only Arabs the tourist ever comes to know, a base-born stock, half bred with negro slaves. I left my horse with the muleteers whom we had caught up on the slope – 'Please God you prosper!' 'Praise be to God! If your Excellency is well we are content' – and ran down the hill into the village. But Jericho was not enough for that first splendid day of the road. I desired eagerly to leave the tourists behind, and the hotels and the picture-postcards. Two hours more and we should reach Jordan bank, and at the head of the wooden bridge that leads from Occident to Orient we might camp in a sheltered place under mud hillocks and among thickets of reed and tamarisk. A halt to buy corn for the horses and the mules and we were off again across the narrow belt of cultivated land that lies round Jericho, and out on to the Ghōr, the Jordan valley.

The Jericho road is bare enough, but the valley of Jordan has an aspect of inhumanity that is almost evil. If the prophets of the Old Testament had fulminated their anathemas against it as they did against Babylon or Tyre, no better proof of their prescience would exist; but they were silent, and the imagination must travel back to flaming visions of Gomorrah and of Sodom, dim legends of iniquity that haunted our own childhood as they haunted the childhood of the Semitic races. A heavy stifling atmosphere weighed upon this lowest level of the earth's surface; the wind was racing across the hilltops above us in the regions where men breathed the natural air, but the valley was stagnant and life-less like a deep sea bottom. We brushed through low thickets of prickly sidr trees, the Spina Christi of which the branches are said to have been twisted into the Crown of Thorns. They are of two kinds these sidr bushes, the Arabs call them zakūm and dōm. From the zakūm they extract a medicinal oil, the dōm bears a small fruit like a crab apple that ripens to a reddish brown not uninviting in appearance. It is a very Dead Sea Fruit, pleasant to look upon and leaving on the lips a taste of sandy bitterness. The sidrs dwindled and vanished, and before us lay a sheet of hard mud on which no green thing grows. It is of a yellow colour, blotched with a venomous grey-white salt: almost unconsciously the eye appreciates its enmity to life. As we rode here a swirl of heavy rain swooped down upon us from the upper world. The muleteers looked grave, and even Mikhāil's face began to lengthen, for in front of us were the Slime Pits of Genesis, and no horse or mule can pass over them except they be dry. The rain lasted a very few minutes, but it was enough. The hard mud of the plain had assumed the consistency of butter, the horses' feet were shod in it up to the fetlocks, and my dog Kurt whined as he dragged his paws out of the yellow glue. So we came to the Slime Pits, the strangest feature of all that uncanny land. A quarter of a mile to the west of Jordan – the belt is much narrower to the east of the stream – the smooth plain resolves itself suddenly into a series of steep mud banks intersected by narrow gullies. The banks are not high, thirty or forty feet at the most, but the crests of them are so sharp and the sides so precipitous that the traveller must find his way across and round them with the utmost care. The shower had made these slopes as slippery as glass, even on foot it was almost impossible to keep upright. My horse fell as I was leading him; fortunately it was on a little ridge between mound and mound, and by the most astonishing gymnastics he managed to recover himself. I breathed a short thanksgiving when I saw my caravan emerge from the Slime Pits: we might, if the rain had lasted, have been imprisoned there for several hours, since if a horseman falls to the bottom of one of the sticky hollows he must wait there till it dries.

Along the river bank there was life. The ground was carpeted with young grass and yellow daisies, the rusty liveries of the tamarisk bushes showed some faint signs of Spring. I cantered on to the great bridge with its trellised sides and roof of beams – the most inspiring piece of architecture in the world, since it is the Gate of the Desert. There was the open place as I remembered it, covered with short turf, sheltered by the high mud banks, and, Heaven be praised! empty. We had had cause for anxiety on this head. The Turkish Government was at that time sending all the troops that could be levied to quell the insurrection in Yemen. The regiments of southern Syria were marched down to the bridge, and so on to 'Ammān, where they were entrained and sent along the Mecca railway to what was then the terminus, Ma'ān near Petra. From Ma'ān they had a horrible march across a sandy waste to the head of the Gulf of 'Akabah. Many hundreds of men and many thousands of camels perished before they reached the gulf, for the wells upon that road are three only (so said the Arabs), and one lies about two miles off the track, undiscoverable to those who are not familiar with the country.

We pitched tents, picketed the horses, and lighted a huge bonfire of tamarisk and willow. The night was grey and still; there was rain on the hills, but none with us – a few inches represents the annual fall in the valley of Jordan. We were not quite alone. The Turkish Government levies a small toll on all who pass backwards and forwards across the bridge, and keeps an agent there for that purpose. He lives in a wattle hut by the gate of the bridge, and one or two ragged Arabs of the Ghōr share his solitude. Among these was a grey-haired negro, who gathered wood for our fire, and on the strength of his services spent the night with us. He was a cheery soul, was Mabūk. He danced with pleasure, round the camp fire, untroubled by the consideration that he was one of the most preposterously mis-shapen of human beings. He told us tales of the soldiery, how they came down in rags, their boots dropping from their feet though it was but the first day's march, half starved too, poor wretches. A Tābūr (900 men) had passed through that morning, another was expected tomorrow – we had just missed them. 'Māsha-'llah!' said Mikhāil, 'your Excellency is fortunate. First you escape from the mud hills and then from the Redīfs.' 'Praise be to God!' murmured Mabūk, and from that day my star was recognised as a lucky one. From Mabūk we heard the first gossip of the desert. His talk was for ever of Ibn er Rashīd, the young chief of the Shammār, whose powerful uncle Muhammad left him so uneasy a legacy of dominion in central Arabia. For two years I had heard no news of Nejd – what of Ibn Sā'oud, the ruler of Riād and Iber Rashīd's rival? How went the war between them? Mabūk had heard many rumours; men did say that Ibn er Rashīd was in great straits, perhaps the Redīfs were bound for Nejd and not for Yemen, who knew? and had we heard that a sheikh of the Sukhūr had been murdered by the 'Ajārmeh, and as soon as the tribe came back from the eastern pasturages… So the tale ran on through the familiar stages of blood feud and camel lifting, the gossip of the desert – I could have wept for joy at listening to it again. There was a Babel of Arabic tongues round my camp fire that evening, for Mikhāil spoke the vulgar cockney of Jerusalem, a language bereft of dignity, and Habīb a dialect of the Lebanon at immense speed, and Muhammad had the Beyrouti drawl with its slow expressionless swing, while from the negro's lips fell something approaching to the virile and splendid speech of the Bedouin. The men themselves were struck by the variations of accent, and once they turned to me and asked which was right. I could only reply, 'God knows! for He is omniscient,' and the answer received a laughing acceptance, though I confess I proffered it with some misgiving.

The dawn broke windless and grey. An hour and a half from the moment I was awakened till the mules were ready to start was the appointed rule, but sometimes we were off ten minutes earlier, and sometimes, alas! later. I spent the time in conversing with the guardian of the bridge, a native of Jerusalem. To my sympathetic ears did he confide his sorrows, the mean tricks that the Ottoman government was accustomed to play on him, and the hideous burden of existence during the summer heats. And then the remuneration! a mere nothing! His gains were larger, however, than he thought fit to name, for I subsequently discovered that he had charged me three piastres instead of two for each of my seven animals. It is easy to be on excellent terms with Orientals, and if their friendship has a price it is usually a small one. We crossed the Rubicon at three piastres a head and took the northern road which leads to Salt. The middle road goes to Heshbān, where lives the great Sheikh of all the Arabs of the Belka, Sultān ibn 'Ali id Diāb ul 'Adwān, a proper rogue, and the southern to Mādeba in Moab. The eastern side of the Ghōr is much more fertile than the western. Enough water flows from the beautiful hills of Ajlūn to turn the plain into a garden, but the supply is not stored, and the Arabs of the 'Adwān tribes content themselves with the sowing of a little corn The time of flowers was not yet. At the end of March the eastern Ghōr is a carpet of varied and lovely bloom, which lasts but a month in the fierce heat of the valley, indeed a month sees the plants through bud and bloom and ripened seed. A ragged Arab showed us the path. He had gone down to join the Redīfs, having been bought as a substitute at the price of fifty napoleons by a well-to-do inhabitant of Salt. When he reached the bridge he found he was too late, his regiment having passed through two days before. He was sorry, he would have liked to march forth to the war (moreover, I imagine the fifty liras would have to be refunded), but his daughter would be glad, for she had wept to see him go. He stopped to extricate one of his leather slippers from the mud.

'Next year,' quoth he, catching me up again, 'please God I shall go to America.'

I stared in amazement at the half-naked figure, the shoes dropping from the bare feet, the torn cloak slipping from the shoulders, the desert headdress of kerchief and camel's hair rope.

'Can you speak any English?' I asked.

'No,' he replied calmly, 'but I shall have saved the price of the journey, and, by God! here there is no advancement.'

I inquired what he would do when he reached the States.

'Buy and sell,' he replied; 'and when I have saved 200 liras I shall return.'

The same story can be heard all over Syria. Hundreds go out every year, finding wherever they land some of their compatriots to give them a helping hand. They hawk the streets with cheap wares, sleep under bridges, live on fare that no freeborn citizen would look at, and when they have saved 200 liras, more or less, they return, rich men in the estimation of their village. East of Jordan the exodus is not so great, yet once in the mountains of the Haurān I stopped to ask my way of a Druze, and he answered me in the purest Yankee. I drew rein while he told me his tale, and at the end of it I asked him if he were going back. He looked round at the stone hovels of the village, knee-deep in mud and melting snow: 'You bet!' he replied, and as I turned away he threw a cheerful 'So long!' after me…

When we had ridden two hours we entered the hills by a winding valley which my friend called Wād el Hassanīyyeh, after the tribe of that name. It was full of anemones and white broom (rattam the Arabs call it), cyclamen, starch hyacinths, and wild almond trees. For plants without a use, however lovely they may be, there is no name in Arabic; they are all hashīsh, grass; whereas the smallest vegetable that can be of service is known and distinguished in their speech. The path – it was a mere bridle track – rose gradually. Just before we entered the mist that covered the top of the hill we saw the Dead Sea below us to the south, lying under the grey sky like a great sheet of clouded glass. We reached Salt at four o'clock in real mountain weather, a wet and driving mist. Moreover, the ground near the village was a swamp, owing to the rain that, passing over us the night before, had fallen here. I hesitated to camp unless I could find no drier lodging. The first thing was to seek out the house of Habīb Effendi Fāris, whom I had come to Salt to see, though I did not know him. My claim upon him (for I relied entirely upon his help for the prosecution of my journey) was in this wise: he was married to the daughter of a native preacher in Haifa, a worthy old man and a close friend of mine. Urfa on the Euphrates was the *Stammplatz* of the family, but Abu Namrūd had lived long at Salt and he knew the desert. The greater part of the hours during which he was supposed to teach me grammar were spent in listening to tales of the Arabs and of his son, Namrūd, who worked with Habīb Fāris, and whose name was known to every Arab of the Belka.

'If ever you wish to enter there,' said Abu Namrūd, 'go to Namrūd.' And to Namrūd accordingly I had come.

A very short inquiry revealed the dwelling of Habīb Fāris. I was received warmly, Habīb was out, Namrūd away (was my luck forsaking me?), but would I not come in and rest? The house was small and the children many: while I debated whether the soaked ground outside would not prove a better bed, there appeared a magnificent old man in full Arab dress, who took my horse by the bridle, declared that he and no other should lodge me, and so led me away. I left my horse at the khān, climbed a long and muddy stair, and entered a stone paved courtyard. Yūsef Effendi hurried forward and threw open the door of his guest-chamber. The floor and the divan were covered with thick carpets, the windows glazed (though many of the panes were broken), a European cheffonier stood against the wall: this was more than good enough. In a moment I was established, drinking Yūsef's coffee, and eating my own cake.

Yūsef Effendi Sukkar (upon him be peace!) is a Christian and one of the richest of the inhabitants of Salt. He is a laconic man, but as a host he has not his equal. He prepared me an excellent supper, and when I had eaten, the remains were set before Mikhāil. Having satisfied my physical needs he could not or would not do anything to allay my mental anxieties as to the further course. Fortunately at this moment Habīb Fāris arrived, and his sister-in-law, Paulina, an old acquaintance, and several other worthies, all hastening to 'honour themselves' at the prospect of an evening's talk. (' God forbid! the honour is mine!') We settled down to coffee, the bitter black coffee of the Arabs, which is better than any nectar. The cup is handed with a 'Deign to accept,' you pass it back empty, murmuring 'May you live!' As you sip someone ejaculates, 'A double health,' and you reply, 'Upon your heart!' When the cups had gone round once or twice and all necessary phrases of politeness had been exchanged I entered upon the business of the evening. How was I to reach the Druze mountains? the Government would probably refuse me permission, at 'Ammān there was a military post on the entrance of the desert road; at Bosrā they knew me,

I had slipped through their fingers five years before, a trick that would be difficult to play a second time from the same place. Habīb Fāris considered, and finally we hammered out a plan between us. He would send me tomorrow to Tneib, his corn land on the edge of the desert; there I should find Namrūd who would despatch word to one of the big tribes, and with an escort from them I could ride up in safety to the hills. Yūsef's two small sons sat listening open-eyed, and at the end of the talk one of them brought me a scrap of an advertisement with the map of America upon it. Thereat I showed them my maps, and told them how big the world was and how fine a place, till at ten the party broke up and Yūsef began spreading quilts for my bed. Then and not till then did I see my hostess. She was a woman of exceptional beauty, tall and pale, her face a full oval, her great eyes like stars. She wore Arab dress, a narrow dark blue robe that caught round her bare ankles as she walked, a dark blue cotton veil bound about her forehead with a red handkerchief and falling down her back almost to the ground. Her chin and neck were tattooed in delicate patterns with indigo, after the manner of the Bedouin women. She brought me water, which she poured over my hands, moved about the room silently, a dark and stately figure, and having finished her ministrations she disappeared as silently as she had come, and I saw her no more. 'She came in and saluted me,' said the poet, he who lay in durance at Mecca, 'then she rose and took her leave, and when she departed my soul went out after her.' No one sees Yūsef's wife. Christian though he be, he keeps her more strictly cloistered than any Moslem woman; and perhaps after all he is right.

The rain beat against the windows, and I lay down on the quilts with Mikhāil's exclamation in my ears: 'Māsha-'llah! your Excellency is fortunate.'

2

The village of Salt is a prosperous community of over 10,000 souls, the half of them Christian. It lies in a rich country famous for grapes and apricots, its gardens are mentioned with praise as far back as the fourteenth century by the Arab geographer Abu'l Fida. There is a ruined castle, of what date I know not, on the hill above the clustered house roofs. The tradition among the inhabitants is that the town is very ancient; indeed, the Christians declare that in Salt was one of the first of the congregations of their faith, and there is even a legend that Christ was His own evangelist here. Although the apricot trees showed nothing as yet but bare boughs the valley had an air of smiling wealth as I rode through it with Habīb Fāris, who had mounted his mare to set me on my way. He had his share in the apricot orchards and the vineyards, and smiled agreeably, honest man, as I commended them. Who would not have smiled on such a morning? The sun shone, the earth glittered with frost, and the air had a sparkling transparency which comes only on a bright winter day after rain. But it was not merely a general sense of goodwill that had inspired my words; the Christians of Salt and of Mādeba are an intelligent and an indus- trious race, worthy to be praised. During the five years since I had visited this district they had pushed forward the limit of cultiva- tion two hours' ride to the east, and proved the value of the land so conclusively that when the Hajj railway was opened through it the Sultan laid hands on a great tract stretching as far south as Ma'ān, intending to convert it into a chiflik, a royal farm. It will yield riches to him and to his tenants, for if he be an indifferent ruler, he is a good landlord. Half an hour from Salt, Habīb left me, committing me to the care of his hind, Yūsef, a stalwart man, who strode by my side with his wooden club (Gunwā, the Arabs call it) over his shoulder. We journeyed through wide valleys, treeless, uninhabited, and almost uncultivated, round the head of the Belka plain, and past the opening of the Wādy Sīr, down which a man may ride through oak woods all the way to the Ghōr. There would be trees on the hills too if the charcoal burners would let them grow – we passed by many dwarf thickets of oak and thorn – but I would have nothing changed in the delicious land east of Jordan. A generation or two hence it will be deep in corn and scattered over with villages, the waters of the Wādy Sīr will turn mill-wheels, and perhaps there will even be roads: praise be to God! I shall not be there to see. In my time the uplands will still continue to be that delectable region of which Omar Khayyām sings: 'The strip of herbage strown that just divides the desert from the sown'; they will still be empty save for a stray shepherd standing over his flock with a long-barrelled rifle; and when I meet the rare horseman who rides over those hills and ask him whence he comes, he will still answer: 'May the world be wide to you! from the Arabs.'

That was where we were going, to the Arabs. In the desert there are no Bedouin, the tent dwellers are all 'Arab (with a fine roll of the initial guttural), just as there are no tents but houses – 'houses of hair' they say sometimes if a qualification be needed, but usually just 'houses' with a supreme disregard for any other significance to the word save that of a black goat's hair roof. You may be *'Arab* after a fashion even if you live between walls. The men of Salt are classed among the tribes of the Belka, with the Abādeh and the Da'ja and the Hassaniyyeh and several more that form the great troup of the 'Adwān. Two powerful rulers dispute the mastership here of the Syrian desert, the Beni Sakhr and the 'Anazeh. There is a traditional friendship, barred by regrettable incidents, between the Sukhūr and the Belka, perhaps that was why I heard in these parts that the 'Anazeh were the more numerous but the less distinguished for courage of the two factions. I have a bowing acquaintance with one of the sons of Talāl ul Fāiz, the head of all the Beni Sakhr. I had met him five years before in these very plains, a month later in the season, by which time his tribe moves Jordan-wards out of the warm eastern pasturages. I was riding, escorted by a Circassian zaptieh, from Mādeba to Mshitta – it was before the Germans had sliced the carved facade from that wonderful building. The plain was covered with the flocks and the black tents of the Sukhūr and as we rode through them three horsemen paced out to intercept us, black-browed, armed to the teeth, menacing of aspect. They threw us the salute from afar, but when they saw the soldier they turned and rode slowly back. The Circassian laughed. 'That was Sheikh Fāiz,' he said, 'the son of Talāl. Like sheep, wāllah! like sheep are they when they meet one of us.' I do not know the 'Anazeh, for their usual seat in winter is nearer the Euphrates, but with all deference to the Sukhūr I fancy that their rivals are the true aristocracy of the desert. Their ruling house, the Beni Sha'alān, bear the proudest name, and their mares are the best in all Arabia, so that even the Shammār, Ibn er Rashīd's people, seek after them to improve their own breed.

From the broken uplands that stand over the Ghōr, we entered ground with a shallow roll in it and many small ruined sites dotted over it. There was one at the head of the Wādy Sīr, and a quarter of an hour before we reached it we had seen a considerable mass of foundations and a big tank, which the Arabs call Birket Umm el 'Amūd (the tank of the Mother of the Pillar). Yūsef said its name was due to a column which used to stand in the middle of it, surrounded by the water; an Arab shot at it and broke it, and its fragments lie at the bottom of the tank. The mound or tell, to give it its native name, of Amēreh is covered with ruins, and further on at Yadūdeh there are rock-hewn tombs and sarcophagi lying at the edge of the tank. All the frontier of the desert is strewn with similar vestiges of a populous past, villages of the fifth and sixth centuries when Mādeba was a rich and flourishing Christian city, though some are certainly earlier still, perhaps pre-Roman. Yadūdeh of the tombs was inhabited by a Christian from Salt, the greatest corn-grower in these parts, who lived in a roughly built farmhouse on the top of the tell; he too is one of the energetic newcomers who are engaged in spreading the skirts of cultivation. Here we left the rolling country and passed out into the edges of a limitless plain, green with scanty herbage, broken by a rounded tell or the back of a low ridge and then the plain once more, restful to the eye yet never monotonous, steeped in the magic of the winter sunset, softly curving hollows to hold the mist, softly swelling slopes to hold the light, and over it all the dome of the sky which vaults the desert as it vaults the sea. The first hillock was that of Tneib. We got in, after a nine hours' march, at 5.30, just as the sun sank, and pitched tents on the southern slope. The mound was thick with ruins, low walls of rough-hewn stones laid without mortar, rock-cut cisterns, some no doubt originally intended not for water but for corn, for which purpose they are used at present, and an open tank filled up with earth. Namrūd had ridden over to visit a neighbouring cultivator, but one of his men set forth to tell him of my arrival and he returned at ten o'clock under the frosty starlight, with many protestations of pleasure and assurances that my wishes were easy of execution. So I went to sleep wrapped in the cold silence of the desert, and woke next day to a glittering world of sunshine and fair prospects.

The first thing to be done was to send out to the Arabs. After consultation, the Da'ja, a tribe of the Belka, were decided to be the nearest at hand and the most likely to prove of use, and a messenger was despatched to their tents. We spent the morning examining the mound and looking through a mass of copper coins that had turned up under Namrūd's ploughshare – Roman all of them, one showing dimly the features of Constantine, some earlier, but none of the later Byzantine period, nor any of the time of the Crusaders, as far as the evidence of coinage goes, Tneib has been deserted since the date of the Arab invasion. Namrūd had discovered the necropolis, but there was nothing to be found in the tombs, which had probably been rifled centuries before. They were rock-cut and of a cistern-like character. A double arch of the solid rock with space between for a narrow entrance on the surface of the ground, a few jutting excrescences on the side walls, footholds to those who must descend, loculi running like shelves round the chambers, one row on top of another, such was their appearance. Towards the bottom of the mound on the south side there were foundations of a building which looked as though it might have been a church. But these were poor results for a day's exploration, and in the golden afternoon we rode out two hours to the north into a wide valley set between low banks. There were ruins strewn at intervals round the edge of it, and to the east some broken walls standing up in the middle of the valley – Namrūd called the spot, Kuseir es Sahl, the Little Castle of the Plain. Our objective was a group of buildings at the western end, Khureibet es Sūk. First we came to a small edifice (41 feet by 39 feet 8 inches, the greatest length being from east to west) half buried in the ground. Two sarcophagi outside pointed to its having been a mausoleum. The western wall was pierced by an arched doorway, the arch being decorated with a flat moulding. Above the level of the arch the walls narrowed by the extent of a small set-back, and two courses higher a moulded cornice ran round the building. A couple of hundred yards west of the Kasr or castle (the Arabs christen most ruins either castle or convent) there is a ruined temple. It had evidently been turned at some period to other uses than those for which it was intended, for there were ruined walls round the two rows of seven columns and inexplicable cross walls towards the western end of the colonnades. There appeared to have been a double court beyond, and still further west lay a complex of ruined foundations. The gateway was to the east, the jambs of it decorated with delicate carving, a fillet, a palmetto, another plain fillet, a torus worked with a vine scroll, a bead and reel, an egg and dart and a second palmetto on the cyma. The whole resembled very closely the work at Palmyra – it could scarcely rival the stone lacework of Mshitta, and besides it had a soberer feeling, more closely akin to classical models, than is to be found there. To the north of the temple on top of a bit of rising ground, there was another ruin which proved to be a second mausoleum. It was an oblong rectangle of masonry, built of large stones carefully laid without mortar. At the south-east corner a stair led into a kind of antechamber, level with the surface of the ground at the east side owing to the slope of the hill. There were column bases on the outer side of this antechamber, the vestiges probably of a small colonnade which had adorned the east façade. Six sarcophagi were placed lengthways, two along each of the remaining walls, north, south and west. Below the base of the columns on either side of the stair ran a moulding, consisting of a bold torus between two fillets, and the same appeared on the inner side of the sarcophagi. The face of the buttress wall on the south side rose in two in-sets, otherwise the whole building was quite plain, though some of the fragments scattered round upon the grass were carved with a flowing vine pattern. This mausoleum recalls the pyramid tomb which is common in northern Syria; I do not remember any other example of it so far south. It may have resembled the beautiful monument with a colonnaded front which is one of the glories of the southern Dana, and the fragments of vine-scroll were perhaps part of the entablature.

When I returned to my tents a little before sunset, I learnt that the boy we had despatched in the morning had lingered by the way and, alarmed by the lateness of the hour, had returned without fulfilling his mission. This was sufficiently annoying, but it was nothing compared with the behaviour of the weather next day. I woke to find the great plain blotted out by mist and rain. All day the south wind drove against us, and the storm beat upon our canvas walls. In the evening Namrūd brought news that his cave had been invaded by guests. There were a few tents of the Sukhūr a mile or two away from us (the main body of the tribe was still far to the east, where the winter climate is less rigorous), and the day's rain had been too much for the male inhabitants. They had mounted their mares and ridden in to Tneib, leaving their women and children to shift for themselves during the night. An hour's society presented attractions after the long wet day, and I joined the company.

Namrūd's cave runs far into the ground, so far that it must penetrate to the very centre of the hill of Tneib. The first large chamber is obviously natural, except for the low sleeping places and mangers for cattle that have been quarried out round the walls. A narrow passage carved in the rock leads into a smaller room, and there are yet others behind which I took on trust, the hot stuffy air and the innumerable swarms of flies discouraging me from further exploration. That evening the cave presented a scene primitive and wild enough to satisfy the most adventurous spirit. The Arabs, some ten or a dozen men clothed in red leather boots and striped cloaks soaked with rain, were sitting in the centre round a fire of scrub, in the ashes of which stood the three coffee-pots essential to desert sociability. Behind them a woman cooked rice over a brighter fire that cast a flickering light into the recesses of the cave, and showed Namrūd's cattle munching chopped straw from the rock-hewn mangers. A place comparatively free from mud was cleared for me in the circle, a cup of coffee prepared, and the talk went forward while a man might smoke an Arab pipe five times. It was chiefly of the iniquities of the government. The arm of the law, or rather the mailed fist of misrule, is a constant menace upon the edges of the desert. This year it had been quickened to baleful activity by the necessities of war. Camels and mares had been commandeered wholesale along the borders without hope of compensation in money or in kind. The Arabs had gathered together such livestock as was left to them and sent them away five or six days to the east, where the soldiery dared not penetrate, and Namrūd had followed their example, keeping only such cattle as he needed for the plough. One after another of my fellow guests took up the tale: the guttural strong speech rumbled round the cave. By God and Muhammad the Prophet of God we called down such curses upon the Circassian cavalry as should make those powerful horsemen reel in their saddles. From time to time a draped head, with black elf locks matted round the cheeks under the striped kerchief, bent forward towards the glow of the ashes to pick up a hot ember for the pipe bowl, a hand was stretched out to the coffee cups, or the cooking fire flashed up under a pile of thorn, the sudden light making the flies buzz and the cows move uneasily. Namrūd was not best pleased to see his hardly gathered store of firewood melt away and his coffee beans disappear by handfuls into the mortar. ('Wāllah! they eat little when they feed themselves, but when they are guests much, they and their horses; and the corn is low at this late season.') But the word 'guest' is sacred from Jordan to Euphrates and Namrūd knew well that he owed a great part of his position and of his security to a hospitality which was extended to all comers, no matter how inopportune. I added my quota to the conviviality of the party by distributing a box of cigarettes, and before I left a friendly feeling had been established between me and the men of the Beni Sakhr.

The following day was little more promising than that which had preceded it. The muleteers were most unwilling to leave the shelter of the caves and expose their animals to such rain in the open desert, and reluctantly I agreed to postpone the journey, and sent them into Mādeba, three hours away, to buy oats for the horses, cautioning them not to mention from whom they came. It cleared a little in the afternoon, and I rode across the plain southwards to Kastal, a fortified Roman camp standing on a mound.

This type of camp was not uncommon on the eastern frontiers of the Empire, and was imitated by the Ghassānids when they established themselves in the Syrian desert, if indeed Mshitta was, as has been surmised, but a more exquisite example of the same kind of building. Kastal has a strong enclosing wall broken by a single gate to the east and by round bastions at the angles and along the sides. Within, there is a series of parallel vaulted chambers leaving an open court in the centre – the plan with slight variations of Kal'at el Beida in the Safa and of the modern caravanserai. To the north there is a separate building, probably the Praetorium, the house of the commander of the fortress. It consists of an immense vaulted chamber, with a walled court in front of it, and a round tower at the south-west corner. The tower has a winding stair inside it and a band of decoration about the exterior, rinceaux above and fluted triglyphs below, with narrow blank metopes between them. The masonry is unusually good, the walls of great thickness; with such defences stretching to his furthest borders, the citizen of Rome might sleep secure o' nights.

When I passed by Kastal, five years before, it was uninhabited and the land round it uncultivated, but a few families of fellahīn had established themselves now under the broken vaults and the young corn was springing in the levels below the walls, circumstances which should no doubt warm the heart of the lover of humanity, but which will send a cold chill through the breast of the archaeologist. There is no obliterator like the plough-share, and no destroyer like the peasant who seeks cut stones to build his hovel. I noted another sign of encroaching civilisation in the shape of two half-starved soldiers, the guard of the nearest halting-place on the Hajj railroad, which is called Zīza after the ruins a few miles to the west of it. The object of their visit was the lean hen which one of them held in his hand. He had reft it from its leaner companions in the fortress court – on what terms it were better not to inquire, for hungry men know no law. I was not particularly eager to have my presence on these frontiers notified to the authorities in 'Ammān, and I left rather hastily and rode eastward to Zīza.

The rains had filled the desert watercourses, they do not often flow so deep or so swiftly as the one we had to cross that afternoon. It had filled, too, to the brim the great Roman tank of Zīza, so that the Sukhūr would find water there all through the ensuing summer. The ruins are far more extensive than those at Kastal: there must have been a great city here, for the foundations of houses cover a wide area. Probably Kastal was the fortified camp guarding this city, and the two together shared the name of Zīza, which is mentioned in the Notitia: 'Equites Dalmatici Illyriciana Zīza.' There is a Saracenic Kal'ah, a fort, which was repaired by Sheikh Soktan of the Sukhūr, and had been furnished by him, said Namrūd, with a splendour unknown to the desert; but it has now fallen to the Sultan, since it stands in the territory selected by him for his chiflik, and fallen also into ruin. The mounds behind are strewn with foundations, among them those of a mosque, the mihrāb of which was still visible to the south. Zīza was occupied by a garrison of Egyptians in Ibrahīm Pasha's time, and it was his soldiers who completed the destruction of the ancient buildings. Before they came, many edifices, including several Christian churches, were still standing in an almost perfect state of preservation, so the Arabs reported. We made our way homewards along the edge of the railway embankment, and as we went we talked of the possible advantages that the land might reap from that same line. Namrūd was doubtful on this subject. He looked askance at the officials and the soldiery, indeed he had more cause to fear official raiders, whose rapacity could not be disarmed by hospitality, than the Arabs, who were under too many obligations to him to do him much harm. He had sent up a few truck-loads of corn to Damascus the year before; yes, it was an easier form of transport than his camels, and quicker, if the goods arrived at all; but generally the corn sacks were so much lighter when they reached the city than when Namrūd packed them into the trucks that the profit vanished. This would improve perhaps in time – at the time when lamps and cushions and all the fittings of the desert railway except the bare seats were allowed to remain in the place for which they were made and bought. We spoke, too, of superstition and of fears that clutch the heart at night. There are certain places, said he, where the Arabs would never venture after dark – haunted wells to which thirsty men dared not approach, ruins where the weary would not seek shelter, hollows that were bad camping grounds for the solitary. What did they fear? Jinn; who could tell what men feared? He himself had startled an Arab almost out of his wits by jumping naked at him from a lonely pool in the half light of the dawn. The man ran back to his tents, and swore that he had seen a jinni, and that the flocks should not go down to water where it abode, till Namrūd came in and laughed at him and told his own tale.

We did not go straight back to my tents. I had been invited out to dine that evening by Sheikh Nahār of the Beni Sakhr, he who had spent the previous night in Namrūd's cave; and after consultation it had been decided that the invitation was one which a person of my exalted dignity would not be compromised by accepting.

'But in general,' added Namrūd, 'you should go nowhere but to a great sheikh's tent, or you will fall into the hands of those who invite you only for the sake of the present you will give. Nahār – well, he is an honest man, though he be Meskīn,' – a word that covers all forms of mild contempt, from that which is extended to honest poverty, through imbecility to the first stages of feeble vice.

The Meskīn received me with the dignity of a prince, and motioned me to the place of honour on the ragged carpet between the square hole in the ground that serves as hearth and the partition that separates the women's quarters from the men's. We had tethered our horses to the long tent ropes that give such wonderful solidity to the frail dwelling, and our eyes wandered out from where we sat over the eastward sweep of the landscape – swell and fall, fall and swell, as though the desert breathed quietly under the gathering night. The lee side of an Arab tent is always open to the air; if the wind shifts the women take down the tent wall and set it up against another quarter, and in a moment your house has changed its outlook and faces gaily to the most favourable prospect. It is so small and so light and yet so strongly anchored that the storms can do little to it; the coarse meshes of the goat's hair cloth swell and close together in the wet so that it needs continuous rain carried on a high wind before a cold stream leaks into the dwelling-place.

The coffee beans were roasted and crushed, the coffee-pots were simmering in the ashes, when there came three out of the East and halted at the open tent. They were thickset, broad-shoul-dered men, with features of marked irregularity and projecting teeth, and they were cold and wet with rain. Room was made for them in the circle round the hearth, and they stretched out their fingers to the blaze, while the talk went on uninterrupted, for they were only three men of the Sherarāt, come down to buy corn in Moab, and the Sherarāt, though they are one of the largest and the most powerful of the tribes and the most famous breeders of camels, are of bad blood, and no Arab of the Belka would inter-marry with them. They have no fixed haunts, not even in the time of the summer drought, but roam the inner desert scarcely caring if they go without water for days together. The conversa-tion round Nahār's fire was of my journey. A negro of the Sukhūr, a powerful man with an intelligent face, was very anxious to come with me as guide to the Druze mountains, but he admitted that as soon as he reached the territory of those valiant hillmen he would have to turn and flee – there is always feud between the Druzes and the Beni Sakhr. The negro slaves of the Sukhūr are well used by their masters, who know their worth, and they have a position of their own in the desert, a glory reflected from the great tribe they serve. I was half inclined to accept the present offer in spite of the possible drawback of having the negro dead upon my hands at the first Druze village, when the current of my thoughts was interrupted by the arrival of yet another guest. He was a tall young man, with a handsome delicate face, a complexion that was almost fair, and long curls that were almost brown. As he approached, Nahār and the other sheikhs of the Sukhūr rose to meet him, and before he entered the tent, each in turn kissed him upon both cheeks. Namrūd rose also, and cried to him as he drew near:

'Good? please God! Who is with you?'

The young man raised his hand and replied:

'God!'

He was alone.

Without seeming to notice the rest of the company, his eye embraced the three sheikhs of the Sherarāt eating mutton and curds in the entrance, and the strange woman by the fire, as with murmured salutations he passed into the back of the tent, refusing Nahār's offer of food. He was Gablān, of the ruling house of the Da'ja, cousin to the reigning sheikh, and, as I subsequently found, he had heard that Namrūd needed a guide for a foreigner – news travels apace in the desert – and had come to take me to his uncle's tents. We had not sat for more than five minutes after his arrival when Nahār whispered something to Namrūd, who turned to me and suggested that since we had dined we might go and take Gablān with us. I was surprised that the evening's gossip should be cut so short, but I knew better than to make any objection, and as we cantered home across Namrūd's ploughland and up the hill of Tneib, I heard the reason. There was blood between the Da'ja and the Sherarāt. At the first glance Gablān had recognised the lineage of his fellow guests, and had therefore retired silently into the depths of the tent. He would not dip his hand in the same mutton dish with them. Nahār knew, as who did not? the difficulty of the situation, but he could not tell how the men of the Sherarāt would take it, and, for fear of accidents, he had hurried us away. But by next morning the atmosphere had cleared (metaphorically, not literally), and a day of streaming rain kept the blood enemies sitting amicably round Namrūd's coffee-pots in the cave.

The third day's rain was as much as human patience could endure. I had forgotten by this time what it was like not to feel damp, to have warm feet and dry bed clothes. Gablān spent an hour with me in the morning, finding out what I wished of him. I explained that if he could take me through the desert where I should see no military post and leave me at the foot of the hills, I should desire no more. Gablān considered a moment.

'Oh lady,' said he, 'do you think you will be brought into conflict with the soldiery? for if so, I will take my rifle.'

I replied that I did not contemplate declaring open war with all the Sultan's chivalry, and that with a little care I fancied that such a contingency might be avoided; but Gablān was of opinion that strategy went further when winged with a bullet, and decided that he would take his rifle with him all the same.

In the afternoon, having nothing better to do, I watched the Sherarāt buying corn from Namrūd. But for my incongruous presence and the lapse of a few thousand years, they might have been the sons of Jacob come down into Egypt to bicker over the weight of the sacks with their brother Joseph. The corn was kept in a deep dry hole cut in the rock, and was drawn out like so much water in golden bucketsful. It had been stored with chaff for its better protection, and the first business was to sift it at the well-head, a labour that could not be executed without much and angry discussion. Not even the camels were silent, but joined in the argument with groans and bubblings, as the Arabs loaded them with the full sacks. The Sheikhs of the Sukhūr and the Sherarāt sat round on stones in the drizzling mist, and sometimes they muttered, 'God! God!' and sometimes they exclaimed, 'He is merciful and compassionate!' Not infrequently the sifted corn was poured back among the unsifted, and a dialogue of this sort ensued:

Namrūd: 'Upon thee! upon thee! oh boy! may thy dwelling be destroyed! may thy days come to harm!'

Beni Sakhr: 'By the face of the Prophet of God! may He be exalted!'

Sherarāt (in suppressed chorus): 'God! and Muhammad the Prophet of God, upon Him be peace!'

A party in bare legs and a sheepskin: 'Cold, cold! Wāllah! rain and cold!'

Namrūd: 'Silence, oh brother! descend into the well and draw corn. It is warm there.'

Beni Sakhr: 'Praise be to God the Almighty!'

Chorus of Camels: 'B-b-b-b-b-dd-G-r-r-o-o-a-a.'

Camel Drivers: 'Be still, accursed ones! may you slip in the mud! may the wrath of God fall on you!'

Sukhūr (in unison): 'God! God! by the light of His Face!'

At dusk I went into the servants' tent and found Namrūd whispering tales of murder over the fire on which my dinner was a-cooking.

'In the days when I was a boy,' said he (and they were not far behind us), 'you could not cross the Ghōr in peace. But I had a mare who walked – wāllah! how she walked! Between sunrise and sunset she walked me from Mezerīb to Salt, and never broke her pace. And besides I was well known to all the Ghawārny (natives of the Ghōr). And one night in summer I had to go to Jerusalem – force upon me! I must ride. The waters of Jordan were low, and I crossed at the ford, for there was no bridge then. And as I reached the further bank I heard shouts and the snap of bullets. And I hid in the tamarisk bushes more than an hour till the moon was low, and then I rode forth softly. And at the entrance of the mud hills the mare started from the path, and I looked down and saw the body of a man, naked and covered with knife wounds. And he was quite dead. And as I gazed they sprang out on me from the mud hills, ten horsemen and I was but one. And I backed against the thicket and fired twice with my pistol, but they surrounded me and threw me from the mare and bound me, and setting me again upon the mare they led me away. And when they came to the halting place they fell to discussing whether they should kill me, and one said: "Wāllah! let us make an end." And he came near and looked into my face, and it was dawn. And he said: "It is Namrūd!" for he knew me, and I had succoured him. And they unbound me and let me go, and I rode up to Jerusalem.'

The muleteers and I listened with breathless interest as one story succeeded another.

'There are good customs and bad among the Arabs,' said Namrūd, 'but the good are many. Now when they wish to bring a blood feud to an end, the two enemies come together in the tent of him who was offended. And the lord of the tent bares his sword and turns to the south and draws a circle on the floor,

145

calling upon God. Then he takes a shred of the cloth of the tent and a handful of ashes from the hearth and throws them in the circle, and seven times he strikes the line with his naked sword. And the offender leaps into the circle, and one of the relatives of his enemy cries aloud: "I take the murder that he did upon me!" Then there is peace. Oh lady! the women have much power in the tribe, and the maidens are well looked on. For if a maiden says: "I would have such an one for my husband," he must marry her lest she should be put to shame. And if he has already four wives let him divorce one, and marry in her place the maiden who has chosen him. Such is the custom among the Arabs.'

He turned to my Druze muleteer and continued:

'Oh Muhammad! have a care. The tents of the Sukhūr are near, and there is never any peace between the Beni Sakhr and the Druzes. And if they knew you, they would certainly kill you – not only would they kill you, but they would burn you alive, and the lady could not shield you, nor could I.'

This was a grim light upon the character of my friend Nahār, who had exchanged with me hospitality against a kerchief, and the little group round the fire was somewhat taken back. But Mikhāil was equal to the occasion.

'Let not your Excellency think it,' said he, deftly dishing up some stewed vegetables; 'he shall be a Christian till we reach the Jebel Druze, and his name is not Muhammad but Tarīf, for that is a name the Christians use.'

So we converted and baptised the astonished Muhammad before the cutlets could be taken out of the frying-pan.

3

There is an Arabic proverb which says: 'Hayyeh rubda wa la daif mudha' – neither ash-grey snake nor midday guest. We were careful not to make a breach in our manners by outstaying our welcome, and our camp was up before the sun. To wake in that desert dawn was like waking in the heart of an opal. The mists lifting their heads out of the hollows, the dews floating in ghostly wreaths from the black tents, were shot through first with the faint glories of the eastern sky and then with the strong yellow rays of the risen sun. I sent a silver and purple kerchief to Fellah ul 'Isa, 'for the little son' who had played solemnly about the hearth, took grateful leave of Namrūd, drank a parting cup of coffee, and, the old sheikh holding my stirrup, mounted and rode away with Gablān. We climbed the Jebel el 'Alya and crossed the wide summit of the range; the landscape was akin to that of our own English border country but bigger, the sweeping curves more generous, the distances further away. The glorious cold air intoxicated every sense and set the blood throbbing to my mind – the saying about the Bay of Naples should run differently. See the desert on a fine morning and die – if you can. Even the stolid mules felt the breath of it and raced across the spongy ground ('Mad! the accursed ones!') till their packs swung round and brought them down, and twice we stopped to head them off and reload. The Little Heart, the highest peak of the Jebel Druze, surveyed us cheerfully the while, glittering in its snow mantle far away to the north.

At the foot of the northern slopes of the 'Alya hills we entered a great rolling plain like that which we had left to the south. We passed many of those mysterious rujm which start the fancy speculating on the past history of the land, and presently we caught sight of the scattered encampments of the Hassaniyyeh, who are good friends to the Da'ja and belong to the same group of tribes. And here we spied two riders coming across the plain and Gablān went out to greet them and remained some time in talk, and then returned with a grave face. The day before, the very day before, while we had been journeying peacefully from Tneib, four hundred horsemen of the Sukhūr and the Howeitāt, leagued in evil, had swept these plains, surprised an outlying group of the Beni Hassan and carried off the tents, together with two thousand head of cattle. It was almost a pity, I thought, that we had come a day too late, but Gablān looked graver still at the suggestion, and said that he would have been forced to join in the fray, yes, he would even have left me, though I had been committed to his charge, for the Da'ja were bound to help the Beni Hassan against the Sukhūr. And perhaps yesterday's work would be enough to break the newborn truce between that powerful tribe and the allies of the 'Anazeh and set the whole desert at war again. There was sorrow in the tents of the Children of Hassan. We saw a man weeping by the tent pole, with his head bowed in his hands, everything he possessed having been swept from him. As we rode we talked much of ghazu (raid) and the rules that govern it. The fortunes of the Arab are as varied as those of a gambler on the Stock Exchange. One day he is the richest man in the desert, and next morning he may not have a single camel foal to his name. He lives in a state of war, and even if the surest pledges have been exchanged with the neighbouring tribes there is no certainty that a band of raiders from hundreds of miles away will not descend on his camp in the night, as a tribe unknown to Syria, the Beni Awājeh, fell, two years ago, on the lands south-east of Aleppo, crossing three hundred miles of desert, Mardūf (two on a camel) from their seat above Baghdad, carrying off all the cattle and killing scores of people. How many thousand years this state of things has lasted, those who shall read the earliest records of the inner desert will tell us, for it goes back to the first of them, but in all the centuries the Arab has bought no wisdom from experience. He is never safe, and yet he behaves as though security were his daily bread. He pitches his feeble little camps, ten or fifteen tents together, over a wide stretch of undefended and indefensible country. He is too far from his fellows to call in their aid, too far as a rule to gather the horsemen together and follow after the raiders whose retreat must be sufficiently slow, burdened with the captured flocks, to guarantee success to a swift pursuit. Having lost all his worldly goods, he goes about the desert and makes his plaint, and one man gives him a strip or two of goat's hair cloth, and another a coffee-pot, a third presents him with a camel, and a fourth with a few sheep, till he has a roof to cover him and enough animals to keep his family from hunger. There are good customs among the Arabs, as Namrūd said. So he bides his time for months, perhaps for years, till at length opportunity ripens, and the horsemen of his tribe with their allies ride forth and recapture all the flocks that had been carried off and more besides, and the feud enters on another phase. The truth is that the ghazu is the only industry the desert knows and the only game. As an industry it seems to the commercial mind to be based on a false conception of the laws of supply and demand, but as a game there is much to be said for it. The spirit of adventure finds full scope in it – you can picture the excitement of the night ride across the plain, the rush of the mares in the attack, the glorious (and comparatively innocuous) popping of rifles and the exhilaration of knowing yourself a fine fellow as you turn homewards with the spoil. It is the best sort of fantasia, as they say in the desert, with a spice of danger behind it. Not that the danger is alarmingly great: a considerable amount of amusement can be got without much bloodshed, and the raiding Arab is seldom bent on killing. He never lifts his hand against women and children, and if here and there a man falls it is almost by accident, since who can be sure of the ultimate destination of a rifle bullet once it is embarked on its lawless course? This is the Arab view of the ghazu; the Druzes look at it otherwise. For them it is red war. They do not play the game as it should be played, they go out to slay, and they spare no one. While they have a grain of powder in their flasks and strength to pull the trigger, they kill every man, woman and child that they encounter.

Knowing the independence of Arab women and the freedom with which marriages are contracted between different tribes of equal birth, I saw many romantic possibilities of mingled love and hatred between the Montagues and the Capulets. 'Lo, on a sudden I loved her,' says 'Antara, 'though I had slain her kin.' Gablān replied that these difficult situations did indeed occur, and ended sometimes in a tragedy, but if the lovers would be content to wait, some compromise could be arrived at, or they might be able to marry during one of the brief but oft-recurring intervals of truce. The real danger begins when blood feud is started within the tribe itself and a man having murdered one of his own people is cast out a homeless, kinless exile to shelter with strangers or with foes. Such was Imr ul Kais, the lonely outlaw, crying to the night: 'Oh long night, wilt thou not bring the dawn? yet the day is no better than thou.'

A few miles further north the Hassaniyyeh encampments had not yet heard of yesterday's misfortune, and we had the pleasure of spreading the ill-news. Gablān rode up to every group we passed and delivered his mind of its burden; the men in buckram multiplied as we went, and perhaps I had been wrong in accepting the four hundred of the original statement, for they had had plenty of time to breed during the twenty-four hours that had elapsed between their departure and our arrival. All the tents were occupied with preparations not for war but for feasting. On the morrow fell the great festival of the Mohammedan year, the Feast of Sacrifice, when the pilgrims in Mecca slaughter their offerings and True Believers at home follow their example. By every tent there was a huge pile of thorns wherewith to roast the camel or sheep next day, and the shirts of the tribe were spread out to dry in the sun after a washing which, I have reason to believe, takes place but once a year. Towards sunset we reached a big encampment of the Beni Hassan, where Gablān decided to spend the night. There was water in a muddy pool near at hand and a good site for our tents above the hollow in which the Arabs lay. None of the great sheikhs were camped there and, mindful of Namrūd's warnings, I refused all invitations and spent the evening at home, watching the sunset and the kindling of the cooking fires and the blue smoke that floated away into the twilight. The sacrificial camel, in gorgeous trappings, grazed among my mules, and after dark the festival was heralded by a prolonged letting off of rifles. Gablān sat silent by the camp fire, his thoughts busy with the merrymakings that were on foot at home. It went sorely against the grain that he should be absent on such a day. 'How many horsemen,' said he, 'will alight tomorrow at my father's tent! and I shall not be there to welcome them or to wish a good feast day to my little son!'

We were off before the rejoicings had begun. I had no desire to assist at the last moments of the camel, and moreover we had a long day before us through country that was not particularly safe. As far as my caravan was concerned, the risk was small. I had a letter in my pocket from Fellah ul 'Isa to Nasīb el Atrāsh, the Sheikh of Salkhad in the Jebel Druze. 'To the renowned and honoured sheikh, Nasīb el Atrāsh,' it ran (I had heard my host dictate it to Namrūd and seen him seal it with his seal), 'the venerated, may God prolong his existence! We send you greetings, to you and to all the people of Salkhad, and to your brother Jada'llah, and to the son of your uncle Muhammad el Atrāsh in Umm er Rummān, and to our friends in Imtain. And further, there goes to you from us a lady of the most noble among the English. And we greet Muhammada and our friends… etc., (here followed another list of names), and this is all that is needful, and peace be with you.' And beyond this letter I had the guarantee of my nationality, for the Druzes have not yet forgotten our interference on their behalf in 1860; moreover I was acquainted with several of the sheikhs of the Turshān, to which powerful family Nasīb belonged. But Gablān was in a different case, and he was fully conscious of the ambiguity of his position. In spite of his uncle's visit to the Mountain, he was not at all certain how the Druzes would receive him; he was leaving the last outposts of his allies, and entering a border land by tradition hostile (he himself had no acquaintance with it but that which he had gathered on raiding expeditions), and if he did not find enemies among the Druzes he might well fall in with a scouring party of the bitter foes of the Da'ja, the Haseneh or their like, who camp east of the hills.

After an hour or two of travel, the character of the country changed completely: the soft soil of the desert came to an end, and the volcanic rocks of the Haurān began. We rode for some time up a gulley of lava, left the last of the Hassaniyyeh tents in a little open space between some mounds, and found ourselves on the edge of a plain that stretched to the foot of the Jebel Druze in an unbroken expanse, completely deserted, almost devoid of vegetation and strewn with black volcanic stones. It has been said that the borders of the desert are like a rocky shore on which the sailor who navigates deep waters with success may yet be wrecked when he attempts to bring his ship to port. This was the landing which we had to effect. Somewhere between us and the hills were the ruins of Umm ej Jemāl, where I hoped to get into touch with the Druzes, but for the life of us we could not tell where they lay, the plain having just sufficient rise and fall to hide them. Now Umm ej Jemāl has an evil name – I believe mine was the second European camp that had ever been pitched in it, the first having been that of a party of American archaeologists who left a fortnight before I arrived – and Gablān's evident anxiety enhanced its sinister reputation. Twice he turned to me and asked whether it were necessary to camp there. I answered that he had undertaken to guide me to Umm ej Jemāl, and that there was no question but that I should go, and the second time I backed my obstinacy by pointing out that we must have water that night for the animals, and that there was little chance of finding it except in the cisterns of the ruined village. Thereupon I had out my map, and after trying to guess what point on the blank white paper we must have reached, I turned my caravan a little to the west towards a low rise from whence we should probably catch sight of our destination. Gablān took the decision in good part and expressed regret that he could not be of better service in directing us. He had been once in his life to Umm ej Jemāl, but it was at dead of night when he was out raiding. He and his party had stopped for half an hour to water their horses and had passed on eastward, returning by another route. Yes, it had been a successful raid, praise be to God! and one of the first in which he had engaged. Mikhāil listened with indifference to our deliberations, the muleteers were not consulted, but as we set off again Habīb tucked his revolver more handily into his belt.

We rode on. I was engaged in looking for the rasīf, the paved Roman road that runs from Kal'at ez Zerka straight to Bosrā, and also in wondering what I should do to protect if necessary the friend and guide whose pleasant companionship had enlivened our hours of travel and who should certainly come to no harm while he was with us. As we drew nearer to the rising ground we observed that it was crowned with sheepfolds, and presently we could see men gathering their flocks together and driving them behind the black walls, their hurried movements betraying their alarm. We noticed also some figures, whether mounted or on foot it was impossible to determine, advancing on us from a hollow to the left, and after a moment two puffs of smoke rose in front of them, and we heard the crack of rifles.

Gablān turned to me with a quick gesture.

'Darabūna!' he said. 'They have fired on us.'

I said aloud: 'They are afraid,' but to myself, 'We're in for it.'

Gablān rose in his stirrups, dragged his fur-lined cloak from his shoulders, wound it round his left arm and waved it above his head, and very slowly he and I paced forward together. Another couple of shots were fired, and still we rode forward, Gablān waving his flag of truce. The firing ceased; it was nothing after all but the accepted greeting to strangers, conducted with the customary levity of the barbarian. Our assailants turned out to be two Arabs, grinning from ear to ear, quite ready to fraternise with us as soon as they had decided that we were not bent on sheep stealing, and most willing to direct us to Umm ej Jemal. As soon as we had rounded the tell we saw it in front of us, its black towers and walls standing so boldly out of the desert that it was impossible to believe it had been ruined and deserted for thirteen hundred years. It was not till we came close that the rents and gashes in the tufa masonry and the breaches in the city wall were visible. I pushed forward and would have ridden straight into the heart of the town, but Gablān caught me up and laid his hand upon my bridle.

'I go first,' he said. 'Oh lady, you were committed to my charge.' And since he was the only person who incurred any risk and was well aware of the fact, his resolution did him credit.

We clattered over the ruined wall, passed round the square monastery tower which is the chief feature of the Mother of Camels (such is the meaning of the Arabic name), and rode into an open place between empty streets, and there was no one to fear and no sign of life save that offered by two small black tents, the inhabitants of which greeted us with enthusiasm, and proceeded to sell us milk and eggs in the most amicable fashion. The Arabs who live at the foot of Haurān mountains are called the Jebeliyyeh, the Arabs of the Hills, and they are of no consideration, being but servants and shepherds to the Druzes. In the winter they herd the flocks that are sent down into the plain, and in the summer they are allowed to occupy the uncultivated slopes with their own cattle.

I spent the hour of daylight that remained in examining the wonderful Nabataean necropolis outside the walls. Monsieur Dussaud began the work on it five years ago; Mr. Butler and Dr. Littmann, whose visit immediately preceded mine, will be found to have continued it when their next volumes are given to the world. Having seen what tombs they had uncovered and noted several mounds that must conceal others, I sent away my companions and wandered in the dusk through the ruined streets of the town, into great rooms and up broken stairs, till Gablān came and called me in, saying that if a man saw something in a fur coat exploring those uncanny places after dark, he might easily take the apparition for a ghoul and shoot at it. Moreover, he wished to ask me whether he might not return to Tneib. One of the Arabs would guide us next day to the first Druze village, and Gablān would as soon come no nearer to the Mountain. I agreed readily, indeed it was a relief not to have his safety on my conscience. He received three napoleons for his trouble and a warm letter of thanks to deliver to Fellah ul 'Isa, and we parted with many assurances that if God willed we would travel together again.

The stony foot of the Jebel Haurān is strewn with villages deserted since the Mohammedan invasion in the seventh century. I visited two that lay not far from my path, Shabha and Shabhīyyeh, and found them to be both of the same character as Umm ej Jemāl From afar they look like well-built towns with square towers rising above streets of three-storied houses. Where the walls have fallen they lie as they fell, and no hand has troubled to clear away the ruins. Monsieur de Vogüé was the first to describe the architecture of the Haurān; his splendid volumes are still the principal source of information. The dwelling-houses are built round a court in which there is usually an outer stair leading to the upper story. There is no wood used in their construction, even the doors are of solid stone, turning on stone hinges, and the windows of stone slabs pierced with open-work patterns. Sometimes there are traces of a colonnaded portico, or the walls are broken by a double window, the arches of which are supported by a small column and a rough plain capital; frequently the lintels of the doors are adorned with a cross or a Christian monogram, but otherwise there is little decoration. The chambers are roofed with stone slabs resting on the back of transverse arches. So far as can be said with any certainty, Nabataean inscriptions and tombs are the oldest monuments that have been discovered in the district; they are followed by many important remains of pagan Rome, but the really flourishing period seems to have been the Christian.

After the Mohammadan invasion, which put an end to the prosperity of the Haurān uplands, few of the villages were re-inhabited, and when the Druzes came about a hundred and fifty years ago, they found no settled population. They made the Mountain their own, rebuilt and thereby destroyed the ancient towns, and extended their lordship over the plains to the south, though they have not established themselves in the villages of that debatable land which remains a happy hunting ground for the archaeologist. The American expedition will make good use of the immense amount of material that exists there, and knowing that the work had been done by better hands than mine, I rolled up the measuring tape and folded the foot-rule. But I could not so far overcome a natural instinct as to cease from copying inscriptions, and the one or two (they were extremely few) that had escaped Dr. Littmann's vigilant eye and come by chance to me were made over to him when we met in Damascus.

To our new guide, Fendi, fell the congenial task of posting me up in the gossip of the Mountain. Death had been busy among the great family of the Turshān during the past five years. Fāiz el Atrāsh, Sheikh of Kreyeh, was gone, poisoned said some, and a week or two before my arrival the most renowned of all the leaders of the Druzes, Shibly Beg el Atrāsh, had died of a mysterious and lingering illness – poison again, it was whispered. There was this war and that on hand, a terrible raid of the Arabs of the Wādy Sīrhan to be avenged, and a score with the Sukhūr to be settled, but on the whole there was prosperity, and as much peace as a Druze would wish to enjoy. The conversation was interrupted by a little shooting at rabbits lying asleep in the sun, not a gentlemanly sport perhaps, but one that helped to fill and to diversify the pot. After a time I left the mules and Fendi to go their own way, and taking Mikhāil with me, made a long circuit to visit the ruined towns. We were just finishing lunch under a broken wall, well separated from the rest of the party, when we saw two horsemen approaching us across the plain. We swept up the remains of the lunch and mounted hastily, feeling that any greeting they might accord us was better met in the saddle. They stopped in front of us and gave us the salute, following it with an abrupt question as to where we were going. I answered: 'To Salkhād, to Nasīb el Atrash,' and they let us pass without further remark. They were not Druzes, for they did not wear the Druze turban, but Christians from Kreyeh, where there is a large Christian community, riding down to Umm ej Jemāl to visit the winter quarters of their flocks, so said Fendi, whom they had passed a mile ahead. Several hours before we reached the present limits of cultivation, we saw the signs of ancient agriculture in the shape of long parallel lines of stones heaped aside from earth that had once been fruitful. They looked like the ridge and furrow of a gigantic meadow, and like the ridge and furrow they are almost indelible, the mark of labour that must have ceased with the Arab invasion. At the foot of the first spur of the hills, Tell esh Shīh (it is called after the grey-white Shīh plant which is the best pasturage for sheep), we left the unharvested desert and entered the region of ploughed fields – we left, too, the long clean levels of the open wilderness and were caught fetlock deep in the mud of a Syrian road. It led us up the hill to Umm er Rummān, the Mother of Pomegranates, on the edge of the lowest plateau of the Jebel Druze, as bleak a little muddy spot as you could hope to see. I stopped at the entrance of the village, and asked a group of Druzes where I should find a camping ground, and they directed me to an extremely dirty place below the cemetery, saying there was no other where I should not spoil the crops or the grass, though the crops, Heaven save the mark! were as yet below ground, and the grass consisted of a few brown spears half covered with melting snow. I could not entertain the idea of pitching tents so near the graveyard, and demanded to be directed to the house of Muhammad el Atrāsh, Sheikh of Umm er Rummān. This prince of the Turshān was seated upon his roof, engaged in directing certain agricultural operations that were being carried forward in the slough below. Long years had made him shapeless of figure and the effect was enhanced by the innumerable garments in which the winter cold had forced him to wrap his fat old body. I came as near as the mud would allow, and shouted:

'Peace be upon you, oh Sheikh!'

'And upon you peace!' he bawled in answer.

'Where in your village is there a dry spot for a camp?'

The sheikh conferred at the top of his voice with his henchmen in the mud, and finally replied that he did not know, by God! While I was wondering where to turn, a Druze stepped forward and announced that he could show me a place outside the town, and the sheikh, much relieved by the shifting of responsibility, gave me a loud injunction to go in peace, and resumed his occupations.

My guide was a young man with the clear-cut features and the sharp intelligent expression of his race. He was endowed, too, like all his kin, with a lively curiosity, and as he hopped from side to side of the road to avoid the pools of mud and slush, he had from me all my story, whence I came and whither I was going, who were my friends in the Jebel Druze and what my father's name – very different this from the custom of the Arabs, with whom it is an essential point of good breeding never to demand more than the stranger sees fit to impart. In At Tabari's history there is a fine tale of a man who sought refuge with an Arab sheikh. He stayed on, and the sheikh died, and his son who ruled in his stead advanced in years, and at length the grandson of the original host came to his father and said: 'Who is the man who dwells with us?' And the father answered: 'My son, in my father's time he came, and my father grew old and died, and he stayed on under my protection, and I too have grown old; but in all these years we have never asked him why he sought us nor what is his name. Neither do thou ask.' Yet I rejoiced to find myself once more among the trenchant wits and the searching kohl-blackened eyes of the Mountain, where every question calls for a quick retort or a brisk parry, and when my interlocutor grew too inquisitive I had only to answer:

'Listen, oh you! I am not "thou", but "Your Excellency",' and he laughed and understood and took the rebuke to heart.

There are many inscriptions in Umm er Rummān, a few Nabataean and the rest Cufic, proving that the town on the shelf of the hills was an early settlement and that it was one of those the Arabs re-occupied for a time after the invasion. A delighted crowd of little boys followed me from house to house, tumbling over one another in their eagerness to point out a written stone built into a wall or laid in the flooring about the hearth. In one house a woman caught me by the arm and implored me to heal her husband. The man was lying in a dark corner of the windowless room, with his face wrapped in filthy bandages, and when these had been removed a horrible wound was revealed, the track of a bullet that had passed through the cheek and shattered the jaw, I could do nothing but give him an antiseptic, and adjure the woman to wash the wound and keep the wrappings clean, and above all not to let him drink the medicine, though I felt it would make small odds which way he used it, Death had him so surely by the heel. This was the first of the long roil of sufferers that must pass before the eyes and catch despairingly at the sympathies of every traveller in wild places. Men and women afflicted with ulcers and terrible sores, with fevers and rheumatisms, children crippled from their birth, the blind and the old, there are none who do not hope that the unmeasured wisdom of the West may find them a remedy. You stand aghast at the depths of human misery and at your own helplessness.

The path of archaeology led me at last to the sheikh's door, and I went in to pay him an official visit. He was most hospitably inclined now that the business of the day was over: we sat together in the mak'ad, the audience room, a dark and dirty sort of outhouse, with an iron stove in the centre of it, and discussed the Japanese War and desert ghazus and other topics of the day, while Selmān, the sheikh's son, a charming boy of sixteen, made us coffee. Muhammad is brother-in-law to Shibly and to Yahya Beg el Atrāsh, who had been my first host five years before when I had escaped to his village of 'Areh from the Turkish Mudir at Bosrā, and Selmān is the only son of his father's old age and the only descendant of the famous 'Areh house of the Turshān, for Shibly died and Yahya lives childless. The boy walked back with me to my camp, stepping lightly through the mud, a gay and eager figure touched with the air of distinction that befits one who comes of a noble stock. He had had no schooling, though there was a big Druze maktab at Kreyeh, fifteen miles away, kept by a Christian of some learning.

'My father holds me so precious,' he explained, 'that he will not let me leave his side.'

'Oh Selmān,' I began.

'Oh God!' he returned, using the ejaculation customary to one addressed by name.

'The minds of the Druzes are like fine steel, but what is steel until it is beaten into a sword blade?'

Selmān answered: 'My uncle Shibly could neither read nor write.'

I said: 'The times are changed. The house of the Turshān will need trained wits if it would lead the Mountain as it did before.'

But that headship is a thing of the past. Shibly is dead and Yahya childless, Muhammad is old and Selmān undeveloped, Fāiz has left four sons but they are of no repute, Nasīb is cunning but very ignorant, there is Mustafa at Imtain, who passes for a worthy man of little intelligence, and Hamūd at Sweida, who is distinguished mainly for his wealth. The ablest man among the Druzes is without doubt Abu Tellāl of Shahba, and the most enlightened Sheikh Muhammad en Nassār.

The night was bitterly cold. My thermometer had been broken, so that the exact temperature could not be registered, but every morning until we reached Damascus the water in the cup by my bedside was a solid piece of ice, and one night a little tumbling stream outside the camp was frozen hard and silent. The animals and the muleteers were usually housed in a khan while the frost lasted. Muhammad the Druze, who had returned to his original name and faith, disappeared the moment camp was pitched, and spent the night enjoying the hospitality of his relations. 'For,' said Mikhāil sarcastically, 'every man who can give him a meal he reckons to be the son of his uncle.'

I was obliged to delay my start next morning in order to profit by the sheikh's invitation to breakfast at a very elastic nine o'clock – two hours after sunrise was what was said, and who knows exactly when it may suit that luminary to appear? It was a pleasant party. We discussed the war in Yemen in all its bearings – theoretically, for I was the only person who had any news, and mine was derived from a *Weekly Times* a month old and then Muhammad questioned me as to why Europeans looked for inscriptions.

'But I think I know,' he added. 'It is that they may restore the land to the lords of it.'

I assured him that the latest descendants of the former owners of the Haurān had been dead a thousand years, and he listened politely and changed the subject with the baffled air of one who cannot get a true answer.

The young man who had shown us our camping ground rode with us to Salkhad, saying he had business there and might as well have company by the way. His name was Sāleh ; he was of a clerkly family, a reader and a scribe. I was so tactless as to ask him whether he were 'ākil, initiated – the Druzes are divided into the initiated and the uninitiated. but the line of demarcation does not follow that of social pre-eminence, since most of the Turshān are uninitiated. He gave me a sharp look, and replied:

'What do you think?' and I saw my error and dropped the subject.

But Sāleh was not one to let slip any opportunity of gaining information. He questioned me acutely on our customs, down to the laws of marriage and divorce. He was vastly entertained at the English rule that the father should pay a man for marrying his daughter (so he interpreted the habit of giving her a marriage portion), and we laughed together over the absurdity of the arrangement. He was anxious to know Western views as to the creation of the world and the origin of matter, and I obliged him with certain heterodox opinions, on which he seized with far greater lucidity than that with which they were offered. We passed an agreeable morning, in spite of the mud and boulders of the road. At the edge of the snow wreaths a little purple crocus had made haste to bloom, and a starry white garlic – the Mountain is very rich in Spring flowers. The views to the south over the great plain we had crossed were enchanting; to the north the hills rose in unbroken slopes of snow, Kuleib, the Little Heart, looking quite Alpine with its frosty summit half veiled in mist. Two hours after noon we reached Salkhad, the first goal of our journey.

4

Salcah, the city of King Og in Bashan, must have been a fortified place from the beginning of history. The modern village clusters round the base of a small volcano, on the top of which, built in the very crater, is the ruined fortress. This fortress and its predecessors in the crater formed the outpost of the Haurān Mountains against the desert, the outpost of the earliest civilisation against the earliest marauders. The ground drops suddenly to the south and east, and, broken only by one or two volcanic mounds in the immediate neighbourhood, settles itself down into the long levels that reach Euphrates stream; straight as an arrow from a bow the Roman road runs out from Salkhad into the desert in a line that no modern traveller has followed beyond the first two or three stages. The caravan track to Nejd begins here and passes by Kāf and Ethreh along the Wādi Sirhan to Jōf and Hāil, a perilous way, though the Blunts pursued it successfully and Euting after them. Euting's description of it, done with all the learning and the minute observation of the German, is the best we have. Due south of Salkhad there is an interesting ruined fort, Kal'at el Azrak, in an oasis where there are thickets full of wild boar: Dussaud visited it and has given an excellent account of his journey. No doubt there is more to be found still; the desert knows many a story that has not yet been told, and at Salkhad it is difficult to keep your feet from turning south, so invitingly mysterious are those great plains.

I went at once to the house of Nasīb el Atrāsh and presented Fellāh ul 'Isa's letter. Nasīb is a man of twenty-seven, though he looks ten years older, short in stature and sleek, with shrewd features of a type essentially Druze and an expression that is more cunning than pleasant. He received me in his mak'ad, where he was sitting with his brother Jada'llah, a tall young man with a handsome but rather stupid face, who greeted me with 'Bonjour,' and then relapsed into silence, having come to the end of all the French he knew. Just as he had borrowed one phrase from a European tongue, so he had borrowed one article of dress from European wardrobes: a high stick-up collar was what he had selected, and it went strangely with his Arab clothes. There were a few Druzes drinking coffee in the mak'ad, and one other whom I instantly diagnosed as an alien. He turned out to be the Mudīr el Māl of the Turkish government – I do not know what his exact functions are, but his title implies him to be an agent of the Treasury. Salkhad is one of three villages in Jebel Druze (the others being Sweida and 'Areh) where the Sultan has a Kāimakām and a telegraph station. Yūsef Effendi, Kāimakām, and Milhēm Iliān, Mudīr el Māl, were considerably surprised when I turned up from the desert without warning or permission; they despatched three telegrams daily to the Vāli of Damascus, recounting all that I did and said, and though I was on the best of terms with both of them, finding indeed Milhēm to be by far the most intelligent and agreeable man in the village, I fear I caused them much perturbation of mind. And here let me say that my experience of Turkish officials leads me to count them among the most polite and obliging of men. If you come to them with the proper certificates there is nothing they will not do to help you; when they stop you it is because they are obliged to obey orders from higher authorities; and even when you set aside, as from time to time you must, refusals that are always couched in language conciliatory to a fault, they conceal their just annoyance and bear you no ill will for the trouble you have caused them. The government agents at Salkhad occupy an uneasy position. It is true that there has been peace in the Mountain for the past five years, but the Druzes are a slippery race and one quick to take offence. Milhēm understood them well, and his appointment to the new post of Salkhad is a proof of the Vāli's genuine desire to avoid trouble in the future. He had been at Sweida for many years before he came to Salkhad; he was a Christian, and therefore not divided from the Druzes by the unbridged gulf of hatred that lies between them and Islam, and he was fully aware that Turkish rule in the Jebel Haurān depends on how little demand is made on a people nominally subject and practically independent. Yūsef Effendi was not far behind him in the strength of his conviction on this head, and he had the best of reasons for realising how shadowy his authority was. There are not more than two hundred Turkish soldiers in all the Mountain; the rest of the Ottoman forces are Druze zaptiehs, well pleased to wear a government uniform and draw government pay, on the rare occasions when it reaches them, though they can hardly be considered a trustworthy guard if serious differences arise between their own people and the Sultan. To all outward appearance Nasīb and his brother were linked by the closest bonds of friendship with the Kāimakām; they were for ever sitting in his mak'ad and drinking his coffee, but once when we happened to be alone together, Yūsef Effendi said pathetically in his stilted Turkish Arabic: 'I never know what they are doing: they look on me as an enemy. And if they wish to disobey orders from

Damascus, they cut the telegraph wire and go their own way. What power have I to prevent them?'

Nevertheless there are signs that the turbulent people of the Mountain have turned their minds to other matters than war with the Osmanli, and among the chief of these are the steam mills that grind the corn of Salkhad and a few villages besides. A man who owns a steam mill is pledged to maintain the existing order. He has built it at considerable expense, he does not wish to see it wrecked by an invading Turkish army and his capital wasted; on the contrary, he hopes to make money from it, and his restless energies find a new and profitable outlet in that direction. My impression is that peace rests on a much firmer basis than it did five years ago, and that the Ottoman government has not been slow to learn the lessons of the last war – if only the Vāli of Damascus could have known how favourable an opinion his recent measures would force on the mind of the intriguing Englishwoman, he might have spared his telegraph clerks several hours' work.

There could scarcely have been a better example of the freedom with which the Druzes control their own affairs than was offered by an incident that took place on the very evening of my arrival. It has already been intimated on the authority of Fendi that the relations between the Mountain and the Desert were fraught with the usual possibilities of martial incident, and we had not spent an afternoon in Salkhad without discovering that the great raid that had occurred some months previously was the topic that chiefly interested Nasīb and his brother. Not that they spoke of it in their conversations with me, but they listened eagerly when we told of the raid on the Hassaniyeh and the part the Sukhūr had played in it, and they drew from us all we knew or conjectured as to the present camping grounds of the latter tribe, how far the raiders had come, and in which direction retreated. The muleteers overheard men whispering at the street corners, and their whispers were of warlike preparations; the groups round Mikhāil's fire, ever a centre of social activity, spoke of injuries that could not be allowed to pass unnoticed, and one of the many sons of Muhammad's uncle had provided that famished Beyrouti with a lunch flavoured with dark hints of a league between the Wādi Sirhan and the Beni Sakhr which must be nipped in the bud ere it had assumed alarming proportions. The wave of the ghazu can hardly reach as far as Salkhad itself, but the harm is done long before it touches that point, especially in the winter when every four-footed creature, except the mare necessary for riding, is far away in the southern plain.

My camp was pitched in a field outside the town at the eastern foot of the castle hill. The slopes to the north were deep in snow up to the ruined walls of the fortress, and even where we lay there were a few detached snowdrifts glittering under the full moon. I had just finished dinner, and was debating whether it were too cold to write my diary, when a sound of savage singing broke upon the night, and from the topmost walls of the castle a great flame leapt up into the sky. It was a beacon kindled to tell the news of the coming raid to the many Druze villages scattered over the plain below, and the song was a call to arms. There was a Druze zaptieh sitting by my camp fire; he jumped up and gazed first at me and then at the red blaze above us. I said:

'Is there permission to my going up?'

He answered: 'There is no refusal. Honour us.'

We climbed together over the half frozen mud, and by the snowy northern side of the volcano, edged our way in the darkness round the castle walls where the lava ashes gave beneath our feet, and came out into the full moonlight upon the wildest scene that eyes could see. A crowd of Druzes, young men and boys, stood at the edge of the moat on a narrow shoulder of the hill. They were all armed with swords and knives and they were shouting phrase by phrase a terrible song. Each line of it was repeated twenty times or more until it seemed to the listener that it had been bitten, as an acid bites the brass, onto the intimate recesses of the mind.

> *Upon them, upon them! oh Lord our God! that the foe may fall in swathes before our swords!*
> *Upon them, upon them! that our spears may drink at their hearts!*
> *Let the babe leave his mother's breast!*
> *Let the young man arise and be gone!*
> *Upon them, upon them! oh Lord our God! that our swords may drink at their hearts. . . .*

So they sang, and it was as though the fury of their anger would never end, as though the castle walls would never cease from echoing their interminable rage and the night never again know silence, when suddenly the chant stopped and the singers drew apart and formed themselves into a circle, every man holding his neighbours by the hand. Into the circle stepped three young Druzes with bare swords, and strode round the ring of eager boys that enclosed them. Before each in turn they stopped and shook their swords and cried:

'Are you a good man? Are you a true man?'

And each one answered with a shout:

'Ha! ha!'

The moonlight fell on the dark faces and glittered on the quivering blades, the thrill of martial ardour passed from hand to clasped hand, and earth cried to heaven: War! red war!

And then one of the three saw me standing in the circle, and strode up and raised his sword above his head, as though nation saluted nation.

'Lady!' he said, 'the English and the Druze are one.'

I said: 'Thank God! we, too, are a fighting race.'

Indeed, at that moment there seemed no finer thing than to go out and kill your enemy.

And when this swearing in of warriors was over, we ran down the hill under the moon, still holding hands, and I, seeing that some were only children not yet full grown, said to the companion whose hand chance had put in mine:

'Do all these go out with you?'

He answered: 'By God! not all. The ungrown boys must stay at home and pray to God that their day may soon come.'

When they reached the entrance of the town, the Druzes leapt on to a flat house roof, and took up their devilish song. The fire had burnt out on the castle walls, the night struck suddenly cold, and I began to doubt whether if Milhēm and the Vāli of Damascus could see me taking part in a demonstration against the Sukhūr they would believe in the innocence of my journey; so I turned away into the shadow and ran down to my tents and became a European again, bent on peaceful pursuits and unacquainted with the naked primitive passions of mankind.

We had certain inquiries to make concerning our journey, and stores to lay in before we set out for the eastern side of the Mountain, where there are no big villages, and therefore we spent two days at Salkhad. The great difficulty of the commissariat is barley for the animals. There had been enough for our needs at Umm er Rammān, but there was none at Salkhad; it is always to be got at Sweida, which is the chief post of the Turkish government, but that was far away across the hills, and we decided to send down to Imtein, the path thither being bare of snow. It is worth recording that in the winter, when all the flocks are several hours away in the plain, it is impossible to buy a sheep in the Mountain, and the traveller has to make shift with such scraggy chickens as he may find. The want of foresight which had left our larder so ill-furnished affected Mikhāil considerably, for he prided himself on the roasting of a leg of mutton, and he asked me how it was that all the books I had with me had not hinted at the absence of the animal that could supply that delicacy. I answered that the writers of these works seemed to have been more concerned with Roman remains than with such weighty matters as roasts and stews, whereat he said firmly:

'When your Excellency writes a book, you will not say: "Here there is a beautiful church and a great castle." The gentry can see that for themselves. But you shall say: "In this village there are no hens." Then they will know from the beginning what sort of country it is.'

The first day of my visit I spent with Nasīb, watching him give orders for the grinding of the corn needed for the coming military expedition (to which we sedulously avoided my allusion), photographing him and the notables of his village, and lunching with him in his mak'ad on gritty brown-paper-like bread and dibs, a kind of treacle made from boiled grape juice, and a particularly nasty sort of soup of sour milk with scraps of fat mixed in it – *kirk* the Druzes call it and hold it in an unwarrantable esteem. In the afternoon Nasīb was riding some ten miles to the south, to settle a dispute that had arisen between two of his villages, and he invited me to accompany him; but I thought that there were probably other matters on hand, in which it might be awkward if a stranger were to assist, and I compromised by agreeing to go with him for an hour and turn aside to visit a shrine on top of a tell, the Weli of El Khudr, who is no other than our St. George. Nasīb rode out in style with twenty armed men by his side, himself arrayed in a long mantle of dark blue cloth embroidered in black, with a pale blue handkerchief tucked into the folds of the white turban that encircled his tarbūsh. The cavalcade looked very gallant, each man wrapped in a cloak and carrying his rifle across his knees. These rifles were handed to me one by one that I might read the lettering on them. They were of many different dates and origins, some antiquated pieces stolen from Turkish soldiers, the most French and fairly modern, while a few came from Egypt and were marked with V.R. and the broad arrow. Nasīb rode with me for a time and catechised me on my social status, whether I would ride at home with the King of England, and what was the extent of my father's wealth. His curiosity was not entirely without a motive; the Druzes are always hoping to find some very rich European whose sympathies they could engage, and who would finance and arm them if another war were to break out with the Sultan; but so contemptuous was he of the modest competence which my replies revealed, that I was roused to ask subsequently, by methods more tactful than those of Nasīb, what was wealth in the Mountain. The answer was that the richest of the Turshān, Hamūd of Sweida, had an income of about 5000 napoleons. Nasīb himself was not so well off. He had some 1000 napoleons yearly. Probably it comes to him mainly in kind; all revenues are derived from land, and vary considerably with the fortunes of the agricultural year. The figures given me were, I should think, liberal, and depended on a reckoning according with the best harvest rather than with the mean.

Presently Nasīb fell behind and engaged in a whispered conversation with an old man who was his chief adviser, while the others crowded round me and told me tales of the desert and of great ruins to the south, which they were prepared to show me if I would stay with them. At the foot of the tell we met a group of horsemen waiting to impart to Nasīb some important news about the Arabs. Mikhāil and I stood aside, having seen our host look doubtfully at us out of the corners of his eyes. That the tidings were not good was all we heard, and no one could have learnt even that from Nasīb's crafty unmoved face and eyes concealed beneath the lids as if he wished to make sure that they should not reveal a single flash of his thoughts. Here we left him, to his evident relief, and rode up the tell. Now there is never a prominent hill in the Jebel Druze but it bears a sanctuary on its summit, and the building is always one of those early monuments of the land that date back to the times before Druze or Turk came into it. What is their history? Were they erected to Nabataean gods of rock and hill, to Drusāra and Allāt and the pantheon of the Semitic inscriptions whom the desert worshipped with sacrifice at the Ka'abah and on many a solitary mound? If this be so the old divinities still bear sway under changed names, still smell the blood of goats and sheep sprinkled on the black doorposts of their dwellings, still hear the prayers of pilgrims carrying green boughs and swathes of flowers. As at the Well of El Khudr, there is always in the interior of the sanctuary an erection like a sarcophagus, covered with shreds of coloured rags, and when you lift the rags and peer beneath you find some queer block of tufa, worn smooth with libations and own brother to the Black Stone at Mecca. Near at hand there is a stone basin for water – the water was iced over that day, and the snow had drifted in through the stone doors and was melting through the roof, so that it lay in muddy pools on the floor.

The next day was exceedingly cold, with a leaden sky and a bitter wind, the forerunner of snow. Milhēm Iliān came down to invite me to lodge with him, but I refused, fearing that I should feel the temperature of my tent too icy after his heated room. He stayed some time and I took the opportunity of discussing with him my plan of riding out into the Safa, the volcanic waste east of the Jebel Druze. He was not at all encouraging, indeed he thought the project impossible under existing conditions, for it seemed that the Ghiāth, the tribe that inhabits the Safa, were up in arms against the Government. They had waylaid and robbed the desert post that goes between Damascus and Baghdad, and were expecting retribution at the hands of the Vāli. If therefore a small escort of zaptiehs were to be sent in with me they would assuredly be cut to pieces. Milhēm agreed, however, that it might be possible to go in alone with the Druzes though anything short of an army of soldiers would be useless, and he promised to give me a letter to Muhammad en Nassār, Sheikh of Sāleh, whom he described as a good friend of his and a man of influence and judgment. The Ghiāth are in the same position with regard to the Druzes as are the Jebeliyyeh; they cannot afford not to be on good terms with the Mountain, since they are dependent on the high pasturages during the summer.

Towards sunset I returned Milhēm's visit. His room was full of people, including Nasīb newly returned from his expedition. They made me tell them of my recent experiences in the desert, and I found that all my friends were counted as foes by the Druzes and that they have no allies save the Ghiāth and the Jebeliyyeh – the Sherarāt, the Da'ja, the Beni Hassan, there was a score of blood against them all.

In the desert the word gōm, foe, is second to none save only that of *daif*, guest, but in the Mountain it comes easily first. I said:

'Oh Nasīb, the Druzes are like those of whom Kureyt ibn Uneif sang when he said: 'A people who when evil bares its teeth against them, fly out to meet it in companies or alone.'

The sheikh's subtle countenance relaxed for a second, but the talk was drifting too near dangerous subjects, and he rose shortly afterwards and took his leave. His place was filled by newcomers (Milhēm's coffee-pots must be kept boiling from dawn till late at night), and presently one entered whom they all rose to salute. He was a Kurdish Agha, a fine old man with a white moustache and a clean-shaven chin, who comes down from Damascus from time to time on some business of his own. Milhēm is a native of Damascus, and had much to ask and hear; the talk left desert topics and swung round to town dwellers and their ways and views.

'Look you, your Excellencies,' said a man who was making coffee over the brazier, 'there is no religion in the towns as there is in country places.'

'Yes,' pursued Milhēm –

'May God make it Yes upon you!' ejaculated the Kurd.

'May God requite you, oh Agha! You may find men in the Great Mosque at Damascus at the Friday prayers and a few perhaps at Jerusalem, but in Beyrout and in Smyrna the mosques are empty and the churches are empty. There is no religion any more.'

'My friends,' said the Agha, 'I will tell you the reason. In the country men are poor and they want much. Of whom should they ask it but of God? There is none other that is compassionate to the poor save He alone. But in the towns they are rich, they have got all they desire, and why should they pray to God if they want nothing? The lady laughs – is it not so among her own people?'

I confessed that there was very little difference in this matter between Europe and Asia and presently left the party to pursue their coffee drinking and their conversation without me.

Late at night someone came knocking at my tent and a woman's voice cried to me:

'Lady, lady! a mother's heart (are not the English merciful?) listen to the sorrow of a mother's heart and take this letter to my son!'

I asked the unseen suppliant where her son was to be found.

'In Tripoli, in Tripoli of the West. He is a soldier and an exile, who came not back with the others after the war. Take this letter, and send it by a sure hand from Damascus, for there is no certainty in the posts of Salkhad.'

I unfastened the tent and took the letter, she crying the while:

'The wife of Nasīb told me that you were generous. A mother's heart, you understand, a mother's heart that mourns!'

So she departed weeping, and I sent the mysterious letter by the English post from Beyrout, but whether it ever reached Tripoli of the West and the Druze exile we shall not know.

The Kāimakām came out to see us off next morning and provided us with a Druze zaptieh to show us the way to Sāleh. The wind was searchingly cold, and the snow was reported to lie very deep on the hills, for which reason we took the lower road by Ormān, a village memorable as the scene of the outbreak of the last war. Milhēm had entrusted my guide, Yūsef, with the mail that had just come in to Salkhad; it consisted of one letter only, and that was for a Christian, an inhabitant of Ormān, whom we met outside the village. It was from Massachusetts, from one of his three sons who had emigrated to America and were all doing well, praise be to God! They had sent him thirty liras between them the year before: he bubbled over with joyful pride as we handed him the letter containing fresh news of them. At Ormān the road turned upwards – I continue to call it a road for want of a name bad enough for it. It is part of the Druze system of defence that there shall be no track in the Mountain wide enough for two to go abreast or smooth enough to admit of any pace beyond a stumbling walk, and it is the part that is the most successfully carried out. We were soon in snow, half melted, half frozen, concealing the holes in the path but not firm enough to prevent the animals from breaking through into them. Occasionally there were deep drifts on which the mules embarked with the utmost confidence only to fall midway and scatter their packs, while the horses plunged and reared till they almost unseated us. Mikhāil, who was no rider, bit the slush several times. The makers of the Palestine Exploration map have allowed their fancy to play freely over the eastern slopes of the Jebel Druze. Hills have hopped along for miles, and villages have crossed ravines and settled themselves on the opposite banks, as, for instance, Abu Zreik, which stands on the left bank of the Wādi Rājil, though the map places it on the right. At the time it all seemed to fit in with the general malevolence of that day's journey, and our misery culminated when we entered on an interminable snow field swept by a blizzard of cutting sleet. At the dim end of it, quite unapproachably far away, we could just see through the sleet the slopes on which Sāleh stands, but as we plodded on mile after mile (it was useless to attempt to ride on our stumbling animals and far too cold besides) we gradually came nearer, and having travelled seven hours to accomplish a four hours' march, we splashed and waded late in the afternoon though the mounds of slush and pools of water that did duty as streets. There was not a dry place in all the village, and the snow was falling heavily; clearly there was nothing to be done but to beat at the door of Muhammad en Nassār, who has an honoured reputation for hospitality, and I made the best of my way up steps sheeted with ice to his mak'ad.

If Providence owed us any compensation for the discomforts of the day, it paid us, or at least it paid me, full measure and running over, by the enchanting evening that I spent in the sheikh's house. Muhammad en Nassār is a man full of years and wisdom who has lived to see a large family of sons and nephews grow up round him, and to train their quick wits by his own courteous and gracious example. All the Druzes are essentially gentlefolk; but the house of the sheikhs of Sāleh could not be outdone in good breeding, natural and acquired, by the noblest of the aristocratic races, Persian or Rajputs, or any others distinguished beyond their fellows. Milhēm's letter was quite unnecessary to ensure me a welcome; it was enough that I was cold and hungry and an Englishwoman. The fire in the iron stove was kindled, my wet outer garments taken from me, cushions and carpets spread on the divans under the sheikh's directions, and all the band of his male relations, direct and collateral, dropped in to enliven the evening. We began well. I knew that Oppenheim had taken his escort from Sāleh when he went into the Safa, and I happened to have his book with me – how often had I regretted that a wise instinct had not directed my choice towards Dussaud's two admirable volumes, rather than to Oppenheim's ponderous work, packed with information that was of little use on the present journey! The great merit of the book lies in the illustrations, and fortunately there was among them a portrait of Muhammad en Nassār with his two youngest children. Having abstracted Kiepert's maps, I was so generous as to present the tome to one of the family who had accompanied the learned German upon his expedition. It has remained at Sāleh to be a joy and a glory to the sheikhs, who will look at the pictures and make no attempt to grapple with the text, and the hole in my bookshelves is well filled by the memory of their pleasure.

We talked without ceasing during the whole evening, with a brief interval when an excellent dinner was brought in. The old sheikh, Yūsef the zaptieh, and I partook of it together, and the eldest of the nephews and cousins finished up the ample remains. The topic that interested them most at Sāleh was the Japanese War – indeed it was in that direction that conversation invariably turned in the Mountain, the reason being that the Druzes believe the Japanese to belong to their own race. The line of argument which has led them to this astonishing conclusion is simple. The secret doctrines of their faith hold out hopes that some day an army of Druzes will burst out of the furthest limits of Asia and conquer the world. The Japanese had shown indomitable courage, the Druzes also are brave; the Japanese had been victorious, the Druzes of prophecy will be unconquerable: therefore the two are one and the same. The sympathy of everyone, whether in Syria or in Asia Minor, is on the side of the Japanese, with the single exception of the members of the Orthodox Church, who look on Russia as their protector. It seems natural that the Ottoman government should rejoice to witness the discomfiture of their secular foes, but it is more difficult to account for the pleasure of Arab, Druze (apart from the secret hope of the Druzes above mentioned), and Kurd, between whom and the Turk there is no love lost. These races are not wont to be gratified by the overthrow of the Sultan's enemies, a class to which they themselves generally belong. At bottom there is no doubt a certain Schadenfreude, and the natural impulse to favour the little man against the big bully, and behind all there is that curious link which is so difficult to classify except by the name of a continent, and the war appeals to the Asiatic because it is against the European. However eagerly you may protest that the Russians cannot be considered as a type of European civilisation, however profoundly you may be convinced that the Japanese show as few common characteristics with Turk or Druze as they show with South Sea Islander or

Esquimaux, East calls to East, and the voice wakes echoes from the China Seas to the Mediterranean.

We talked also of the Turk. Muhammad had been one of the many sheikhs who were sent into exile after the Druze war; he had visited Constantinople, and his experiences embraced Asia Minor also, so that he was competent to hold an opinion on Turkish characteristics. In a blind fashion, the fashion in which the Turk conducts most of his affairs, the wholesale carrying off of the Druze sheikhs and their enforced sojourn for two or three years in distant cities of the Empire, has attained an end for which far-sighted statesmanship might have laboured in vain. Men who would otherwise never have travelled fifty miles from their own village have been taught perforce some knowledge of the world; they have returned to exercise a semi-independence almost as they did before, but their minds have received, however reluctantly, the impression of the wide extent of the Sultan's dominions, the infinite number of his resources, and the comparative unimportance of Druze revolts in an empire which yet survives though it is familiar with every form of civil strife. Muhammad had been so completely convinced that there was a world beyond the limits of the Mountain that he had attempted to push two of his six sons out into it by putting them into a Government office in Damascus. He had failed because, even with his maxims in their ears, the boys were too headstrong. Some youthful neglect of duty, followed by a sharp rebuke from their superior, had sent them hurrying back to the village where they could be independent sheikhs, idle and respected. Muhammad took in a weekly sheet published in Damascus, and the whole family followed with the keenest interest such news of foreign politics, of English politics in particular, as escaped the censor's pencil. Important events sometimes eluded their notice – or that of the editor – for my hosts asked after Lord Salisbury and were deeply grieved to hear he had been dead some years. The other name they knew, besides Lord Cromer's, which is known always and everywhere, was that of Mr. Chamberlain, and thus there started in the mak'ad at Sāleh an animated debate on the fiscal question, lavishly illustrated on my part with examples drawn from the Turkish gumruk, the Custom House. It may be that my arguments were less exposed to contradiction than those which most free traders are in a position to use, for the whole of Sāleh rejected the doctrines of protection and retaliation (there was no halfway-house here) with unanimity.

There was only one point which was not settled with perfect satisfaction to all, and that was my journey to the Safa. I have a shrewd suspicion that Milhēm's letter, which had been handed to me sealed, so that I had not been able to read it, was of the nature of that given by Praetus to Bellerophon when he sent him to the King of Lycia, and that if Muhammad was not commanded to execute the bearer on arrival, he was strongly recommended to discourage her project. At any rate, he was of opinion that the expedition could not be accomplished unless I would take at least twenty Druzes as escort, which would have involved so much preparation and expense that I was obliged to abandon the idea.

At ten o'clock I was asked at what hour I wished to sleep, and, to the evident chagrin of those members of the company who had not been riding all day in the snow, I replied that the time had come. The sons and nephews took their departure, wadded quilts were brought in and piled into three beds, one on each of the three sides of the immense divan, the sheikh, Yūsef and I tucked ourselves up, and I knew no more till I woke in the sharp frost of the early dawn. I got up and went out into the fresh air. Sāleh was fast asleep in the snow; even the little stream that tumbled in and out of a Roman fountain in the middle of the village was sleeping under a thick coat of ice. In the clear cold silence I watched the eastern sky redden and fade and the sun send a long shaft of light over the snow field through which we had toiled the day before. I put up a short thanksgiving appropriate to fine weather, roused the muleteers and the mules from their common resting place under the dark vaults of the khan, ate the breakfast which Muhammad en Nassār provided, and took a prolonged and most grateful farewell of my host and his family. No better night's rest and no more agreeable company can have fallen to the lot of any wanderer by plain and hill than were accorded to me at Sāleh.

5

When I had come to Damascus five years before, my chief counsellor and friend – a friend whose death will be deplored by many a traveller in Syria – was Lütticke, head of the banking house of that name and honorary German consul. It was a chance remark of his that revealed to me the place that the town had and still has in Arab history. 'I am persuaded,' said he, 'that in and about Damascus you may see the finest Arab population that can be found anywhere. They are the descendants of the original invaders who came up on the first great wave of the conquest, and they have kept their stock almost pure.'

Above all other cities Damascus is the capital of the desert. The desert stretches up to its walls, the breath of it is blown in by every wind, the spirit of it comes through the eastern gates with every camel driver. In Damascus the sheikhs of the richer tribes have their town houses; you may meet Muhammad of the Haseneh or Bassān of the Beni Rashīd peacocking down the bazaars on a fine Friday, in embroidered cloaks and purple and silver kerchiefs fastened about their brows with camels' hair ropes bound with gold. They hold their heads high, these Lords of the Wilderness, striding through the holiday crowds, that part to give them passage, as if Damascus were their own town. And so it is, for it was the first capital of the Bedouin khalifs outside the

Hejāz, and it holds and remembers the greatest Arab traditions. It was almost the first of world-renowned cities to fall before the irresistible chivalry of the desert which Muhammad had called to arms and to which he had given purpose and a battle-cry, and it was the only one which remained as important under the rule of Islam as it had been under the empire of Rome. Mu'āwiyah made it his capital, and it continued to be the chief city of Islam until the fall of the house of Ummayah ninety years later. It was the last of Moslem capitals that ruled in accordance with desert traditions. Persian generals placed the Beni Abbās upon their throne in Mesopotamia, Persian and Turkish influences were dominant in Baghdad, and with them crept in the fatal habits of luxury which the desert had never known, nor the early khalifs who milked their own goats and divided the spoils of their victories among the Faithful. The very soil of Mesopotamia exhaled emanations fatal to virility. The ancient ghosts of Babylonian and Assyrian palace intrigue rose from their muddy graves, mighty in evil, to overthrow the soldier khalif, to strip him of his armour and to tie him hand and foot with silk and gold. Damascus had been innocent of them; Damascus, swept by the clean desert winds, had ruled the empire of the Prophet with some of the Spartan vigour of early days. She was not a parvenue like the capitals on the Tigris; she had seen kings and emperors within her walls, and learnt the difference between strength and weakness, and which path leads to dominion and which to slavery.

When I arrived I was greeted with the news that my journey in the Haurān had considerably agitated the mind of his Excellency Nāzim Pasha, Vāli of Syria; indeed it was currently reported that this much exercised and delicately placed gentleman had been vexed beyond reason by my sudden appearance at Salkhad and that he had retired to his bed when I had departed beyond the reach of Yūsef Effendi's eye, though some suggested that the real reason for his Excellency's sudden indisposition was a desire to avoid taking part in the memorial service to the Archduke Serge. Be that as it may, he sent me on the day of my arrival a polite message expressing his hope that he might have the pleasure of making my acquaintance.

I confess my principal feeling was one of penitence when I was ushered into the big new house that the Vāli has built for himself at the end of Salahiyyeh, the suburb of Damascus that stretches along the foot of the bare hills to the north of the town. I had a great wish to apologise, or at any rate to prove to him that I was not to be regarded as a designing enemy. These sentiments were enhanced by the kindness with which he received me, and the respect with which he inspires those who come to know him. He is a man of a nervous temperament, always on the alert against the difficulties with which his vilayet is not slow to provide him, conscientious, and I should fancy honest, painfully anxious to reconcile interests that are as easy to combine as oil with vinegar, the corner of his eye fixed assiduously on his royal master who will take good care that so distinguished a personality as Nāzim Pasha shall be retained at a considerable distance from the shores of the Bosphorus. The Vāli has been eight years in Damascus, the usual term of office being five, and he has evidently made up his mind that in Damascus he will remain, if no ill luck befall him, for he has built himself a large house and planned a fine garden, the laying out of which distracts his mind, let us hope, from pre-occupations that can seldom be pleasant. One of his safeguards is that he has been actively concerned with the construction of the Hejāz railway, in which the Sultan takes the deepest interest, and until it is completed or abandoned he is sufficiently useful to be kept at his post. The bazaar, that is public opinion, does not think that it will be abandoned, in spite of the opposition of the Sherīf of Mecca and all his clan, who will never be convinced of the justice of the Sultan's claim to the khalifate of Islam nor willing to bring him into closer touch with the religious capitals. The bazaar backs the Sultan against the Sherīf and all other adversaries, sacred or profane. The wheels of the Turk grind slowly and often stop, but in the end they grind small, especially when the grist is Arab tribes rendered peculiarly brittle by their private jealousies and suspicions and pretensions. Turkish policy is like that of which Ibn Kulthūm sang when he said:

> *When our mill is set down among a people they are as flour before our coming.*

> *Our meal cloth is spread eastwards of Nejd and the grain is the whole tribe of Kuda'a.*

> *Like guests you alighted at our door and we hastened our hospitality lest you should turn on us.*

> *We welcomed you and hastened the welcoming: yea, before the dawn, and our mills grind small.*

Nāzim Pasha, though he has been eight years in Syria, talks no Arabic. We in Europe, who speak of Turkey as though it were a homogeneous empire, might as well when we speak of England intend the word to include India, the Shan States, Hong Kong and Uganda. In the sense of a land inhabited mainly by Turks there is not such a country as Turkey. The parts of his dominions where the Turk is in a majority are few; generally his position is that of an alien governing, with a handful of soldiers and an empty purse, a mixed collection of subjects hostile to him and to each other. He is not acquainted with their language, it is absurd to expect of him much sympathy for aspirations political and religious which are generally made known to him amid a salvo of musketry, and if the bullets happen to be directed, as they often are, by one unruly and unreasonable section of the vilayet at another equally unreasonable and unruly, he is hardly likely to feel much regret at the loss of life that may result. He himself, when he is let alone, has a strong sense of the comfort of law and order. Observe the internal arrangements of a Turkish village, and you shall see that the Turkish peasant knows how to lay down rules of conduct and how to obey them. I believe that the best of our own native local officials in Egypt are Turks who have brought to bear under the new regime the good sense and the natural instinct for government for which they had not much scope under the old. It is in the upper grades that the hierarchy of the Ottoman Empire has proved so defective, and the upper grades are filled with Greeks, Armenians, Syrians, and personages of various nationalities generally esteemed in the East (and not without reason) untrustworthy. The fact that such men as these should inevitably rise to the top, points to the reason of the Turk's failure. He cannot govern on wide lines, though he can organise a village community; above all he cannot govern on foreign lines, and unfortunately he is brought more and more into contact with foreign nations. Even his own subjects have caught the infection of progress. The Greeks and Armenians have become merchants and bankers, the Syrians merchants and landowners; they find themselves hampered at every turn by a government which will not realise that a wealthy nation is made up of wealthy subjects. And yet, for all his failure, there is no one who would obviously be fitted to take his place. For my immediate purpose I speak only of Syria, the province with which I am the most familiar. Of what value are the pan-Arabic associations and the inflammatory leaflets that they issue from foreign printing presses? The answer is easy: they are worth nothing at all. There is no nation of Arabs; the Syrian merchant is separated by a wider gulf from the Bedouin than he is from the Osmanli, the Syrian country is inhabited by Arabic speaking races all eager to be at each other's throats, and only prevented from fulfilling their natural desires by the ragged half-fed soldier who draws at rare intervals the Sultan's pay. And this soldier, whether he be Kurd or Circassian or Arab from Damascus, is worth a good deal more than the hire he receives. Other armies may mutiny, but the Turkish army will stand true to the khalif; other armies may give way before suffering and privation and untended sickness, but that of the Sultan will go forward as long as it can stand, and fight as long as it has arms, and conquer as long as it has leaders. There is no more wonderful and pitiful sight than a Turkish regiment on the march: greybeards and half-fledged youths, ill-clad and often barefoot, pinched and worn – and indomitable. Let such as watch them salute them as they pass: in the days when war was an art rather than a science, of that stuff the conquerors of the world were made.

But I have left the Governor of Syria waiting far too long. We talked, then, in French, a language with which he was imperfectly acquainted, and from time to time a Syrian gentleman helped him in Turkish over the stiles and pitfalls of the foreign tongue. The Syrian was a rich Maronite landowner of the Lebanon, who happened to be in good odour at Government House though he had but recently spent a year in prison. He had accompanied me upon my visit and was then and there appointed by the

Vāli to be my cicerone in Damascus; Selīm Beg was his name. The talk was principally of archaeology, I purposely insisting on my interest in that subject as compared with the politics of the Mountain and the Desert, to which we thus avoided any serious allusion. The Vāli was affability itself. He presented me with certain photographs of the priceless manuscripts of the Kubbet el Khazneh in the Great Mosque, now closed for ever to the public eye, and promised me the rest of the series. To that end a bowing personage took my English address and noted it carefully in a pocket book, and I need scarcely say that that was the last anyone heard of the matter. Presently the Vāli announced that Madame Pasha and the children were waiting to see me, and I followed him upstairs into a sunny room with windows opening on to a balcony from which you could see all Damascus and its gardens and the hills beyond. There is only one Madame Pasha, and she is a pretty, sharp-featured Circassian, but there was another (gossip says the favourite) who died a year ago. The children were engaging. They recited French poems to me, their bright eyes quick to catch and to respond to every expression of approbation or amusement; they played tinkling polkas, sitting very upright on the music stool with their pigtails hanging down their velvet backs. The Pasha stood in the window and beamed upon them, the Circassian wife smoked cigarettes and bowed whenever she caught my eye, a black slave boy at the door grinned from ear to ear as his masters and mistresses, who were also his schoolmates and his playfellows, accomplished their tasks. I came away with a delightful impression of pretty smiling manners and vivacious intelligence, and expressed my pleasure to the Pasha as we went downstairs.

'Ah!' said he politely, 'if I could have them taught English! But what will you? we cannot get an Englishwoman to agree with our customs, and I have only the Greek lady whom you saw to teach them French.'

I had indeed noticed the Greek woman, an underbred little person, whose bearing could not escape attention in the graceful company upstairs, but I was not slow to expatiate on the excellence of the French she spoke – may Heaven forgive me! The Pasha shook his head.

'If I could get an Englishwoman!' said he. Unfortunately I had no one to suggest for the post, nor would he have welcomed a suggestion.

Before I left, two distinguished personages arrived to have audience of the Vāli. The first was a man by complexion almost a negro, but with an unmistakable look of race and a sharp quick glance. He was the Amīr 'Abdullah Pasha, son of 'Abd ul Kādir, the great Algerian, by a negro slave. The second was Sheikh Hassan Nakshibendi, hereditary chief pope, I had almost said of an orthodox order of Islam famous in Damascus, where its principal Tekyah is situated. (Now a Tekyah is a religious institution for the housing of mendicant dervishes and other holy persons, something like a monastery, only that there is no vow of chastity imposed upon its members, who may have as many wives as they choose outside the Tekyah; Sheikh Hassan himself had the full complement of four.) All the wily ecclesiastic's astuteness shone from the countenance of this worthy. I do not know that his wits were especially remarkable, but his unscrupulousness must have supplemented any deficiencies, or his smile belied him. The meeting with these two accomplished my introduction to Damascus society. Both of them extended to me a warm invitation to visit them in their houses, the Tekyah or anywhere I would, and I accepted all, but I went to the Amīr 'Abdullah first.

Or rather, I went first to the house of his elder brother, the Amīr 'Ali Pasha, because it was there that 'Abd ul Kādir had lived, and there that he had sheltered, during the black days of the massacres in 1860, a thousand Christians. About his name there lingers a romantic association of courage and patriotism, crowned by a wise and honoured age full of authority and the power lent by wealth, for the 'Abd ul Kādir family own all the quarter in which they reside. The house, like any great Damascus house, made no show from the outside. We entered through a small door in a narrow winding street by a dark passage, turned a couple of corners and found ourselves in a marble court with a fountain in the centre and orange trees planted round. All the big rooms opened into this court, the doors were thrown wide to me, and coffee and sweetmeats were served by the groom of the chambers, while I admired the decoration of the walls and the water that bubbled up into marble basins and flowed away by marble conduits. In this and in most of the Damascene palaces every window sill has a gurgling pool in it, so that the air that blows into the room may bring with it a damp freshness. The Amīr 'Ali was away, but his major domo, who looked like a servant *de bonne maison* and had the respectful familiarity of manner that the Oriental dependant knows so well how to assume, showed us his master's treasures, the jewelled sabre presented to the old Amīr by Napoleon III, 'Abd ul Kādir's rifles, and a pair of heavy, silver-mounted swords sent as a gift last year by 'Abd ul 'Aziz ibn er Rashīd – there is a traditional friendship, I learnt, between the Algerian family and the Lords of Hāil. He showed us, too, pictures of 'Abd ul Kādir; the Amīr leading his cavalry, the Amīr at Versailles coming down the steps of the palace with Napoleon, bearing himself as one who wins and not as one who loses, the Amīr as an old man in Damascus, always in the white Algerian robes that he never abandoned, and always with the same grave and splendid dignity of countenance. And last I was led over a little bridge, that crossed a running stream behind the main court, into a garden full of violets, through which we passed to stables as airy, as light and as dry as the best European stables could have been. In the stalls stood two lovely Arab mares from the famous studs of the Ruwalla and a well-bred mule almost as valuable as they. There was a sad-looking man who accompanied us upon our round, though he did not seem to belong to the establishment; his face was so gloomy that it arrested my attention, and I asked Selīm Beg who he was. A Christian, he answered, of a rich family, who had been persecuted to change his religion and had sought sanctuary with the Amīr 'Ali. I heard no more of his story, but he fitted into the picture that 'Abd ul Kādir's dwelling-place left upon the mind: the house of gentlefolk, well kept by well-trained servants, provided with the amenities of life and offering protection to the distressed.

On the following morning I went to see the Amīr 'Abdullah, who lived next door to his brother. I found there a nephew of 'Abdullah's, the Amīr Tahir, son of yet another brother, and my arrival was greeted with satisfaction because there happened to be staying with them a distinguished guest whom I should doubtless like to see. He was a certain Sheikh Tāhir ul Jezāiri, a man much renowned for his learning and for his tempestuous and revolutionary politics. Summoned hastily into the divanned and carpeted upper room in which we were sitting, he entered like a whirlwind, and establishing himself by my side poured into my ear, and into all other ears in the vicinity, for he spoke loud, his distress at not being permitted by the Vāli to associate freely with gifted foreigners such as the American archaeologists or even myself ('God forbid! ' I murmured modestly), and a great many other grievances besides. When this topic had run comparatively dry, he sent the Amīr Tāhir to seek for some publications of his own with which he presented me. They dealt with Arabic and the allied languages such as Nabataean, Safaitic and Phoenician, the alphabetical signs of which he had arranged very carefully and well in comparative tables, though he had not an idea of the signification of any one of the tongues except his own. A curious and typical example of oriental scholarship was Sheikh Tāhir, but from the samples I had of his conversation I am not sure that the sympathies of those who respect peace and order would not be with the Vāli. Presently another notable dropped in, Mustafa Pasha el Barāzi, a member of one of the four leading families of Hamāh, and the whole company fell to talking of their own concerns, Syrian politics and other matters, while I listened and looked out of the window over the Amīr's garden and the stream at its foot, and wondered what had made me so fortunate as to be taking part in a Damascene morning call. At length the Amīr 'Abdullah and his nephew took me aside and discussed long and earnestly a great project which I had broached to them and which I will not reveal here. And when the visit was over Selīm and Mustafa and I went out and lunched at an excellent native restaurant in the Greek bazaar, sitting cheek by jowl with a Bedouin from the desert and eating the best of foods and the choicest of Damascus cream tarts for the sum of eighteenpence between the three of us, which included the coffee and a liberal tip.

There was another morning no less pleasant when I went with the faithful Selīm to pay my respects on a charming old man, the most famous scribe in all the city, Mustafa el Asbā'i was his name. He lived in a house decorated with the exquisite taste of

195

two hundred years ago inlaid with coloured marbles and overlaid with gesso duro worked in patterns like the frontispiece of an illuminated Persian manuscript and painted in soft rich colours in which gold and golden brown predominated. We were taken through the reception rooms into a little chamber on an upper floor where Mustafa was wont to sit and write those texts that are the pictures of the Moslem East. It was hung round with examples from celebrated hands ancient and modern, among which I recognised that of my friend Muhammad 'Ali, son of Beha Ullah the Persian prophet, to my mind the most skilful penman of our day, though Oriental preference goes out to another Persian of the same religious sect, Mushkin Kalam, and him also I count among my friends. We sat on cushions and drank coffee, turning over the while exquisite manuscripts of all dates and countries, some written on gold and some on silver, some on brocade and some on supple parchment (several of these last being pages of Kufic texts abstracted from the Kubbet el Khazneh before it was closed), and when we rose to go Mustafa presented me with three examples of his own art, and I carried them off rejoicing.

Later in the afternoon we drove out to the valley of the Barada, Selīm and I, and called on a third son of 'Abd ul Kādir: 'Amir Omar, prince d'Abd ul Kādir' ran his visiting card, printed in the Latin character. He is the country gentleman of the family. 'Ali has been carried into spheres of greater influence by his marriage with a sister of 'Izzet Pasha, the mighty Shadow behind the Throne in Constantinople: 'Abdullah has always a thousand schemes on hand that keep him to the town, but 'Umar is content to hunt and shoot and tend his garden and lead the simple life. So simple was it that we found him in a smoking cap and a dressing gown and carpet slippers walking the garden alleys. He took us into his house, which, like the other houses of his family, was full of flowers, and up to a pavilion on the roof, whither his pointer followed us with a friendly air of companionship. There amid pots of hyacinths and tulips we watched the sun set over the snowy hills and talked of desert game and sport.

Nor let me, amid all this high company, forget my humbler friends: the Afghan with black locks hanging about his cheeks, who gave me the salute every time we met (the Amīr of Afghanistan has an agent in Damascus to look after the welfare of his subjects on the pilgrimage); the sweetmeat seller at the door of the Great Mosque, who helped me once or twice through the mazes of the bazaars and called to me each time I passed him: 'Has your Excellency no need of your Dragoman today?'; or the dervishes of Sheikh Hassan's Tekyah, who invited me to attend the Friday prayers. Not least the red-bearded Persian who keeps a tea shop in the Corn Market and who is a member of the Beha'i sect among which I have many acquaintances. As I sat drinking glasses of delicious Persian tea at his table, I greeted him in his own tongue and whispered: 'I have been much honoured by the Holy Family at Acre.' He nodded his head and smiled and answered: 'Your Excellency is known to us,' and when I rose to go and asked his charge he replied: 'For you there is never anything to pay.' I vow there is nothing that so warms the heart as to find yourself admitted into the secret circle of Oriental beneficence – and few things so rare.

Upon a sunny afternoon I escaped from the many people who were always in waiting to take me to one place or another and made my way alone through the bazaars, ever the most fascinating of loitering grounds, till I reached the doors of the Great Mosque. It was the hour of the afternoon prayer. I left my shoes with a bedridden negro by the entrance and wandered into the wide cloister that runs along the whole of the west side of the Mosque.

A fire some ten years ago, and the reparations that followed it, have robbed the Mosque of much of its beauty, but it still remains the centre of interest to the archaeologist, who puzzles over the traces of church and temple and Heaven knows what besides that are to be seen embedded in its walls and gates. The court was half full of afternoon shadow and half of sun, and in the golden light troops of little boys with green willow switches in their hands were running to and fro in noiseless play, while the Faithful made their first prostrations before they entered the Mosque. I followed them in and watched them fall into long lines down nave and aisle from east to west. All sorts and grades of men stood side by side, from the learned doctor in a fur-lined coat and silken robes to the raggedest camel driver from the desert, for Islam is the only republic in the world and recognises no distinctions of wealth or rank. When they had assembled to the number of three or four hundred the chant of the Imam began. 'God!' he cried, and the congregation fell with a single movement upon their faces and remained a full minute in silent adoration till the high chant began again. 'The Creator of this world and the next, of the heavens and of the earth, He who leads the righteous in the true path and the wicked to destruction: God!' And as the almighty name echoed through the colonnades where it had sounded for near two thousand years, the listeners prostrated themselves again, and for a moment all the sanctuary was silence.

That night I went to an evening party at the invitation of Shekīb el Arslān, a Druze of a well known family of the Lebanon and a poet foreby – have I not been presented with a copy of his latest ode? The party was held in the Maidān at the house of some corn merchants, who are agents to the Haurān Druzes in the matter of corn selling and know the politics of the Mountain well. There were twelve or fourteen persons present. Shekīb and I and the corn merchants (dressed as befits well-to-do folk in blue silk robes and embroidered yellow turbans) and a few others, I know not who they were. The room was blessedly empty of all but carpets and a divan and a brazier, and this was noteworthy, for not even the 'Abd ul Kādir houses are free from blue and red glass vases and fringed mats that break out like a hideous disease in the marble embrazures and on the shelves of the gesso duro cupboards. Shekīb was a man of education and had experience of the world; he had even travelled once as far as London. He talked in French until one of our hosts stopped him with:

'Oh, Shekib! you know Arabic, the lady also. Talk therefore that we can understand.'

His views on Turkish politics were worth hearing.

'My friends,' said he, 'the evils under which we suffer are due to the foreign nations who refuse to allow the Turkish empire to move in any direction. When she fights they take the fruits of her victory from her, as they did after the war with the Greeks. What good is it that we should conquer the rebellious Albanians? the Bulgarians alone would gain advantage and the followers of our Prophet (*sic*, though he was a Druze) could not live under the hand of the Bulgarians as they would not live under the hand of the Greeks in Crete. For look you, the Moslems of Crete are now dwelling at Salahiyyeh as you know well, and Crete has suffered by their departure.'

There was so much truth in this that I who listened wished that the enemies of Turkey could hear and would deeply ponder the point of view of intelligent and well-informed subjects of the Ottoman Empire.

My last day in Damascus was a Friday. Now Damascus on a fine Friday is a sight worth travelling far to see. All the male population dressed in their best parade the streets, the sweetmeat sellers and the auctioneers of second-hand clothes drive a roaring trade, the eating shops steam with dressed meats of the most tempting kind, and splendidly caparisoned mares are galloped along the road by the river Abana. Early in the afternoon I had distinguished visitors. The first to wait on me was Muhammad Pasha, Sheikh of Jerūd, an oasis halfway upon the road to Palmyra. Jerūdi is the second greatest brigand in all the land, the greatest (no one disputes him the title) being Fayyād Agha of Karyatein, another oasis on the Palmyra road. Fayyād, I fancy, is an evil rogue, though he had been polite enough to me when I had passed his way, but Jerūdi's knavery is of a different brand. He is a big, powerful man with a wall eye; he was a mighty rider and raider in his day, for he has Arab blood in his veins, and his grandfather was of the high stock of the 'Anazeh, but he has grown old and heavy and gouty, and his desire is for peace, a desire difficult to attain, what with his antecedents and the outlying position of Jerūd, which makes it the natural resort of all the turbulent spirits of the desert. He must keep on terms both with his Arab kin and with the government, each trying to use his influence with the other, and he the while seeking to profit from both, with his wall eye turned towards the demands of the law, and his good eye fixed on his own advantage, if I understand him. Justly irate consuls have several times demanded of the Vāli his immediate execution; but the Vāli, though he not infrequently signifies his disapproval of some markedly outrageous deed by a term of imprisonment, can never be brought to take the further step, saying that the government has before now found Jerūdi a useful man, and no doubt the Vāli is the best judge. To his great sorrow Muhammad Pasha has no sons to inherit his very considerable wealth, and the grasshopper, in the shape of a tribe of expectant nephews, has come to be a burden on his years. Recently he married a daughter of Fayyad's house, a girl of fifteen, but she has not brought him children. A famous tale about him is current in Damascus, a tale to which men do not, however, allude in his presence. At the outbreak of the last Druze war Jerūdi happened to be enjoying one of his interludes of adhesion to the powers that be, and because he knew the Mountain well he was sent with thirty or forty men to scout and report, the army following upon his heels. It happened that as he passed through a hamlet near Ormān, his old acquaintance, the sheikh of the village, saw him, and invited him in to eat. And as he sat in the mak'ad awaiting his dinner he heard the Druzes discussing outside whether they had not better profit by this opportunity to kill him as an officer of the Turkish army; and he desired earnestly to go away from that place, but he could not, the rules of polite society making it incumbent upon him to stay and eat the dinner that was a-cooking. So when it came he despatched it with some speed, for the discussion outside had reached a stage that inspired him with the gravest anxiety, and having eaten he mounted his horse and rode away before the Druzes had reached a conclusion. And as he went he found himself suddenly between two fires; the Turkish army had come up and the first battle of the war had begun. He and his men, discouraged and perplexed, took refuge behind some rocks, and, as best they might, they made their way back one by one to the extreme rear of the Turkish troops. The Druzes have composed a song about this incident; it begins:

> *Jerūdi's golden mares are famed,*
> *And fair the riders in their stumbling flight!*
> *Muhammad Pasha, tell thy lord*
> *Where are his soldiers, where his arms!*

This piece is not often sung before him.

My next visitor was Sheikh Hassan Nakshibendi, he of the sleek and cunning clerical face. He contrived to make good use even of the ten minutes he spent in the inn parlour, for noticing a gaudy ring on Selīm Beg's finger he asked to see it, and liked it so well that he put it in his pocket saying that Selīm would certainly wish to give a present to his khānum, the youngest of his wives, whom he had married a year or two before. Selīm replied that in that case we must go at once to his house in Salahiyyeh that the present might be offered, and both Sheikh Hassan and Muhammad Pasha having their victorias at the door, we four got into them and drove off to Salahiyyeh through the bright holiday streets. At the door of the house Selīm announced that I ought first to take leave of the Vāli, who lived close at hand, and borrowed Jerūdi's carriage that we might go in style. Then said Selīm to Muhammad Pasha:

'Are you not coming with us?' But the question was put in sarcasm, for he knew well that Jerūdi was going through a period of disgrace and that he had but recently emerged from a well-merited imprisonment.

Jerūdi shook his head and drawing near to us, seated in his victoria, he whispered:

'Say something in my favour to the Pasha.'

We laughed and promised to speak for him, though Selīm confided to me as we drove away that when he had been in disgrace ('entirely owing to the intrigues of my enemies'), not a man had come forward to help him, while now that he was in favour every one begged for his intervention; and he drew his frock coat round him and leant back against the cushions of Jerūdi's carriage with the air of one who is proudly conscious that he is in a position to fulfil scriptural injunctions to the letter.

Nāzim Pasha was on his doorstep taking leave of the commander-in-chief. When he saw us he came down the steps and called us in with the utmost friendliness. The second visit to his house (he had been to see me in between) was much less formal than the first. We talked of the Japanese War, a topic never far from the lips of my interlocutors, great or small, and I made bold to ask him his opinion.

'Officially,' said he, 'I am neutral.'

'But between friends?'

'Of course I am on the side of the Japanese,' he answered. And then he added: 'It is you who have gained by their victory.'

I replied: 'But will you not also gain?'

He answered gloomily: 'We have not gained as yet. Not at all in Macedonia.'

Then he asked how I had enjoyed my visit to Damascus. Selīm replied hastily:

'Today she has had a great disappointment.'

The Vāli looked concerned.

'Yes,' continued Selīm,' she had hoped to see a chief of brigands, and she has found only a peaceful subject of your Excellency.'

'Who is he?' said Nāzim

'Muhammad Pasha Jerūdi,' answered Selīm. The good word had been spoken very skilfully.

When we returned to Sheikh Hassan's house we related this conversation to the subject of it, and Jerūdi pulled a wry face, but expressed himself satisfied. Sheikh Hassan then took me to see his wife – his fifth wife, for he had divorced one of the legal four to marry her. He has the discretion to keep a separate establishment for each, and I do not question that he is repaid by the resulting peace of his hearths. There were three women in the inner room, the wife and another who was apparently not of the household, for she hid her face under the bedclothes when Sheikh Hassan came in, and a Christian, useful in looking after the male guests (there were others besides Jerūdi and Selīm) and in doing commissions in the bazaars, where she can go more freely than her sister Moslems. The harem was shockingly untidy. Except when the women folk expect your visit and have prepared for it, nothing is more forlornly unkempt than their appearance. The disorder of the rooms in which they live may partly be accounted for by the fact that there are neither cupboards nor drawers in them, and all possessions are kept in large green and gold boxes, which must be unpacked when so much as a pocket-handkerchief is needed, and frequently remain unpacked. Sheikh Hassan's wife was a young and pretty woman, though her hair dropped in wisps about her face and neck, and a dirty dressing-gown clothed a figure which had, alas! already fallen into ruin.

But the view from Nakshibendi's balcony is immortal. The great and splendid city of Damascus, with its gardens and its domes and its minarets, lies spread out below, and beyond it the desert, the desert reaching almost to its gates. And herein is the heart of the whole matter.

This is what I know of Damascus; as for the churches and the castles, the gentry can see those for themselves.

6

We left next day at an early hour, but the people of Homs got up to see us off. Nothing save the determination to afford them no more amusement than I could help kept me outwardly calm. In a quarter of an hour we had passed beyond the Tripoli Gate, and the Roman brickwork, and beyond the range of vision of the furthest sighted of the little boys; the peaceful beauty of the morning invaded our senses, and I turned to make the acquaintance of the companions with whom the Kāimakām had provided me. They were four in number, and two of them were free and two were bound. The first two were Kurdish zaptiehs; one was charged to show me the way to Kal'at el Husn, and the other to guard over the second pair of my fellow travellers, a couple of prisoners who had been on the Kāimakām's hands for some days past, waiting until he could find a suitable opportunity, such as that afforded by my journey, to send them to the fortress in the Jebel Nosairiyyeh, and so to the great prison at Tripoli. They were clad, poor wretches, in ragged cotton clothes and handcuffed together. As they trudged along bravely through dust and mud, I proffered a word of sympathy, to which they replied that they hoped God might prolong my life, but as for them it was the will of their lord the Sultan that they should tramp in chains. One of the Kurds interrupted with the explanation:

'They are deserters from the Sultan's army: may God reward them according to their deeds! Moreover, they are Ismailis from Selemiyyeh, and they worship a strange god who lives in the land of Hind. And some say she is a woman, and for that reason they worship her. And every year she sends an embassy to this country to collect the money that is due to her, and even the poorest of the Ismailis provide her with a few piastres. And yet they declare that they are Muslims: who knows what they believe? Speak, oh Khudr, and tell us what you believe.'

The prisoner thus addressed replied doggedly:

'We are Muslims;' but the soldier's words had given me a clue which I was able to follow up when the luckless pair crept close to my horse's side and whispered:

'Lady, lady! have you journeyed to the land of Hind?'

'Yes,' said I.

'May God make it Yes upon you! Have you heard there of a great king called the King Muhammad?'

Again I was able to reply in the affirmative, and even to add that I myself knew him and had conversed with him, for their King Muhammad was no other than my fellow subject the Agha Khān, and the religion of the prisoners boasted a respectable antiquity, having been founded by him whom we call the Old Man of the Mountain. They were the humble representatives of the dreaded (and probably maligned) sect of the Assassins.

Khudr caught my stirrup with his free hand and said eagerly:

'Is he not a great king?'

But I answered cautiously, for though the Agha Khān is something of a great king in the modern sense, that is to say he is exceedingly wealthy, it would have been difficult to explain to his disciples exactly what the polished, well-bred man of the world was like whom I had last met at a London dinner party, and who had given me the Marlborough Club as his address. Not that these things, if they could have understood them, would have shocked them; the Agha Khān is a law unto himself, and if he chose to indulge in far greater excesses than dinner parties his actions would be sanctified by the mere fact that they were his. His father used to give letters of introduction to the Angel Gabriel, in order to secure for his clients a good place in Paradise; the son, with his English education and his familiarity with European thought, has refrained from exercising this privilege, though he has not ceased to hold, in the opinion of his followers, the keys of heaven. They show their belief in him in a substantial manner by subscribing, in various parts of Asia and Africa, a handsome income that runs yearly into tens of thousands.

We rode for about an hour through gardens, meeting bands of low-caste Arabs jogging into Homs on their donkeys with milk and curds for the market, and then we came to the plain beyond the Orontes, which is the home of these Arabs. The plain had a familiar air; it was not dissimilar from the country in the Druze hills, and like the Haurān it was covered with black volcanic stones. It is a vast quarry for the city of Homs. All the stones that are used for building are brought from beyond the river packed on donkeys. They are worth a metalīk in the town (now a metalīk is a coin too small to possess a European counterpart), and a man with a good team can earn up to ten piastres a day. In the Spring the only Arabs who camp in the Wa'r Homs, the Stony Plain of Homs, are a despised race that caters for the needs of the city, for, mark you, no Bedouin who respected himself would earn a livelihood by selling curds or by any other means except battle; but in the summer the big tribes such as the Haseneh settle there for a few months, and after the harvest certain of the 'Anazeh who feed their camels upon the stubble. These great folk are much like salmon in a trout stream coming in from the open sea and bullying the lesser fry. When we passed in March there was a good deal of standing water in the plain, and grass and flowers grew between the stones; and as we journeyed westward, over ground that rose gradually towards the hills, we came into country that was like an exquisite garden of flowers. Pale blue hyacinths lifted their clustered bells above the tufa blocks, irises and red anemones and a yellow hawksweed and a beautiful purple hellebore dotted the grass – all the bounties of the Syrian Spring were scattered on that day beneath our happy feet. For the first five hours we followed the carriage road that leads to Tripoli, passing the khān that marks the final stage before the town of Homs, and the boundary line between the vilayets of Damascus and of Beyrout; then we turned to the right and entered a bridle-path that lay over a land of rolling grass, partly cultivated and fuller of flowers than the edges of the road had been. The anemones were of every shade of white and purple, small blue irises clustered by the path and yellow crocuses by the banks of the stream. In the eyes of one who had recently crossed southern Syria the grass was even more admirable than the flowers. The highest summits of the Jebel Nosairiyyeh are clad with a verdure that no fertile slope in Samaria or Judaea can boast. The path mounted a little ridge and dropped down to a Kurdish village, half Arab tent and half mud-built wall. The inhabitants must have been long in Syria, for they had forgotten their own tongue and spoke nothing but Arabic, though, like the two zaptiehs, they spoke with the clipped accent of the Kurd. Beyond the village a plain some three miles wide, the Bkei'a, stretched to the foot of the steep buttress of the Nosairiyyeh hills, and from the very top of the mountain frowned the great crusader fortress towards which we were going. The sun shone on its turrets, but a black storm was creeping up behind it; we could hear the thunder rumbling in the hills, and jagged lightning shot through the clouds behind the castle. The direct road across the Bkei'a was impassable for horsemen, owing to the flooded swamps, which were deep enough, said the villagers, to engulf a mule and its load; we turned therefore reluctantly to the right, and edged round the foot of the hills. Before we had gone far we met two riders sent out to welcome us by the Kāimakām of Kal'at el Husn, and as they joined us the storm broke and enveloped us in sheets of rain. Splashing through the mud and drenched with rain we reached the foot of the hills at five o'clock, and here I left my caravan to follow the road, and with one of the Kāimakām's horsemen climbed by a steep and narrow bridle-path straight up to the hilltop. And so at sunset we came to the Dark Tower and rode through a splendid Arab gateway into a vaulted corridor, built over a winding stair. It was almost night within; a few loopholes let in the grey dusk from outside and provided the veriest apology for daylight. At intervals we passed doorways leading into cavernous blackness. The stone steps were shallow and wide but much broken; the horses stumbled and clanked over them as we rode up and up, turned corner after corner, and passed under gateway after gateway until the last brought us out into the courtyard in the centre of the keep. I felt as though I were riding with some knight of the Fairy Queen, and half expected to see written over the arches: 'Be bold!' 'Be bold!' 'Be not too bold!' But there was no magician in the heart of the castle – nothing but a crowd of villagers craning their necks to see us, and the Kāimakām, smiling and friendly, announcing that he could not think of letting me pitch a camp on such a wet and stormy night, and had prepared a lodging for me in the tower.

The Kāimakām of Kal'at el Husn is a distinguished man of letters. His name is 'Abd ul Hamid Beg Rāfi'a Zādeh, and his family comes from Egypt, where many of his cousins are still to be found. He lives in the topmost tower of the keep, where he had made ready a guest chamber commodiously fitted with carpets and a divan, a four-post bedstead and a mahogany wardrobe with looking-glass doors of which the glass had been so splintered in the journey a-camel back from Tripoli that it was impossible to see the smallest corner of one's face in it. I was wet through, but the obligations of good society had to be fulfilled, and they demanded that we should sit down on the divan and exchange polite phrases while I drank glasses of weak tea. My host was preoccupied and evidently disinclined for animated conversation for a good reason, as I subsequently found – but on my replying to his first greeting he heaved a sigh of relief, and exclaimed:

'Praise be to God! your Excellency speaks Arabic. We had feared that we should not be able to talk with you, and I had already invited a Syrian lady who knows the English tongue to spend the evening for the purpose of interpreting.'

We kept up a disjointed chat for an hour while the damp soaked more and more completely through my coat and skirt, and it was not until long after the mules had arrived and their packs had been unloaded that the Kāimakām rose and took his departure, saying that he would leave me to rest. We had, in fact, made a long day's march; it had taken the muleteers eleven hours to reach Kal'at el Husn. I had barely had time to change my wet clothes before a discreet knocking at the inner door announced the presence of the womenfolk. I opened at once and admitted a maid servant, and the wife of the Kāimakām, and a genteel lady who greeted me in English of the most florid kind. This last was the Sitt Ferīdeh, the Christian wife of the Government land surveyor, who is also a Christian. She had been educated at a missionary school in Tripoli, and I was not long left in ignorance of the fact that she was an authoress, and that her greatest work was the translation of *The Last Days of Pompeii* into Arabic. The Kāimakām's wife was a young woman with apple cheeks, who would have been pretty if she had not been inordinately fat. She was his second wife; he had married her only a month or two before, on the death of his first, the mother of his children. She was so shy that it was some time before she ventured to open her lips in my presence, but the Sitt Ferīdeh carried off the situation with a gushing volubility, both in English and in Arabic, and a cheerful air of emphasising by her correct demeanour the fervour of her Christianity. She was a pleasant and intelligent woman, and I enjoyed her company considerably more than that of my hostess. The first word that the Khānum ventured to utter was, however, a welcome one, for she asked when I would please to dine. I replied with enthusiasm that no hour could be too early for me, and we crossed a muddy courtyard and entered a room in which a bountiful meal had been spread out. Here we were joined by an ancient dame who was presented to me as 'a friend who has come to gaze upon your Excellency', and we all sat down to the best of dinners eaten by one at least of the party with the best of sauces. A thick soup and four enormous dishes of meat and vegetables, topped by a rice pudding, composed the repast. When dinner was over we returned to my room, a brazier full of charcoal was brought in, together with hubble-bubbles for the ladies, and we settled ourselves to an evening's talk. The old woman refused to sit on the divan, saying that she was more accustomed to the floor, and disposed herself neatly as close as possible to the brazier, holding out her wrinkled hands over the glowing coals. She was clad in black, and her head was covered by a thick white linen cloth, which was bound closely above her brow and enveloped her chin, giving her the air of some aged prioress of a religious order. Outside the turret room the wind howled; the rain beat against the single window, and the talk turned naturally to deeds of horror and such whispered tales of murder and death as must have startled the shadows in that dim room for many and many a century. A terrible domestic tragedy had fallen upon the Kāimakām ten days before: his son had been shot by a schoolfellow at Tripoli in some childish quarrel – the women seemed to think it not unusual that a boy's sudden anger should have such consequences. The Kāimakām had been summoned by telegraph; he had ridden down the long mountain road with fear clutching at his heart, only to find the boy dead, and his sorrow had been almost more than he could bear. So said the Sitt Ferīdeh.

The ancient crone rocked herself over the brazier and muttered:

'Murder is like the drinking of milk here! God! there is no other but Thou.'

A fresh gust of wind swept round the tower, and the Christian woman took up the tale.

'This Khānum,' said she, nodding her head towards the figure by the brazier, 'knows also what it is to weep. Her son was but now murdered in the mountains by a robber who slew him with his knife. They found his body lying stripped by the path.'

The mother bent anew over the charcoal, and the glow flushed her worn old face.

'Murder is like the spilling of water!' she groaned.

'Oh Merciful!'

It was late when the women left me. One of them offered to pass the night in my room, but I refused politely and firmly.

Next day I was wakened by thunder and by hailstones rattling against my shutters. There was nothing for it but to spend another twenty-four hours under the Kāimakām's roof and be thankful that we had a roof to spend them under. I explored the castle from end to end, with immense satisfaction to the eternal child that lives in the soul of all of us and takes more delight in the dungeons and battlements of a fortress than in any other relic of antiquity. Kal'at el Husn is so large that half the population of the village is lodged in the vaulted substructures of the keep, while the garrison occupies the upper towers. The walls of the keep rise from a moat inside the first line of fortifications, the line through which we had passed the night before by the vaulted gallery. The butcher of the castle lodged by the gateway of the inner wall; every morning he killed a sheep on the threshold, and those who went out stepped across a pool of blood as though some barbaric sacrifice were performed daily at the gate. The keep contained a chapel, now converted into a mosque, and a banquet hall with Gothic windows, the tracery of which was blocked with stones to guard those who dwelt within against the cold. The tower in which I was lodged formed part of the highest of the defences and rose above three stories of vaults. A narrow passage from it along the top of the wall led into a great and splendid chamber, beyond which was a round tower containing a circular room roofed by a fourfold vault, and lighted by pointed windows with rosettes and mouldings round the arches. The castle is the 'Kerak of the Knights' of Crusader chronicles. It belonged to the Hospitallers, and the Grand Master of the Order made it his residence. The Egyptian Sultan Malek ed Dāher took it from them, restored it, and set his exultant inscription over the main gate. It is one of the most perfect of the many fortresses which bear witness to the strange jumble of noble ardour, fanaticism, ambition and crime that combined to make the history of the Crusades – a page whereon the Christian nations cannot look without a blush nor read without the unwilling pity exacted by vain courage. For to die in a worthless cause is the last extremity of defeat. Kerak is closely related to the military architecture of southern France, yet it bears traces of an Oriental influence from which the great Orders were not immune, though the Templars succumbed to it more completely than the Hospitallers. Like the contemporary Arab fortresses the walls increased in thickness towards the foot to form a sloping bastion of solid masonry which protected them against the attacks of sappers, but the rounded towers with their great projection from the line of the wall were wholly French in character. The Crusaders are said to have found a castle on the hilltop and taken it from the Moslems, but I saw no traces of earlier work than theirs. Parts of the present structure are later than their time, as, for instance, a big building by the inner moat, on the walls of which were carved lions not unlike the Seljuk lion.

After lunch I waded down the muddy hill to the village and called on the Sitt Ferīdeh and her husband. There were another pair of Christians present, the man being the Sāhib es Sandūk, which I take to be a kind of treasurer. The two men talked of the condition of the Syrian poor. No one, said the land surveyor, died of hunger, and he proceeded to draw up the yearly budget of the average peasant. The poorest of the fellahīn may earn from 1000 to 1500 piastres a year (£7 to £11), but he has no need of any money except to pay the capitation tax and to buy himself a substitute for military service. Meat is an unknown luxury; a cask of semen (rancid butter) costs 8s. or 10s. at most; it helps to make the burghul and other grains palatable, and it lasts several months. If the grain and the semen run low the peasant has only to go out into the mountains or into the open country, which is no man's land, and gather edible leaves or grub up roots. He builds his house with his own hands, there are no fittings or furniture in it, and the ground on which it stands costs nothing. As for clothing, what does he need? a couple of linen shirts, a woollen cloak every two or three years, and a cotton kerchief for the head. The old and the sick are seldom left uncared for; their families look after them if they have families, and if they are without relations they can always make a livelihood by begging, for no one in the East refuses to give something when he is asked, though the poor can seldom give money. Few of the fellahīn own land of their own; they work for hire on the estates of richer men. The chief landowners round Kal'at el Husn are the family of the Danādisheh, who come from Tripoli. Until quite recently the government did not occupy the castle; it belongs to the family of the Zā'bieh, who have owned it for two hundred years, and still live in some rooms on the outer wall. The Treasurer broke in here and said that even the Moslem population hated the Ottoman government, and would infinitely rather be ruled by a foreigner, what though he were an infidel – preferably by the English, because the prosperity of Egypt had made so deep an impression on Syrian minds.

That evening the Kāimakām sent me a message asking whether I would choose to dine alone or whether I would honour him and his wife, and I begged to be allowed to take the latter alternative. In spite of a desire, touchingly evident, to be a good host, he was sad and silent during the earlier stages of the dinner, until we hit upon a subject that drew him from the memory of his sorrow. The mighty dead came out to help us with words upon their lips that have lifted the failing hearts of generations of mankind. The Kāimakām was well acquainted with Arabic literature; he knew the poets of the Ignorance by heart, and when he found that I had a scanty knowledge of them and a great love for them he quoted couplet after couplet. But his own tastes lay with more modern singers; the tenth-century Mutanabbi was evidently one of his favourite authors. Some of the old fire still smoulders in Mutanabbi's verse; it burnt again as the Kāimakām recited the famous ode in which the poet puts from him the joys of youth:

> *Oft have I longed for age to still the tumult in my brain,*
> *And why should I repine when my prayer is fulfilled?*
> *We have renounced desire save for the spear-points,*
> *Neither do we dally, except with them.*
> *The most exalted seat in the world is the saddle of a swift*
> *horse,*
> *And the best companion for all time is a book.*

'Your Excellency,' concluded the Kāimakām, 'must surely hold that couplet in esteem.'

When we returned to the guest chamber he asked whether he should not read his latest poem, composed at the request of the students of the American College at Beyrout (the most renowned institution of its kind in Syria) to commemorate an anniversary they were about to celebrate. He produced first the students' letter, which was couched in flattering terms, and then his sheets of manuscript, and declaimed his verses with the fine emphasis of the Oriental reciter, pausing from time to time to explain the full meaning of a metaphor or to give an illustration to some difficult couplet. His subject was the praise of learning, but he ended inconsequently with a fulsome panegyric on the Sultan, a passage of which he was immensely proud. As far as I could judge it was not very great poetry, but what of that? There is no solace in misfortune like authorship, and for a short hour the Kāimakām forgot his grief and entered into regions where there is neither death nor lamentation. I offered him sympathy and praise at suitable points and could have laughed to find myself talking the same agreeable rubbish in Arabic that we all talk so often in English. I might have been sitting in a London drawing-room, instead of between the bare walls of a Crusader tower, and the world is after all made of the one stuff throughout.

It was still raining on the following morning and I had dressed and breakfasted in the lowest spirits when of a sudden someone waved a magic wand, the clouds were cleared away, and we set off at half-past seven in exquisite sunshine. At the bottom of the steep hill on which the castle stands there lies in an olive grove a Greek monastery. When I reached it I got off my horse and went in, as was meet, to salute the Abbot, and, behold! he was an old acquaintance whom I had met at the monastery of Ma'alūla five years earlier on my return from Palmyra. There were great rejoicings at this fortunate coincidence, and much jam and water and coffee were consumed in the celebration of it. The monastery has been rebuilt, except for a crypt-like chapel, which they say is 1200 years old. The vault is supported by two pairs of marble columns, broken off below the capital and returned into the wall, a scheme more curious than attractive. The capitals are in the form of lily heads of a Byzantine type. By the altar screen, a good piece of modern wood carving, there are some very beautiful Persian tiles. In the western wall of the monastery I was shown a door so narrow between the jambs that it is scarcely possible to squeeze through them, impossible, said the monks, for anyone except he be pure of heart. I did not risk my reputation by attempting to force the passage.

We rode on through shallow wooded valleys full of flowers; the fruit trees were coming into blossom and the honeysuckle into leaf, and by a tiny graveyard under some budding oaks we stopped to lunch. Before us lay the crucial point of our day's march. We could see the keep of Sāfīta Castle on the opposite hill, but there was a swollen river between, the bridge had been swept away, and report said that the ford was impassable. When we reached the banks of the Abrash we saw the river rushing down its wide channel, an unbroken body of swirling water through which no loaded mule could pass. We rode near two hours downstream, and were barely in time with the second bridge, the Jisr el Wād, which was in the last stage of decrepitude, the middle arch just holding together. The hills on the opposite bank were covered with a low scrub, out of which the lovely iris stylosa lifted its blue petals, and the scene was further enlivened by a continuous procession of white-robed Nosairis making their way down to the bridge. I had a Kurdish zaptieh with me, 'Abd ul Mejīd, who knew the mountains well, and all the inhabitants of them. Though he was a Mohammedan he had no feeling against the Nosairis, whom he had always found to be a harmless folk, and everyone greeted him with a friendly salutation as we passed. He told me that the white-robed companies were going to the funeral feast of a great sheikh much renowned for piety, who had died a week ago. The feast on such occasions is held two days after the funeral, and when the guests have eaten of the meats each man according to his ability pays tribute to the family of the dead, the sums varying from one lira upwards to five or six. To have a reputation for holiness in the Jebel Nosairiyyeh is as good as a life insurance with us.

Owing to our long circuit we did not reach Sāfīta till four. I refused the hospitality of the Commandant, and pitched my tents on a ridge outside the village. The keep which we had seen from afar is all that remains of the White Castle of the Knights

Templars. It stands on the top of the hill with the village clustered at its foot, and from its summit are visible the Mediterranean and the northern parts of the Phoenician coast. I saw a Phoenician coin among the antiquities offered me for sale, and the small bronze figure of a Phoenician god – Sāfita was probably an inland stronghold of the merchant nation. The keep was a skilful architectural surprise. It contained, not the vaulted hall or refectory that might have been expected, but a great church which had thus occupied the very heart of the fortress. A service was being held when we entered and all the people were at their prayers in a red glow of sunset that came through the western doors. The inhabitants of Sāfita are most of them Christians, and many speak English with a strong American accent picked up while they were making their small fortunes in the States. Besides the accent, they had acquired a familiarity of address that did not please me, and lost some of the good manners to which they had been born.' Abd ul Mejīd, the smart non-commissioned officer, accompanied me through the town, saved me from the clutches of the Americanised Christians, twirled his fierce military moustaches at the little boys who thought to run after us, and followed their retreat with extracts from the finest vocabulary of objurgation that I have been privileged to hear.

Late in the evening two visitors were announced, who turned out to be the Zābit (Commandant) and another official sent by the Kāimakām of Drekish to welcome me and bring me down to his village. We three rode off together in the early morning with a couple of soldiers behind us, by a winding path through the hills, and after two hours we came to a valley full of olive groves, with the village of Drekish on the slopes above them. At the first clump of olive trees we found three worthies in frock coats and tarbushes waiting to receive us; they mounted their horses when we approached and fell into the procession, which was further swelled as we ascended the village street by other notables on horseback, till it reached the sum total of thirteen. The Kāimakām met us at the door of his house, frock-coated and ceremonious, and led me into his audience-room where we drank coffee. By this time the company consisted of some thirty persons of importance. When the official reception was over my host took me into his private house and introduced me to his wife, a charming Damascene lady, and we had a short conversation, during which I made his better acquaintance. Riza Beg el 'Ābid owes his present position to the fact that he is cousin to 'Izzet Pasha, for there is not one of that great man's family but he is at least Kāimakām. Riza Beg might have climbed the official ladder unaided; he is a man of exceptionally pleasant manners, amply endowed with the acute intelligence of the Syrian. The family to which he and 'Izzet belong is of Arab origin. The members of it claim to be descended from the noble tribe of the Muwāli, who were kin to Harūn er Rashīd, and when you meet 'Izzet Pasha it is as well to congratulate him on his relationship with that Khalif, though he knows, and he knows also that you know, that the Muwāli repudiate his claims with scorn and count him among the descendants of their slaves, as his name 'Ābid (slave), may show. Slaves or freemen, the members of the 'Ābid house have climbed so cleverly that they have set their feet upon the neck of Turkey, and will remain in that precarious position until 'Izzet falls from favour. Riza Beg pulled a grave face when I alluded to his high connection, and observed that power such as that enjoyed by his family was a serious matter, and how gladly would he retire into a less prominent position than that of Kāimakām! Who knew but that the Pasha too would not wish to exchange the pleasures of Constantinople for a humbler and a safer sphere – a supposition that I can readily believe to be well grounded, since 'Izzet, if rumour speaks the truth, has got all that a man can reasonably expect from the years during which he has enjoyed the royal condescension. I assured the Kāimakām that I should make a point of paying my respects to the Pasha when I reached Constantinople, a project that I ultimately carried out with such success that I may now reckon myself, on 'Izzet's own authority, as one of those who will enjoy his lifelong friendship.

By this time lunch was ready, and the Khānum having retired, the other guests were admitted to the number of four, the Zābit, the Kādi and two others. It was a copious, an excellent and an entertaining meal. The conversation flowed merrily round the table, prompted and encouraged by the Kāimakām, who handled one subject after the other with the polished ease of a man of the world. As he talked I had reason to observe once more how fine and subtle a tongue is modern Syrian Arabic when used by a man of education. The Kādi's speech was hampered by his having a reputation for learning to uphold, which obliged him to confine himself to the dead language of the Kur'an. As I took my leave the Kāimakām explained that for that night I was still to be his guest. He had learnt, said he, that I wished to camp at the ruined temple of Husn es Suleimān, and had despatched my caravan thither under the escort of a zaptieh, and sent up servants and provisions, together with one of his cousins to see to my entertainment. I was to take the Zābit with me, and Rā'ib Effendi el Helu, another of the luncheon party, and he hoped that I should be satisfied. I thanked him profusely for his kindness, and declared that I should have known his Arab birth by his generous hospitality.

Our path mounted to the top of the Nosairiyyeh hills and followed along the crests, a rocky and beautiful track. The hills were extremely steep, and bare of all but grass and flowers except that here and there, on the highest summits, there was a group of big oaks with a white-domed Nosairi mazār shining through their bare boughs. The Nosairis have neither mosque nor church, but on every mountain top they build a shrine that marks a burial-ground. These high-throned dead, though they have left the world of men, have not ceased from their good offices, for they are the protectors of the trees rooted among their bones, trees which, alone among their kind, are allowed to grow untouched.

Husn es Suleimān lies at the head of a valley high up in the mountains. A clear spring breaks from under its walls and flows round a natural platform of green turf, on which we pitched our tents. The hills rise in an amphitheatre behind the temple, the valley drops below it, and the gods to whom it was dedicated enjoy in solitude the ruined loveliness of their shrine. The walls round the temenos are overgrown with ivy, and violets bloom in the crevices. Four doorways lead into the court, in the centre of which stand the ruins of the temple, while a little to the south of the cella are the foundations of an altar, bearing in fine Greek letters a dedication that recounts how a centurion called Decimus of the Flavian (?) Legion, with his two sons and his daughter, raised an altar of brass to the god of Baitocaicē and placed it upon a platform of masonry in the year 444. The date is of the Seleucid era and corresponds to A.D. 132. It is regrettable that Decimus did not see fit to mention the name of the god, which remains undetermined in all the inscriptions. The northern gateway is a triple door, lying opposite to a second rectangular enclosure, which contains a small temple in antis at the south-east corner, and the apse of a sanctuary in the northern wall. This last sheltered perhaps the statue of the unknown god, for there are steps leading up to it and the bases of columns on either side. As at Ba'albek, the Christians sanctified the spot by the building of a church, which lay across the second enclosure at right angles to the northern sanctuary. The masonry of the outer walls of both courts is very massive, the stones being sometimes six or eight feet long. The decoration is much more austere than that of Ba'albek, but certain details so intimately recall the latter that I am tempted to conjecture that the same architect may have been employed at both places, and that it was he who cut on the underside of the architraves of Baitocaicē the eagles and cherubs that he had used to adorn the architrave of the Temple of Jupiter. The peasants say that there are deep vaults below both temple and court. The site must be well worthy of careful excavation, though no additional knowledge will enhance the beauty of the great shrine in the hills.

The Kāimakām had not fallen short of his word. Holocausts of sheep and hens had been offered up for us, and after my friends and I had feasted, the soldiers and the muleteers made merry in their turn. The campfires blazed brightly in the clear sharp mountain air, the sky was alive with stars, the brook gurgled over the stones; and the rest was silence, for Kurt was lost. Somewhere among the hills he had strayed away, and he was gone never to return. I mourned his loss, but slept the more peacefully for it ever after.

All my friends and all the soldiers rode with us next day to the frontier of the district of Drekish and there left us after having hounded a reluctant Nosairi out of his house at 'Ain esh Shems and bidden him help the zaptieh who accompanied us to find the extraordinarily rocky path to Masyād. After they had gone I summoned Mikhāil and asked him what he had thought of our day's entertainment. He gave the Arabic equivalent for a sniff and said:

'Doubtless your Excellency thinks that you were the guest of the Kāimakām. I will tell you of whom you were the guest. You saw those fellahīn of the Nosairiyyeh, the miserable ones, who sold you anticas at the ruins this morning? They were your hosts. Everything you had was taken from them without return. They gathered the wood for the fires, the hens were theirs, the eggs were theirs, the lambs were from their flocks, and when you refused to take more saying, I have enough,' the soldiers seized yet another lamb and carried it off with them. And the only payment the fellahīn received were the metalīks you gave them for their old money. But if you will listen to me,' added Mikhāil inconsequently, 'you shall travel through the land of Anatolia and never take a quarter of a mejīdeh from your purse. From Kāimakām to Kāimakām you shall go, and everywhere they shall offer you hospitality – that sort does not look for payment, they wish your Excellency to say a good word for them when you come to Constantinople. You shall sleep in their houses, and eat at their tables, as it was when I travelled with Sacks...'

But if I were to tell all that happened when Mikhāil travelled with Mark Sykes I should never get to Masyād. The day was rendered memorable by the exceptional difficulty of the paths and by the beauty of the flowers. On the hilltops grew the alpine cyclamen, crocuses, yellow, white and purple, and whole slopes of white primroses; lower down, irises, narcissus, black and green orchids, purple orchis and the blue many-petalled anemone in a boscage of myrtle. When we reached the foot of the steepest slopes I sent the unfortunate Nosairi home with a tip, which was a great deal more than he expected to get out of an adventure that had begun with a command from the soldiery. At three we reached Masyād and camped at the foot of the castle.

Now Masyād was a disappointment. There is indeed a great castle, but, as far as I could judge, it is of Arab workmanship, and the walls round the town are Arab also. A Roman road from Hamah passes through Masyād, and there must be traces of Roman settlement in the town, but I saw none. I heard of a castle at Abu Kbesh on the top of the hills, but it was said to be like Masyād, only smaller, and I did not go up to it. The castle of Masyād has an outer wall and an inner keep reached by a vaulted passage like that of Kal'at el Husn. The old keep is almost destroyed, and has been replaced by jerry-built halls and chambers erected by the Ismailis some hundreds of years ago when they held the place, so I was told by an old man called the Emir Mustafa Milhēm, who belonged to the sect and served me as guide. He also said that his family had inhabited the castle for seven or eight hundred years, but possibly he lied, though it is true that the Ismailis have held it as long. Built into the outer gateways are certain capitals and columns that must have been taken from Byzantine structures. There are some old Arabic inscriptions inside the second gate which record the names of the builders of that part of the fortifications, but they are much broken. I was told afterwards that I ought to have visited a place called Deir es Sleb, where there are two churches and a small castle. It is not marked in the map, and I heard nothing of it until I had left it far behind. I saw bits of the rasīf, the Roman road, as I travelled next day to Hamāh. At the bridge over the river Sarut, four and a half hours from Masyād, there is a curious mound faced to the very top with a rough wall of huge stones. Mikhāil found a Roman coin in the furrows of the field at the foot of it. From the river we had two and a half hours of tedious travel that were much lightened by the presence of a charming old Turk, a telegraph official, who joined us at the bridge and told me his story as we rode.

'Effendim, the home of my family is near Sofia. Effendim, you know the place? Māsha'llah, it is a pleasant land! Where I lived it was covered with trees, fruit trees and pines in the mountains and rose gardens in the plain. Effendim, many of us came here after the war with the Muscovite for the reason that we would not dwell under any hand but that of the Sultan, and many returned again after they had come. Effendim? for what cause? They would not live in a country without trees; by God, they could not endure it.' Thus conversing we reached Hamāh.

7

The next day's journey is branded on my mind by an incident which I can scarcely dignify with the name of an adventure – a misadventure let me call it. It was as tedious while it was happening as a real adventure (and no one but he who has been through them knows how tiresome they frequently are), and it has not left behind it that remembered spice of possible danger that enlivens fireside recollections. We left Kal'at el Mudīk at eight in pouring rain, and headed northwards to the Jebel Zāwiyyeh, a cluster of low hills that lies between the Orontes valley and the broad plain of Aleppo. This range contains a number of ruined towns, dating mainly from the fifth and sixth centuries, partially re-inhabited by Syrian fellahīn, and described in detail by de Vogüé and Butler. The rain stopped as we rode up a low sweep of the hills where the red earth was all under the plough and the villages set in olive groves. The country had a wide bare beauty of its own, which was heightened by the dead towns that were strewn thickly over it. At first the ruins were little more than heaps of cut stones, but at Kefr Anbīl there were some good houses, a church, a tower and a very large necropolis of rock-cut tombs. Here the landscape changed, the cultivated land shrank into tiny patches, the red earth disappeared and was replaced by barren stretches of rock, from out of which rose the grey ruins like so many colossal boulders. There must have been more cultivation when the district supported the very large population represented by the ruined towns, but the rains of many winters have broken the artificial terracings and washed the earth down into the valleys, so that by no possibility could the former inhabitants draw from it now sufficient produce to sustain them. North-east of Kefr Anbīl, across a labyrinth of rocks, appeared the walls of a wonderful village, Khirbet Hass, which I was particularly anxious to see. I sent the mules straight to El Bārah, our halting place that night, engaged a villager as a guide over the stony waste, and set off with Mikhāil and Mahmūd. The path wound in and out between the rocks, a narrow band of grass plentifully scattered with stones; the afternoon sun shone hot upon us, and I dismounted, took off my coat, bound it (as I thought) fast to my saddle, and walked on ahead amid the grass and flowers. That was the beginning of the misadventure. Khīrbet Hāss was quite deserted save for a couple of black tents. The streets of the market were empty, the walls of the shops had fallen in, the church had long been abandoned of worshippers, the splendid houses were as silent as the tombs, the palisaded gardens were untended, and no one came down to draw water from the deep cisterns. The charm and the mystery of it kept me loitering till the sun was near the horizon and a cold wind had risen to remind me of my coat, but, lo! when I returned to the horses it was gone from my saddle. Tweed coats do not grow on every bush in north Syria, and it was obvious that some effort must be made to recover mine. Mahmūd rode back almost to Kefr Anbīl, and returned after an hour and a half empty-handed. By this time it was growing dark; moreover a black storm was blowing up from the east, and we had an hour to ride through very rough country. We started at once, Mikhāil, Mahmūd and I, picking our way along an almost invisible path. As ill luck would have it, just as the dusk closed in the storm broke upon us, the night turned pitch dark, and with the driving rain in our faces we missed that Medea-thread of a road. At this moment Mikhāil's ears were assailed by the barking of imaginary dogs, and we turned our horses' heads towards the point from which he supposed it to come. This was the second stage of the misadventure, and I at least ought to have remembered that Mikhāil was always the worst guide, even when he knew the direction of the place towards which he was going. We stumbled on; a watery moon came out to show us that our way led nowhere, and being assured of this we stopped and fired off a couple of pistol shots, thinking that if the village were close at hand the muleteers would hear us and make some answering signal. None came, however, and we found our way back to the point where the rain had blinded us, only to be deluded again by that phantom barking and to set off again on our wild dog chase. This time we went still further afield, and Heaven knows where we should ultimately have arrived if I had not demonstrated by the misty moon that we were riding steadily south, whereas El Bārah lay to the north. At this we turned heavily in our tracks, and when we had ridden some way back we dismounted and sat down upon a ruined wall to discuss the advisability of lodging for the night in an empty tomb, and to eat a mouthful of bread and cheese out of Mahmūd's saddle-bags. The hungry horses came nosing up to us; mine had half my share of bread, for after all he was doing more than half the share of work. The food gave us enterprise; we rode on and found ourselves in the twinkling of an eye at the original branching off place. From it we struck a third path, and in five minutes came to the village of El Bārah, round which we had been circling for three hours. The muleteers were fast asleep in the tents; we woke them somewhat rudely, and asked whether they had not heard our signals. Oh yes, they replied cheerfully, but concluding that it was a robber taking advantage of the stormy night to kill someone, they had paid small attention. This is the whole tale of the misadventure; it does credit to none of the persons concerned, and I blush to relate it. It has, however, taught me not to doubt the truth of similar occurrences in the lives of other travellers whom I have now every reason to believe entirely veracious.

Intolerable though El Bārah may be by night, by day it is most marvellous and most beautiful. It is like the dream city which children create for themselves to dwell in between bed-time and sleep-time, building palace after palace down the shining ways of the imagination, and no words can give the charm of it nor the magic of the Syrian spring. The generations of the dead walk with you down the streets, you see them flitting across their balconies, gazing out of windows wreathed with white clematis, wandering in palisaded gardens that are still planted with olive and with vine and carpeted with iris, hyacinth and anemone. Yet you may search the chronicles for them in vain; they played no part in history, but were content to live in peace and to build themselves great houses in which to dwell and fine tombs to lie in after they were dead. That they became Christian the hundreds of ruined churches and the cross carved over the doors and windows of their dwellings, would be enough to show; that they were artists their decorations prove; that they were wealthy their spacious mansions, their summer houses and stables and outhouses testify. They borrowed from Greece such measure of cultivation and of the arts as they required, and fused with them the spirit of Orient magnificence which never breathed without effect on the imagination of the West; they lived in comfort and security such as few of their contemporaries can have known, and the Mahommadan invasion swept them off the face of the earth.

I spent two days at El Bārah and visited five or six of the villages round about, the Sheikh of El Bārah and his son serving me as guides. The Sheikh was a sprightly old man called Yūnis, who had guided all the distinguished archaeologists of his day, remembered them, and spoke of them by name or rather by names of his own, very far removed from the originals. I contrived to make out those of de Vogüé and Waddington, and another that was quite unintelligible was probably intended for Sachau. At Serjilla, a town with a sober and solid air of respectability that would be hard to match, though it is roofless and quite deserted, he presented me with a palace and its adjacent tomb that I might live and die in his neighbourhood, and when I left he rode with me as far as Deir Sanbīl to put me on my way. He was much exercised that day by a disturbance that had arisen in a village near at hand. A man had been waylaid by two others of a neighbouring village who desired to rob him. Fortunately a fellow townsman had come to his assistance and together they had suceeded in beating off the attack, but in the contest the friend had lost his life. His relations had raided the robbers' village and carried off all the cattle. Mahmūd was of opinion that they should not have taken the law into their own hands.

'By God!' said he, 'they should have laid the case before the Government.'

But Yūnis replied, with unanswerable logic:

'Of what use was it to go to the Government? They wanted their rights.'

In the course of conversation I asked Yunīs whether he ever went to Aleppo.

'By God!' said he. 'And then I sit in the bazaars and watch the consuls walking, each with a man in front clothed in a coat worth two hundred piastres, and the ladies with as it were flowers upon their heads.' (The fashionable European hat, I imagine.) 'I always go to Aleppo when my sons are in prison there,' he explained. 'Sometimes the gaoler is soft-hearted and a little money will get them out.'

I edged away from what seemed to be delicate ground by asking how many sons he had.

'Eight, praise be to God! Each of my wives bore me four sons and two daughters.'

'Praise be to God!' said I.

'May God prolong your life!' said Yūnis. 'My second wife cost me a great deal of money,' he added.

'Yes?' said I.

'May God make it Yes upon you, oh lady! I took her from her husband, and by God (may His name be praised and exalted!) I had to pay two thousand piastres to the husband and three thousand to the judge.'

This was too much for Hajj Mahmūd's sense of the proprieties.

'You took her from her husband?' said he. 'Wāllah! that was the deed of a Nosairi or an Ismaili. Does a Moslem take away a man's wife? It is forbidden.'

'He was my enemy,' explained Yunīs. 'By God and the Prophet of God, there was enmity between us even unto death.'

'Had she children?' inquired Mahmūd.

'Ey wāllah!' assented the Sheikh, a little put about by Mahmūd's disapproval. 'But I paid two thousand piastres to the husband and three thousand –'

'By the Face of God!' exclaimed Mahmūd, still more outraged, 'it was the deed of an infidel.'

And here I put an end to further discussion of the merits of the case by asking whether the woman had liked being carried off.

'Without doubt,' said Yūnis. 'It was her wish.'

We may conclude, therefore, that ethics did not have much to do with the matter, though he indemnified so amply both the husband and the judge.

This episode led us to discuss the usual price paid for a wife.

'For such as we,' said Yūnis, with an indescribable air of social pre-eminence, 'the girl will not be less than four thousand piastres, but a poor man who has no money will give the father a cow or a few sheep, and he will be content.'

After he left us I rode round by Ruweihā that I might see the famous church by which stands the domed tomb of Bizzos. This church is the most beautiful in the Jebel Zāwiyyeh, with its splendid narthex and carved doorways, its stilted arches and the wide-spanned arcades of its nave – how just was the confidence in his own mastery over his material which encouraged the builder to throw those great arches from pier to pier is proved by the fact that one of them stands to this day. The little tomb of Bizzos is almost as perfect as it was when it was first built. By the doorway an inscription is cut in Greek:

'Bizzos son of Pardos. I lived well, I die well and well I rest. Pray for me.' The strangest features in all the architecture of North Syria are the half-remembered classical motives that find their way into mouldings that are almost Gothic in their freedom, and the themes of a classical entablature that grace church window or architrave. The scheme of Syrian decoration was primarily a row of circles or wreaths filled with whorls or with the Christian monogram; but as the stonecutters grew more skilful they ran their circles together into a hundred exquisite and fanciful shapes of acanthus and palm and laurel, making a flowing pattern round church or tomb as varied as the imagination could contrive. The grass beneath their feet, the leaves on the boughs above their heads, inspired them with a wealth of decorative design much as they inspired William Morris twelve hundred years later.

There is another church at Ruweihā scarcely less perfect than the Bizzos church, but not so splendid in design. It is remarkable for a monument standing close to the south wall, which has been explained as a bell tower, or a tomb, or a pulpit, or not explained at all. It is constructed of two stories, the lower one consisting of six columns supporting a platform, from the low wall of which rise four corner piers to carry the dome or canopy. The resemblance to some of the North Italian tombs, as, for instance, to the monument of Rolandino, in Bologna, is so striking that the beholder instinctively assigns a similar purpose to the graceful building at Ruweihā.

We camped that night at Dāna, a village that boasts a pyramid tomb with a porch of four Corinthian columns, as perfect in execution and in balanced proportion as anything you could wish to see. On our way from Ruweihā we passed a mansion which I would take as a type of the domestic architecture of the sixth century. It stood apart, separated by a mile or two of rolling country from any village, with open balconies facing towards the west and a delightful gabled porch to the north, such a porch as might adorn any English country house of today. You could fancy the sixth-century owner sitting on the stone bench within and watching for his friends – he can have feared no enemies, or he would not have built his dwelling far out in the country and guarded it only with a garden palisade. At Kasr el Banāt, the Maidens' Fortress as the Syrians call it, I was impressed more than at any other place with the high level that social order had reached in the Jebel Zāwiyyeh, for here were security and wealth openly displayed, and leisure wherein to cultivate the arts; and as I rode away I fell to wondering whether civilisation is indeed, as we think it in Europe, a resistless power sweeping forward and carrying upon its crest those who are apt to profit by its advance; or whether it is not rather a tide that ebbs and flows, and in its ceaseless turn and return touches ever at the flood the self-same place upon the shore.

Late at night one of Sheikh Yūnis's sons rode in to ask us whether his father were still with us. On leaving us that enterprising old party had not, it seemed, returned to the bosom of his anxious family, and I have a suspicion that his friendly eagerness to set us on our way was but part of a deep-laid plot by means of which he hoped to be able to take a hand in those local disturbances that had preoccupied him during the morning. At any rate he had made off as soon as we were out of sight, and the presumption was that he had hastened to join in the fray. What happened to him I never heard, but I am prepared to wager that whoever bit the dust at the village of El Mughāra it was not Sheikh Yūnis.

Three rather tedious days lay between us and Aleppo. We might have made the journey in two, but I had determined to strike a little to the east in order to avoid the carriage road, which was well known, and to traverse country which, though it might not be more interesting, was at least less familiar. Five hours' ride from Dāna across open rolling uplands brought us to Tarutīn. We passed several ancient sites, re-occupied by half-settled Arabs of the Muwāli tribes, though the old buildings were completely ruined. All along the western edges of the desert the Bedouin are beginning to cultivate the soil, and are therefore forced to establish themselves in some fixed spot near their crops. 'We are become fellahīn,' said the Sheikh of Tarutīn. In some distant age, when all the world is ploughed and harvested, there will be no nomads left in Arabia. In the initial stages these new-made farmers continue to live in tents, but the tents are stationary, the accompanying dirt cumulative, and the settlement unpleasing to any of the senses. The few families at Tarutīn had not yet forgotten their desert manners, and we found them agreeable people, notwithstanding the accuracy with which the above remarks applied to their village of hair.

I had not been in camp an hour before there was a great commotion among my men, and Mikhāil came to my tent shouting, 'The Americans! the Americans!' It was not a raid, but the Princeton archaeological expedition, which, travelling from Damascus by other ways than ours, was now making for the Jebel Zāwiyyeh; and a fortunate encounter my camp thought it, for each one of us found acquaintances among the masters or among the muleteers, and had time to talk, as people will talk who meet by chance upon an empty road. Moreover, the day I spent at Tarutīn provided me with an admirable object lesson in archaeology. As the members of the expedition planned the ruins and deciphered the inscriptions, the whole fifth-century town rose from its ashes and stood before us – churches, houses, forts, rock-hewn tombs with the names and dates of death of the occupants carved over the door. Next day we had a march of ten hours. We went north, passing a small mud-village called Helbān, and another called Mughāra Merzeh, where there were the remains of a church and rock-cut tombs of a very simple kind. (None of these places are marked on Kiepert's map.) Then we turned to the east and reached Tulūl, where we came upon an immense expanse of flood water, stretching south at least twelve miles from the Matkh, the swamp in which the River

Kuwēk rises. At Tulūl some Arab women were mourning over a new-made grave. For three days after the dead are buried they weep thus at the grave side; only at Mecca and at Medīna, said Mahmūd, there is no mourning for those who are gone. There when breath leaves the body the women give three cries, to make known to the world that the soul has fled; but beyond these cries there is no lamentation, for it is forbidden that tears should fall upon the head of the corpse. The Lord has given and He has taken away. So we went south along the edge of the high ground to a little hill called Tell Selma, where we turned east again and rounded the flood water and rode along its margin to a big village, Moyemāt, half tents and half beehive huts built of mud. There is no other material but mud in which to build; from the moment we left the rocky ground on which Tarutīn stands we never saw a stone – never a stone and never a tree, but an endless unbroken cornfield, with the first scarlet tulips coming into bloom among the young wheat. It was heavy going, though it was soft to the horses' feet. If there were a little more earth upon the hills of Syria and a few more stones upon the plain, travelling would be easier in that country; but He, than whom there is none other, has ordered differently. From Moyemāt we rode north-east until we came to a village called Hober, at the foot of a spur of the Jebel el Hāss, and here we tried to camp, but could get neither oats nor barley, nor even a handful of chopped straw; and so we went on to Kefr 'Abīd, which is marked on the map, and pitched tents at six o'clock. The villages unknown to Kiepert are probably of recent construction, indeed many of them are still half camp. They are exceedingly numerous; about Hober I counted five within a radius of a mile or two. The Arabs who inhabit them retain their nomad habits of feud. Each village has its allies and its blood enemies, and political relations are as delicate as they are in the desert. My diary contains the following note at the end of the day: 'Periwinkles, white irises of the kind that were blue at El Bārah, red and yellow ranunculus, storks, larks.' These were all that broke the monotony of the long ride.

About half an hour to the north of Kefr 'Abīd there is a little beehive village which contains a very perfect mosaic of geometrical patterns. The fragments of other mosaics are to be found scattered through the village, some in the houses, and some in the courtyards, and the whole district needs careful exploration while the new settlers are turning up the ground and before they destroy what they may find. We reached Aleppo at midday, approaching it by an open drain. Whether it were because of the evil smell or because of the heavy sky and dust-laden wind I do not know, but the first impression of Aleppo was disappointing. The name, in its charming Europeanised form, should belong to a more attractive city, and attractive Aleppo certainly is not, for it is set in a barren, treeless, featureless world, the beginning of the great Mesopotamian flats. The site of the town is like a cup and saucer, the houses lie in the saucer and the castle stands on the upturned cup, its minaret visible several hours away while no vestige of the city appears until the last mile of the road. I stayed two days, during which time it rained almost ceaselessly, therefore I do not know Aleppo – an Oriental city will not admit you into the circle of its intimates unless you spend months within its walls, and not even then if you will not take pains to please – but I did not leave without having perceived dimly that there was something to be known. It has been a splendid Arab city; as you walk down the narrow streets you pass minarets and gateways of the finest period of Arab archi-tecture; some of the mosques and baths and khāns (especially those half ruined and closed) are in the same style, and the castle is the best example of twelfth-century Arab workmanship in all Syria, with iron doors of the same period – they are dated – and beautiful bits of decoration. There must be some native vitality still that corresponds to these signs of past greatness, but the town has fallen on evil days. It has been caught between the jealousies of European concession hunters, and it suffers more than most Syrian towns from the strangling grasp of the Ottoman Government. It is slowly dying for want of an outlet to the sea, and neither the French nor the German railway will supply its need. Hitherto the two companies have been busily engaged in thwarting one another. The original concession to the Rayak-Hamāh railway extended to Aleppo and north to Birijik – I was told that the tickets to Birijikwere printed off when the first rails were laid at Rayak. Then came Germany, with her great scheme of a railway to Baghdad. She secured a concession for a branch line from Killiz to Aleppo, and did what she could to prevent the French from advancing beyond Hamāh, on the plea that the French railway would detract from the value of the German concession – my information, it may be well imagined, is not from the Imperial Chancery, but from native sources in Aleppo itself.

Since I left, the French have taken up their interrupted work on the Rayak-Hamāh line, though it is to be carried forward, I believe, not to Birijik, but only as far as Aleppo. It will be of no benefit to the town. Aleppo merchants do not wish to send their goods a three days' journey to Beyrout; they want a handy seaport of their own, which will enable them to pocket all the profits of the trade, and that port should be Alexandretta. Neither does the Baghdad railway, if it be continued, offer any prospect of advantage. By a branch line already existing (it was built by English and French capitalists, but has recently passed under German control) the railway will touch the sea at Mersina, but Mersina is as far from Aleppo as is Beyrout. That a line should be laid direct from Aleppo to Alexandretta is extremely improbable, since the Sultan fears above all things to connect the inland caravan routes with the coast, lest the troops of the foreigner, and particularly of England, should find it perilously easy to land from their warships and march up country. Aleppo should be still, as it was in times past, the great distributing centre for the merchandise of the interior, but traffic is throttled by the fatal frequency with which the Government commandeers the baggage camels. Last year, with the Yemen war on hand and the consequent necessity of transporting men and military stores to the coast that they might be shipped to the Red Sea, this grievance had become acute. For over a month trade had been stagnant and goods bound for the coast had lain piled in the bazaar – a little more and they would cease to come at all, the camel owners from the East not daring to enter the zone of danger to their beasts. Here, as in all other Turkish towns, I heard the cry of official bankruptcy. The Government had no funds wherewith to undertake the most necessary works, the treasuries were completely empty.

Though my stay was short I was not without acquaintances, among whom the most important was the Vāli. Kiāzim Pasha is a man of very different stamp from the Vāli of Damascus. To the extent that the latter is, according to his lights, a real statesman, in so far is Kiāzim nothing but a *farceur*. He received me in his harem, for which I was grateful when I saw his wife, who is one of the most beautiful women that it is possible to behold. She is tall and stately, with a small dark head, set on magnificent shoulders, a small straight nose, a pointed chin and brows arching over eyes that are like dark pools – I could not take mine from her face while she sat with us. Both she and her husband are Circassians, a fact that had put me on my guard before the Vāli opened his lips. They both spoke French, and he spoke it very well. He received me in an offhand manner, and his first remark was:

'Je suis le jeune pasha qui a fait la paix entre les églises.'

I knew enough of his history to realise that he had been Muteserrif of Jerusalem at a time when the rivalries between the Christian sects had ended in more murders than are customary, and that some kind of uneasy compromise had been reached, whether through his ingenuity or the necessities of the case I had not heard.

'How old do you think I am?' said the pasha.

I replied tactfully that I should give him thirty-five years.

'Thirty-six!' he said triumphantly. 'But the consuls listened to me. Mon Dieu! that was a better post than this, though I am Vāli now. Here I have no occasion to hold conferences with the consuls, and a man like me needs the society of educated Europeans.'

(Mistrust the second: an Oriental official, who declares that he prefers the company of Europeans.)

'I am very Anglophil,' said he.

I expressed the gratitude of my country in suitable terms.

'But what are you doing in Yemen?' he added quickly.

'Excellency,' said I, 'we English are a maritime people, and there are but two places that concern us in all Arabia.'

'I know,' he interpolated. 'Mecca and Medīna.'

'No,' said I. 'Aden and Kweit.'

'And you hold them both,' he returned angrily – yes, I am bound to confess that the tones of his voice were not those of an Anglo-maniac.

Presently he began to tell me that he alone among pashas had grasped modern necessities. He meant to build a fine metalled road to Alexandretta – not that it will be of much use, thought I, if there are no camels to walk in it – like the road he had built from Samaria to Jerusalem. That was a road like none other in Turkey – did I know it? I had but lately travelled over it, and seized the opportunity of congratulating the maker of it; but I did not think it necessary to mention that it breaks off at the bottom of the only serious ascent and does not begin again till the summit of the Judaean plateau is reached.

This is all that need be said of Kiăzim Pasha's methods.

A far more sympathetic acquaintance was the Greek Catholic Archbishop, a Damascene educated in Paris and for some time curé of the Greek Catholic congregation in that city, though he is still comparatively young. I had been given a letter to him, on the presentation of which he received me with great affability in his own house. We sat in a room filled with books, the windows opening on to the silent courtyard of his palace, and talked of the paths into which thought had wandered in Europe; but I found to my pleasure that for all his learning and his long sojourn in the West, the Archbishop had remained an Oriental at heart.

'I rejoiced,' said he, 'when I was ordered to return from Paris to my own land. There is much knowledge, but little faith in France; while in Syria, though there is much ignorance, religion rests upon a sure foundation of belief.'

The conclusion that may be drawn from this statement is not flattering to the Church, but I refrained from comment.

He appeared in the afternoon to return my call – from the Văli downwards all must conform to this social obligation – wearing his gold cross and carrying his archiepiscopal staff in his hand. From his tall brimless hat a black veil fell down his back, his black robes were edged with purple, and an obsequious chaplain walked behind him. He found another visitor sitting with me in the inn parlour, Nicola Homsi, a rich banker of his own congregation. Homsi belongs to an important Christian family settled in Aleppo, and his banking house has representatives in Marseilles and in London. He and the Archbishop between them were fairly representative of the most enterprising and the best educated classes in Syria. It is they who suffer at the hands of the Turk – the ecclesiastic, because of a blind and meaningless official opposition that meets the Christian at every turn; the banker, because his interests call aloud for progress, and progress is what the Turk will never understand. I therefore asked them what they thought would be the future of the country. They looked at one another, and the Archbishop answered:

'I do not know. I have thought deeply on the subject, and I can see no future for Syria, whichever way I turn.'

That is the only credible answer I have heard to any part of the Turkish question.

The air of Aleppo is judged by the Sultan to be particularly suitable for pashas who have fallen under his displeasure at Constantinople. The town is so full of exiles that even the most casual visitor can scarcely help making acquaintance with a few of them. One was lodged in my hotel, a mild-mannered dyspeptic, whom no one would have suspected of revolutionary sympathies. Probably he was indeed without them, and owed his banishment merely to some chance word, reported and magnified by an enemy or a spy. I was to see many of these exiles scattered up and down Asia Minor, and none that I encountered could tell me for what cause they had suffered banishment. Some, no doubt, must have had a suspicion, and some were perfectly well aware of their offence, but most of them were as innocently ignorant as they professed to be. Now this has a wider bearing on the subject of Turkish patriotic feeling than may at first appear; for the truth is that these exiled pashas are very rarely patriots paying the price of devotion to a national ideal, but rather men whom an unlucky turn of events has alienated from the existing order. If there is any chance that they may be taken back into favour you will find them nervously anxious, even in exile, to refrain from action that would tend to increase official suspicion; and it is only when they have determined that there is no hope for them as long as the present Sultan lives, that they are willing to associate freely with Europeans or to speak openly of their grievances. There is, so far as I can see, no organised body of liberal opinion in Turkey, but merely individual discontents, founded on personal misfortune. It seems improbable that when the exiles return to Constantinople on the death of the Sultan they will provide any scheme of form or show any desire to alter a system under which, by the natural revolution of affairs, they will again find themselves persons of consideration.

There is another form of exile to be met with in Turkey, the honourable banishment of a distant appointment. To this class, I fancy, belongs Nāzim Pasha himself, and so does my friend Muhammad 'Ali Pasha of Aleppo. The latter is an agreeable man of about thirty, married to an English wife. He accompanied me to the Vāli's house, obtained permission that I should see the citadel, and in many ways contrived to make himself useful. His wife was a pleasant little lady from Brixton; he had met her in Constantinople and there married her, which may, for ought I know, have been partly the reason of his fall from favour, the English nation not being a *gens grata* at Yildiz Kiosk. Muhammad 'Ali Pasha is a gentleman in the full sense of the word, and he seems to have made his wife happy; but it must be clearly understood that I could not as a general rule recommend Turkish pashas as husbands to the maidens of Brixton. Though she played tennis at the Tennis Club, and went to the sewing parties of the European colony, she was obliged to conform to some extent to the habits of Moslem women. She never went into the streets without being veiled; 'because people would talk if a pasha's wife were to show her face,' said she.

We reached the citadel in the one hour of sunlight that shone on Aleppo during my stay, and were taken round by polite officers, splendid in uniforms and clanking swords and spurs, who were particularly anxious that I should not miss the small mosque in the middle of the fortress, erected on the very spot where Abraham milked his cow. The very name of Aleppo, said they, is due to this historic occurrence, and there can be no doubt that its Arabic form, Haleb, is composed of the same root letters as those that form the verb to milk. In spite of the deep significance of the mosque, I was more interested in the view from the top of the minaret. The Mesopotamian plain lay outspread before us, as flat as a board – Euphrates stream is visible from that tower on a clear day, and indeed you might see Baghdad but for the tiresome way in which the round earth curves, for there is no barrier to the eye in all that great level. Below us, were the clustered roofs of bazaar and khān, with here and there a bird's-eye glimpse of marble courtyards, and here and there the fine spire of a minaret. Trees and water were lacking in the landscape, and water is the main difficulty in Aleppo itself. The sluggish stream that flows out of the Matkh dries up in the summer, and the wells are brackish all the year round. Good drinking water must be brought from a great distance and costs every household at least a piastre a day, a serious addition to the cost of living. But the climate is good, sharply cold in winter and not over hot for more than a month or two in the summer. Such is Aleppo, the great city with the high-sounding name and the traces of a splendid past.

8

We started from Bāsufān at eight o'clock on the morning of April 4, and rode south by incredibly stony tracks, leaving Kal'at Sim'ān to the west and skirting round the eastern flanks of the Jebel Sheikh Barakāt. Musa declared that he must accompany us on the first part of our way, and came with us to Deiret 'Azzeh, a large Mohammadan village of from three hundred to four hundred houses. Here he left us, and we went down into the fertile plain of Sermeda, ringed round with the slopes of the Jebel Halakah. At midday we reached the large village of Dāna, and lunched by the famous third-century tomb that de Vogüé published, to my mind the loveliest of the smaller monuments of North Syria and worthy in its delicate simplicity to stand by the Choragic Monument of Lysicrates at Athens. There was nothing else to detain us at Dāna, and having waited for the baggage animals to come up I sent them on with Mikhāil and a local guide, bidding them meet Najīb and me at the ruins of Dehes. After some consultation Najīb and the local man decided on the spot, known to me only from the accounts of travellers, and it was not till we had reached it that I discovered that we were at Mehes instead of Dehes. It was all one, however, since we had met and found the place to be a convenient camping-ground. From Dāna, Najīb took me north along the Roman road by a

Roman triumphal arch, the Bāb el Hawa, finely situated at the entrance of a rocky valley. We rode along this valley for a mile or two, passing a ruined church, and struck up the hills to the west by a gorge that brought us out on to a wide plateau close to the deserted village of Ksejba. We went on to the village of Bābiska, through country which was scattered with flowers and with groups of ruined houses and churches: the heart leapt at the sight of such lonely and unravished beauty. On these hilltops it was difficult to say where stood Bākirha, the town I wished to visit, but near Bābiska we found a couple of shepherd tents, and from one of the inhabitants inquired the way. The shepherd was a phlegmatic man; he said there was no road to Bākirha, and that the afternoon had grown too late for such an enterprise, moreover he himself was starting off in another direction with a basket of eggs and could not help us. I, however, had not ridden so many miles in order to be defeated at the last, and, with some bullying and a good deal of persuasion we induced the shepherd to show us the way to the foot of the hill on which Bākirha stands. He walked with us for an hour or so, then pointed towards the summit of the Jebel Bārisha and saying, 'There is Bākirha,' he left us abruptly and returned to his basket of eggs.

High up on the mountainside we saw the ruins bathed in the afternoon sun, and having looked in vain for a path we pushed our horses straight in among the boulders and brakes of flowering thorn. But there is a limit to the endurance even of Syrian horses, and ours had almost reached it after a long day spent in clambering over stones. We had still to get into camp, Heaven alone knew how far away; yet I could not abandon the shining walls that were now so close to us upon the hill, and I told the reluctant Najīb to wait below with the horses while I climbed up alone. The day was closing in, and I climbed in haste; but for all my haste the scramble over those steep rocks, half-buried in flowers and warm with the level sun, is a memory that will not easily fade. In half an hour I stood at the entrance of the town, below a splendid basilica rich in varied beauty of decoration and design. Beyond it the ruined streets, empty of all inhabitants, lay along the mountainside, houses with carved balconies and deep-porched doorways, columned marketplaces, and the golden sunlight over all. But I was bent upon another pilgrimage. A broad and winding road led up above the town until it reached the boundary of the flowered slopes, and nothing except a short rocky face of hill lay between the open ground where the path ended and the summit of the range. The mountain was cleft this way and that by precipitous gorges, enclosing between their escarpments prospects of sunlit fertile plain, and at the head of the gorges on a narrow shelf of ground stood a small and exquisite temple. I sat down by the gate through which the worshippers had passed into the temple court. Below me lay the northern slopes of the Jebel Bārisha and broad fair valleys and the snow-clad ranks of the Giour Dāgh veiled in a warm haze. Temple and town and hillside were alike deserted save that far away upon a rocky spur a shepherd boy piped a wild sweet melody to his scattered flocks. The breath of the reed is the very voice of solitude; shrill and clear and passionless it rose to the temple gate, borne on deep waves of mountain air that were perfumed with flowers and coloured with the rays of the low sun. Men had come and gone, life had surged up the flanks of the hills and retreated again, leaving the old gods to resume their sway over rock and flowering thorn, in peace and loneliness and beauty.

So at the gate of the sanctuary I offered praise, and having given thanks went on my way rejoicing.

Najīb welcomed me back with expressions of relief.

'By God!' said he, 'I have not smoked a single cigarette since I lost sight of your Excellency, but all this hour I said: "Please God she will not meet with a robber among the rocks."'

Therewith, to make up for lost opportunity, he lighted the cigarette that his anxiety had not prevented him from rolling during my absence, and though I will not undertake to affirm that it was indeed the only one, the sentiment was gratifying. I thought at the time (but next day's march proved me to be wrong) that we rode down to the plain of Sermeda by the roughest track in the world. When we got to the foot of the hill we turned up a valley to the south, a narrow ribbon of cultivation winding between stony ranges. Presently it widened, and we passed a large modern village, where we received the welcome news that our camp had been seen ahead; at a quarter past six we struggled into Mehes or Dehes, whichever it may have been, feeling that our horses would have been put to it if they had been asked to walk another mile. An enchanting camp was Mehes. It was not often that I could pitch tents far from all habitation. The muleteer pined for the sour curds and other luxuries of civilisation, and indeed I missed the curds too, but the charm of a solitary camp went far to console me. The night was still and clear, we were lodged in the ruined nave of a church, and we slept the sleep of the blessed after our long ride.

There was one more ruin that I was determined to visit before I left the hills. It was the church of Kalb Lōzeh, which from descriptions seemed to be (as indeed it is) the finest building after Kal'at Sim'ān in all North Syria. I sent the baggage animals round by the valleys, with strict, but useless, injunctions to Fāris that he was not to dawdle, and set out with Mikhāil and Najīb to traverse on horseback two mountain ranges, the Jebel Bārisha and the Jebel el 'Ala. It is best to do rock climbing on foot; but if anyone would know the full extent of the gymnastic powers of a horse, he should ride up the Jebel el 'Ala to Kalb Lōzeh. I had thought myself tolerably well versed in the subject, but I found that the expedition widened my experience not a little. We rode straight up an intolerably stony hill to the west of Mehes, and so reached the summit of the Jebel Bārisha. The ground here was much broken by rocks, but between them were tiny olive groves and vineyards and tiny, scattered cornfields. Every ledge and hollow was a garden of wild flowers; tall blue irises unfurled their slender buds under sweet-smelling thickets of bay, and the air was scented with the purple daphne. This paradise was inhabited by a surly peasant, the least obliging and the most taciturn of men. After much unsuccessful bargaining (the price he set on any service he might render us was preposterous, but we were in his hands and he obliged us to give way) he agreed to guide us to Kalb Lōzeh, and conducted us forthwith down the Jebel Bārisha by a precipitous path cut out of the living rock. It was so steep and narrow that when we met a party of women coming up from the lower slopes with bundles of brushwood – brushwood! it was flowering daphne and bay – we had great difficulty in edging past them. At the bottom of this breakneck descent there was a deep valley with a lake at one end of it, and in front of us rose the Jebel el 'Ala, to the best of my judgment a wall of rock, quite impossible for horses to climb. The monosyllabic peasant who directed us – I am glad I do not remember his name – indicated that our path lay up it, and Najīb seeming to acquiesce, I followed with a sinking heart. It was indescribable. We jumped and tumbled over the rock faces and our animals jumped and tumbled after us, scrambling along the edge of little precipices, where, if they had fallen they must have broken every bone. Providence watched over us and we got up unhurt into a country as lovely as that which we had left on top of the Jebel Bārisha. At the entrance of an olive grove our guide turned back, and in a few moments we reached Kalb Lōzeh.

Whether there was ever much of a settlement round the great church I do not know; there are now but few remains of houses, and it stands almost alone. It stands too very nearly unrivalled among the monuments of Syrian art. The towered narthex, the wide bays of the nave, the apse adorned with engaged columns, the matchless beauty of the decoration and the justice of proportion preserved in every part, are the features that first strike the beholder; but as he gazes he becomes aware that this is not only the last word in the history of Syrian architecture, spoken at the end of many centuries of endeavour, but that it is also the beginning of a new chapter in the architecture of the world. The fine and simple beauty of Romanesque was born in North Syria. It is curious to consider to what developments the genius of these architects might have led if they had not been checked by the Arab invasion. Certain it is that we should have had an independent school of great builders, strongly influenced perhaps by classical tradition and yet more strongly by the East, but everywhere asserting an unmistakable personality as bold as it was imaginative and delicate. There is little consolation in the reflection that the creative vigour that is evident at Kalb Lōzeh never had time to pass into decadence.

I had heard or read that in the mountains near Kalb Lōzeh were to be found a few Druze villages, inhabited by emigrants from the Lebanon, but as I had not yet come upon them I had almost forgotten their existence. Near the church stood half a dozen hovels, the inhabitants of which came out to watch me as I photographed. Almost unconsciously I was struck by some well-known look in the kohl-blackened eyes and certain peculiarities of manner that are difficult to specify but that combine to form an impression of easy and friendly familiarity with perhaps a touch of patronage in it. When the women joined the little crowd my eye was caught by the silver chains and buckles that they wore, which I remembered vaguely to have remarked elsewhere. As we were about to leave, an oldish man came forward and offered to walk with us for an hour, saying that the way down to Hārim was difficult to find, and we had not walked fifty yards together before I realised the meaning of my subconscious recognition.

'Māsha'llah!' said I, 'you are Druzes.'

The man looked round anxiously at Najīb and Mikhāil, following close on our heels, bent his head and walked on without speaking.

'You need not fear,' said I. 'The soldier and my servant are discreet men.'

He took heart at this and said:

'There are few of us in the mountains, and we dread the Mohammadans and hide from them that we are Druzes, lest they should drive us out. We are not more than two hundred houses in all.'

'I have been hoping to find you,' said I, 'for I know the sheikhs in the Haurān, and they have shown me much kindness. Therefore I desire to salute all Druzes wherever I may meet with them.'

'Allah!' said he. 'Do you know the Turshān?'

'By God!' said I.

'Shibly and Yahya his brother?'

'Yahya I know, but Shibly is dead.'

'Dead!' he exclaimed. 'Oh Merciful! Shibly dead!' And with that he drew from me all the news of the Mountain and listened with rapt attention to tales for which I had not thought to find a willing ear so far from Salkhad. Suddenly his questions stopped and he swerved off the path towards a vineyard in which a young man was pruning the vines.

'Oh my son!' he cried. 'Shibly el Atrāsh is dead! Lend me thy shoes, that I may walk with the lady towards Hārim, for mine are worn.'

The young man approached, kicking off his red leather slippers as he came.

'We belong to God!' said he. 'I saw Shibly but a year ago.' And the news had to be repeated to him in detail.

We journeyed on along the stony mountain tops, brushing through purple daphne that grew in wonderful profusion, and talking as we went as though we had been old friends long parted. When we came to the lip of the Jebel el 'Ala we saw Hārim below us, and I insisted that my companion should spare himself the labour of walking further. He agreed, with great reluctance, to turn back, and stood pouring out blessings on me for full five minutes before he would bid me farewell, and then returned to us again that he might be sure we had understood the way.

'And next time you come into the Jebel el 'Ala,' said he, 'you must bring your camp to Kalb Lōzeh and stay at least a month, and we will give you all you need and show you all the ruins. And now may you go in peace and safety, please God; and in peace and in health return next year.'

'May God prolong your life,' said I, 'and give you peace!'

So we separated, and my heart was warm with an affection for his people which it is never difficult to rekindle. Cruel in battle they may be – the evidence against them is overwhelming; some have pronounced them treacherous, others have found them grasping; but when I meet a Druze I do not hesitate to greet a friend, nor shall I until my confidence has been proved to have been misplaced.

Hārim castle stands on a mound at the entrance of one of the few gorges that give access to the Jebel el 'Ala. Beyond it lies the great Orontes plain that was a granary in old days to the city of Antioch. Much of the northern part of the plain was under water, the swampy lake which the Syrians call El Bahra having been extended by the recent rains to its fullest limit. We turned south from Hārim and rode along the foot of the slopes of the Jebel el 'Ala to Salkīn, a memorable ride by reason of the exceeding beauty of the land through which we passed. I have seen no such abundant fertility in all Syria. Groves of olive and almond shared the fat ground with barley and oats; tangled thickets of gorse and broom, daphne and blackberry, edged the road, and every sunny spot was blue with iris stylosa. Salkīn itself lay in a wooded valley amid countless numbers of olive trees that stretched almost to the Orontes, several miles away. We dismounted before we reached the town in an open spot between olive-gardens. It was five o'clock, but Fāris had not arrived, and we disposed ourselves comfortably under the trees to wait for him. Our advent caused some excitement among the people who were sitting on the grass enjoying the evening calm; before long one, who was evidently a person of consideration, strolled up to us, accompanied by a servant, and invited me to come and rest in his house. He was a portly man, though he had barely touched middle age, and his countenance was pleasant; I accepted his invitation, thinking I might as well see what Salkīn had to offer. Opportunities of enlarging the circle of your acquaintance should always be grasped, especially in foreign parts.

I soon found that I had fallen into the hands of the wealthiest inhabitant of the town. Muhammad 'Ali Agha is son to Rustum Agha, who is by birth a Circassian and was servant in the great Circassian family of Kakhya Zādeh of Hamadān – that is their

Arabic name, the Persians call them Kat Khuda Zādeh. The Kakhya Zādehs migrated to Aleppo two centuries back; by such transactions as are familiar to Circassians, they grew exceedingly rich and are now one of the most powerful families in Aleppo. Their servants shared in their prosperity, and Rustum Agha, being a careful man, laid by enough money to buy land at Salkīn near his master's large estate in the Orontes valley. Fortune favoured him so well that the hand of a daughter of the Kakhya house was accorded to his son. I did not learn all these details at once, and was astonished while I sat in Muhammad 'Ali's harem to observe the deference with which he treated his wife, wondering why the sharp-featured, bright-eyed little lady who had borne him no sons should be addressed by her husband with such respect, for I did not then know that she was sister to Reshīd Agha Kakhya Zādeh. Muhammad 'Ali's only child, a girl of six years old, what though she were of so useless a sex, was evidently the apple of her father's eye. He talked to me long of her education and prospects, while I ate the superlatively good olives and cherry jam that his maid servants set before me. The Khānum was so gracious as to prepare the coffee with her own hands, and to express admiration of the battered felt hat that lay, partly concealed by its purple and silver kerchief, on the divan beside me.

'Oh, the beautiful European hat!' said she. 'Why do you wear a mendīl over it when it is so pretty?'

And with that she stripped it of the silk scarf and camel's hair rope, and placing it in all its naked disreputableness on her daughter's black curls, she declared that it was the most becoming head-dress in the world.

At six o'clock news was brought that my baggage animals had arrived, but before I could be allowed to return to my tents

Rustum Agha had to be visited. He was lying on a couch heaped with wadded silken coverlets in an upper chamber overlooking the beautiful rushing stream and the two great cypresses that add much to the picturesqueness of Salkīn. These trees stand like tall black sentinels before the gate of the house, which is the first and the largest in the winding village street. Rustum Agha was very old and very sick. His face lay like the face of a corpse upon the pale primrose silk of the bedclothes. He seemed to be gratified by my visit, though when he opened his lips to greet me he was seized with such an intolerable fit of coughing that his soul was almost shaken out of his body. As soon as he recovered he asked for the latest tidings of Russia and Japan, and I marvelled that he, who seemed so near his end, had the patience to ask anything of us, but whether we could see the lagging garnerer with the scythe hobbling up between the cypresses at the door.

As I sat down to dinner in my tent two of Muhammad 'Ali's servants staggered into camp bearing a large jar of olives grown in the gardens of Salkīn and preserved in their own oil. They brought too a request from their master that he might come and spend an hour with me, and I sent back a message praying that he would honour me. He appeared later, with one or two people in attendance to carry his hubble-bubble, and settled himself for a comfortable chat to the gurgling accompaniment of the water pipe, a soothing and an amicable sound conducive to conversation. He told me that Salkīn was one of the many Seleucias, and that it had been founded by Seleucus I himself as a summer resort for the inhabitants of Antioch. The spot on which I was camped, said he, and the graveyard beyond it, formed the site of the Seleucid town, 'and whenever we dig a grave we turn up carved stones and sometimes writing.' It seems not unnatural that the fertile foothills should have been selected by the people of Antioch for their country houses, but I have no further evidence to support the statement. He said also that his brother-in-law, Reshīd Agha, was staying with him, and he expressed a hope that I would call on him before I left next day.

If Reshīd Agha Kakhya Zādeh is the chief magnate of the district he is also the chief villain. I found him sitting in the early morning under the cypresses by the foaming stream, and a more evil face in a sweeter setting and lighted by a fairer sun it would have been hard to picture. He was a tall man with an over-bearing manner; his narrow forehead sheltered a world of vicious thoughts, his eyes squinted horribly, his thick sensuous lips spluttered as they enunciated the vain boastings and the harsh commands that formed the staple of his conversation He was wrapped in a pale silk robe, and he smoked a hubble bubble with a jewelled mouthpiece. By his side lay a bunch of Spring flowers, which he lifted and smelt at as he talked, finally offering the best of them to me. It is one of the privileges of the irresponsible traveller that he is not called upon to eschew the company of rogues, and when I found that my friend Muhammad 'Ali was about to accompany Reshīd Agha to the latter's house at Alāni and that this lay upon my path, I agreed to their suggestion that we should start together. The animals were brought out, we mounted under the cypresses and trotted off through olive-groves towards the Orontes valley. Reshīd Agha rode a splendid Arab mare; her black livery shone with the grooming she had received, she was lightly bitted, her headstall was a silver chain, her bridle was studded with silver ornaments, her every movement was a pleasure to behold. Her master appealed repeat-edly to Muhammad 'Ali, who jogged along by his side on a fine mule, for admiration of his mount, and when the latter had replied obsequiously with the required praise, his words were taken up and reinforced by an old fat man who rode with us upon a lean pony. He was jester and flatterer in ordinary to the Kakhya Zādeh, and, if his countenance spoke truly, panderer to his employer's vices and conniver at his crimes – among such strange company I had fallen that April morning. Hājj Najīb trotted along contentedly enough behind us; but Mikhāil, whose sense of the proprieties was strong, could barely conceal his disapproval, and answered in monosyllables when the jester or Reshīd Agha addressed him, though he unbent to Muhammad 'Ali, whom he judged (and rightly) to be of another clay. We rode for an hour over soft springy ground, Reshīd pointing out the beauties of his property as we went.

'All these olive-gardens are mine,' said he, 'by God and the Prophet of God! there are no such olives in the land. Every year I come out from Aleppo and see to the olive harvest with my own eyes lest the knaves who work for me should cheat me, God curse them! And therefore I have built myself a house at Alāni – God knows a man should make himself comfortable and live decently. But you shall see it, for you must eat with me; my table is spread for all comers. And around the house I have planted fields of mulberry trees; ten thousand stripling trees I have set in the last five years. I shall raise silkworks, please God! in great number. Oh Yūsef! show her the boxes of eggs that came from the land of France.'

The jester drew out of his breast a little cardboard box marked with the brand of a French firm; but before I could express my respect for the Agha's industry his attention had been distracted by some peasants who were pruning the olives not to his liking, and he spurred his mare up to the trees and poured out volleys of oaths and execrations upon the unfortunate men, after which he returned to my side and resumed the tale of his own prowess.

The house was large and new, and furnished throughout with plush and gilt-framed mirrors. Nothing would satisfy the Agha but that I should see and admire every corner, and the jester gave me the lead in praise and congratulation. From him I gathered that I was chiefly called upon to exalt the merits of the iron stoves that were prominent in each of the rooms – no doubt they added to the comfort if not to the picturesqueness of the establishment. This over we sat down on a divan to wait till lunch was ready. The Agha employed the time in relating to me with an over-emphasised indignation his struggles against the corrupt and oppressive government under which he lived, but he omitted to mention that what he suffered at the hands of those above him he passed on with interest to those below.

'By God!' he spluttered, 'you have seen how I labour among my olive trees, how I plant mulberries and send for the silkworm eggs from afar, that I may make a new trade at Alāni. Is the Vāli grateful? No, by the Prophet! He sends his men and they say: "Stop! till we see how much more we can tax you!" And when I would have set up a mill by the river for the grinding of my corn, they said: "Stop! it is not lawful." Then they sent for me in the middle of the harvest, and I rode hastily to Aleppo, and day by day and week by week they kept me waiting, and forbade me to leave the city. And by God!' shouted the Agha, thumping on a little inlaid table with his fist, 'I baffled them! I went to the Kādi, and said: "From whom is the order?" He said: "From the Vāli." Then I went to the Vāli and said: "From whom is the order?" And he answered: "I know not; perchance from the Kādi." And I bade them put it in writing, but they dared not, and so they let me go.'

In the middle of these tales three visitors were announced. They took a deferential seat on the opposite divan, and expended themselves in salutations and compliments. The Agha received them as an emperor might receive his subjects, and one of them presently seized the opportunity of saying to me in a stage whisper audible to all:

'You have seen what manner of man is the Agha? He is like a king in this country.' Whereat the Agha grew yet more regally gracious.

We sat down at last to a board loaded with every variety of Syrian delicacy, and few cuisines can beat the Syrian at its best. The Agha talked and ate with equal eagerness, and pressed one dish after another upon his guests. When the feast was in full swing a servant came to him and said that there was a certain fellāh who wished to speak with him.

'Let him come!' said the Agha indifferently. A ragged peasant figure appeared in the doorway and gazed with eyes half sullen, half frightened at the company, and the profusion of delicate meats.

'Peace be upon you, oh Agha!' he began.

But as soon as he saw the suppliant the Agha started to his feet in a very fury of passion. His face became purple, his squinting eyes started from his head, and he thumped the table with his clenched fist while he cried:

'Begone! and may God curse you and your offspring, and destroy your father's house! Begone, I tell you, and bring the money, or I will send you to prison with your wife and your family, and you shall starve there till you die.'

'Oh Agha!' said the man, with a certain dignity that faced the other's rage, 'a little time. Grant me a little time.'

'Not a day! not an hour!' yelled the Agha. 'Away! go! and tonight you shall bring me the money.'

The peasant vanished from the doorway without another word, the Agha sat down and continued his interrupted conversation and his interrupted meal; the other guests ate on as if nothing had happened, but I felt a little ashamed of my place at Reshīd's right hand, and I was not sorry to bid him farewell.

The Agha sent us down to the Orontes and caused us to be conveyed across the stream in his own ferry-boat. When we reached the other side Mikhāil ostentatiously took a crust from his pocket and began to eat it.

'Have you not eaten at Alāni?' said I.

'I do not eat with such as he,' replied Mikhāil stiffly.

At this Najīb, whom no such scruple had withheld from enjoying the unwonted luxury of an ample meal, nodded his head and said:

'The Agha is an evil man, may God reward him according to his deeds! He squeezes their last metalīk from the poor, he seizes their land, and turns them out of their houses to starve.'

'And worse than that,' said Mikhāil darkly.

'By God!' said Najīb. 'Every man who has a fair wife or a fair daughter stands in fear of him, for he will never rest until the woman is in his hands. By God and Muhammad the Prophet of God! many a man has he killed that he might take his wife into his own harem, and no one is hated more than he.'

'Cannot the law prevent him?' said I.

'Who shall prevent him?' said Najīb. 'He is rich – may God destroy his dwelling!'

'Oh Mikhāil!' said I as we picked our way across the muddy fields. 'I have travelled much in your country and I have seen and known many people, and seldom have I met a poor man whom I would not choose for a friend nor a rich man whom I would not shun. Now how is this? Does wealth change the very heart in Syria? For, look you, in my country not all the powerful are virtuous, but neither are they all rogues. And you and the Druze of Kalb Lōzeh and Mūsa the Kurd, would you too, if you had means, become like Reshīd Agha?'

'Oh lady,' said Mikhāil, 'the heart is the same, but in your country the government is just and strong and every one of the English must obey it, even the rich; whereas with us there is no justice, but the big man eats the little, and the little man eats the less, and the government eats all alike. And we all suffer after our kind and cry out to God to help us since we cannot help ourselves. But at least I did not eat the bread of Reshīd Agha,' concluded Mikhāil rather sententiously; and at this Najīb and I hung our heads.

Then followed five hours of the worst travelling. It may have been a judgment upon Najīb and me for sitting at the table of the wicked, but, like most of the judgments of Providence, it fell impartially on the just and the unjust, for Mikhāil endured as much as we. All that we had suffered the day before from the rocks we now suffered at the opposite end of the scale from the mud. The torture was a thousand times more acute. For five hours we crossed hills of earth on which there was never a stone, but the sticky slime of the slopes alternated with deep sloughs, where our horses sank up to their girths, and when at last we emerged from this morass into the Orontes valley man and beast were exhausted. The rising ground, which we had left, now rose into rocky ridges and peaks, the broad valley lay on our right hand, half full of flood water, and beyond it stood a splendid range of mountains. It was not long before we caught sight of the Byzantine towers and walls crowning the ridges to the left, and between hedges of flowering bay we stumbled along the broken pavement of the Roman road that led to Antioch. The road was further occupied by a tributary of the Orontes, which flowed merrily over the pavement. It was with some excitement that I gazed on the city of Antioch, which was for so many centuries a cradle of the arts and the seat of one of the most gorgeous civilisations that the world has known. Modern Antioch is like the pantaloon whose clothes are far too wide for his lean shanks; the castle walls go climbing over rock and hill, enclosing an area from which the town has shrunk away. But it is still one of the loveliest of places, with its great ragged hill behind it, crowned with walls, and its clustered red roofs stretching down to the wide and fertile valley of the Orontes. Earthquakes and the changing floods of the stream have overturned and covered with silt the palaces of the Greek and of the Roman city, yet as I stood at sunset on the sloping swad of the Nosairiyyeh graveyard below Mount Silpius, where my camp was pitched, and saw the red roofs under a crescent moon, I recognised that beauty is the inalienable heritage of Antioch.

9

A further acquaintance with Antioch did not destroy the impressions of the first evening. The more I wandered through the narrow paved streets the more delightful did they appear. Except the main thoroughfare, which is the bazaar, they were almost empty; my footsteps on the cobblestones broke through years of silence. The shallow gables covered with red tiles gave a charming and very distinctive note to the whole city, and shuttered balconies jutted out from house to house. Of the past there is scarcely a vestige. Two fine sarcophagi, adorned with putti and garlands and with the familiar and, I fancy, typically Asiatic motive of lions devouring bulls, stand in the Serāya, and one similar to these, but less elaborate, by the edge of the Daphne road. I saw, too, a fragment of a classical entablature in the courtyard of a Turkish house, and a scrap of wall in the main street that may certainly be dated earlier than the Mohammadan invasion – its courses of alternate brick and stone resembled the work on the Acropolis. For the rest the Antioch of Seleucus Nicator is a city of the imagination only. The island on which it was built has disappeared owing to the changing of the river bed, but tradition places it above the modern town. The banks of the Orontes must have been lined with splendid villas; I was told that the foundations of them were brought to light whenever a man dug deep enough through the silt, and that small objects of value, such as coins and bronzes, were often unearthed. Many such were brought to me for sale, but I judged them to be forgeries of an unskilful kind, and I was confirmed in my opinion by a Turkish pasha, Rifa't Agha, who has occupied his leisure in making a collection of antiquities. He possesses a fine series of Seleucid coins, the earlier nearly as good as the best Sicilian, the later nearly as bad as the worst Byzantine, and a few bronze lamps, one of which, in the shape of a curly-haired Eros head, is a beautiful example of Roman work. The Agha presented me with a small head, which I take to have been a copy of the head of Antioch with the high crown, and though it was but roughly worked, it possessed some distinction borrowed from a great original.

Forty years ago the walls and towers of the Acropolis were still almost perfect; they are now almost destroyed. The inhabitants of Antioch declare that the city is rocked to it foundations every half-century, and they are in instant expectation of another upheaval, the last having occurred in 1862; but it is prosperity not earthquake that has wrought the havoc in the fortress. The town is admirably situated in its rich valley, and connected with the port of Alexandretta by a fairly good road; it might easily become a great commercial centre, and even under Turkish rule it has grown considerably in the past fifty years, and grown at the expense of the Acropolis. To spare himself the trouble of quarrying, the Oriental will be deterred by no difficulty, and in spite of the labour of transporting the dressed stones of the fortress to the foot of the exceedingly steep hill on which it stands, all the modern houses have been built out of materials taken from it. The work of destruction continues; the stone facing is quickly disappearing from the walls, leaving only a core of a rubble and mortar which succumbs in a short time to the action of the weather. I made the whole circuit of the fortress one morning, and it took me three hours. To the west of the summit of Mount Silpius a rocky cleft seamed the hillside. It was full of rock-cut tombs, and just above my camp an ancient aqueduct spanned it. On the left hand of the cleft the line of wall dropped by precipitous rocks to the valley. Where large fragments remained it was evident that the stone facing had alternated with bands of brick, and that sometimes the stone itself had been varied by courses of smaller and larger blocks. The fortifications embraced a wide area, the upper part leading by gentle slopes, covered with brushwood and ruined foundations, to the top of the hill. In the west wall there was a narrow massive stone door, with a lintel of jointed blocks and a relieving arch above it. The south wall was broken by towers; the main citadel was at the south-east corner. From here the walls dropped down again steeply to the city and passed some distance to the east of it. They can be traced, I believe, to the Orontes. I did not follow their course, but climbed down from the citadel by a stony path into a deep gorge that cuts through the eastern end of the hill. The entrance to this gorge is guarded by a strong wall of brick and stone, which is called the Gate of Iron, and beyond it the fortifications climb the opposite side of the ravine and are continued along the hilltop. I do not know how far they extend; the ground was so rough and so much overgrown with bushes that I lost heart and turned back. There was a profusion of flowers among the rocks, marigold, asphodel, cyclamen and iris.

Beyond the gorge of the Iron Gate, on the hillside facing the Orontes, there is a cave which tradition calls the cave of St. Peter. The Greek communion has erected a little chapel at its mouth. Yet further along the hill is a still more curious relic of ancient

Antioch, the head of a Sphinx carved in relief upon a rock some twenty feet high. Folded about her brow she wears a drapery that falls on either side of her face and ends where the throat touches the bare breast. Her featureless countenance is turned slightly up the valley, as though she watched for one that shall yet come out of the East. If she could speak she might tell us of great kings and gorgeous pageants, of battle and of siege, for she has seen them all from her rock on the hillside. She still remembers that the Greeks she knew marched up from Babylonia, and since even the Romans did not teach her that the living world lies westward, I could not hope to enlighten her, and so left her watching for some new thing out of the East.

There was another pilgrimage to be made from Antioch: it was to Daphne, the famous shrine that marked the spot where the nymph baffled the desire of the god, the House of the Waters it is called in Arabic. It lies to the west of the town, about an hour's ride along the foot of the hills, and in the Spring a more enchanting ride could not be found. The path led through an exquisite boscage of budding green, set thickly with flowering hawthorn and with the strange purple of the Judas tree; then it crossed a low spur and descended into a steep valley through which a stream tumbled towards the Orontes.

No trace remains of the temples that adorned this fairest of all sanctuaries. Earthquakes and the mountain torrents have swept them down the ravine. But the beauty of the site has not diminished since the days when the citizens of the most luxurious capital in the East dallied there with the girls who served the god. The torrent does not burst noisily from the mountainside; it is born in a deep still pool that lies, swathed in a robe of maidenhair fern, in thickets 'annihilating all that's made to a green thought in a green shade'. From the pool issues a translucent river, unbroken of surface, narrow and profound; it runs into swirls and eddies and then into foaming cataracts and waterfalls that toss their white spray into the branches of mulberry and plane. Under the trees stand eleven water-mills; the ragged millers are the only inhabitants of Apollo's shrine. They brought us walnuts to eat by the edge of the stream, and small antique gems that had dropped from the ornaments of those who sought pleasures less innocent perhaps than ours by the banks of that same torrent.

It is impossible to travel in North Syria without acquiring a keen interest in the Seleucid kings, backed by a profound respect for their achievements in politics and in the arts; I was determined therefore to visit before I pushed north the site of Seleucia Pieria, the port of Antioch and the burial-place of Seleucus Nicator. Inland capital and seaport sprang into being at the same moment, and were both part of one great conception that turned the lower reaches of the Orontes into a rich and populous market – in those days kings could create world-famous cities with a wave of the sceptre, and the Seleucids were not backward in following the example Alexander had set them. Like Apamea, Seleucia has shrunk to the size of a hamlet, or perhaps it would be truer to say that it has split up into several hamlets covered by the name of Sweidiyyeh. (The nomenclature is confusing, as each group of farms or huts has a separate title.) The spacing of the population at the mouth of the Orontes is due to the occupation in which the inhabitants of the villages are engaged. They are raisers of silk-worms, an industry that requires during about a month in the Spring such continuous attention that every man must live in the centre of his mulberry-groves, and is consequently separated by the extent of them from his neighbours. After three hours' ride through a delicious country of myrtle thickets and mulberry gardens we reached Sweidiyyeh, a military post and the most important of the scattered villages. Here for the first and only time on my journey I was stopped by an officer, the worse for 'arak, who demanded my passport. Now passport I had none; I had lost it in the Jebel Zāwiyyeh when I lost my coat, and it is a proof of how little bound by red tape the Turkish official can show himself to be that I travelled half the length of the Ottoman Empire without a paper to my name. On this occasion the zaptieh who was with me demonstrated with some heat that he would not have been permitted to accompany me if I had not been a respectable and accredited person, and after a short wrangle we were allowed to pursue our way. The reason of this meticulous exactitude was soon made clear: the villages on the coast contain large colonies of Armenians; they are surrounded by military stations, to prevent the inhabitants from escaping either inland to other parts of the empire or by sea to Cyprus, and the comings and goings of strangers are carefully watched. One of the objects that the traveller should ever set before himself is to avoid being drawn into the meshes of the Armenian question. It was the tacit conviction of the learned during the Middle Ages that no such thing as an insoluble question existed. There might be matters that presented serious difficulties, but if you could lay them before the right man – some Arab in Spain, for instance, omniscient by reason of studies into the details of which it was better not to inquire – he would give you a conclusive answer. The real trouble was only to find your man. We, however, have fallen from that faith. We have proved by experience that there are, alas! many problems insoluble to the human intelligence, and of that number the Turkish empire owns a considerable proportion.

The Armenian question is one of them, and the Macedonian question is another. In those directions madness lies.

It was with the determination not to waver in a decision that had contributed, largely, I make no doubt, to happy and prosperous journeyings, that I rode down to Chaulīk, the port of ancient Seleucia. I found my resolve the less difficult to observe because the Armenians talked little but Armenian and Turkish, at any rate the few words of Arabic that some of them possessed were not sufficient to enable them to enter into a detailed account of their wrongs. He who served me that afternoon as a guide was a man of so cheerful a disposition that he would certainly have selected by preference a different topic. His name was Ibrahīm, he was bright-eyed and intelligent, and his cheerfulness was deserving of praise, since his yearly income amounted to no more than 400 piastres, under £2 of English money. From this he proposed to save enough to bribe the Turkish officials at the port that they might wink at his escape in an open boat to Cyprus: 'for,' said he, 'there is no industry here but the silkworms, and they give me work for two months in the year, and for the other ten I have nothing to do and no way of earning money.' He also informed me that the Nosairis who inhabited the adjoining villages were unpleasant neighbours.

'There is feud between you?' said I.

'Ey wāllah!' said he with emphatic assent, and related in illustration the long story of a recent conflict which, as far as it was comprehensible, seemed to have been due entirely to the aggressions of the Armenians.

'But you began the stealing,' said I when he had concluded.

'Yes,' said he. 'The Nosairis are dogs.' And he added with a smile: 'I was imprisoned in Aleppo for two years afterwards.'

'By God! you deserved it,' said I.

'Yes,' said he, as cheerfully as ever.

And this, I rejoice to say, was all that Ibrahīm contributed to the store of evidence on the Armenian question.

The Bay of Seleucia is not unlike the Bay of Naples and scarcely less beautiful. A precipitous ridge of the hills, honey-combed with rock-hewn tombs and chambers, forms a background to the mulberry-gardens, and, sweeping round, encloses the bay to the north. Below it lie the walls and water-gates of the port, silted up with earth and separated from the sea by a sandy beach. The Orontes flows through sand and silt farther to the south, and the view is closed by a steep range of hills culminating at the southern point in the lovely peak of Mount Cassius, which takes the place of Vesuvius in the landscape. I pitched my camp near the northern barrier in a little cove divided from the rest of the bay by a low spur which ran out into a ruin-covered headland that commanded the whole sweep of the coast, and I pleased myself with the fancy that it was on this point that the temple and tomb of Seleucus Nicator had stood, though I do not know whether its exact situation has ever been determined. Below it on the beach lay an isolated rock in which a columned hall had been excavated. This hall was fragrant of the sea and fresh with the salt winds that blew through it: a very temple of nymphs and tritons. Ibrahīm took me up and down the face of the precipitous cliffs by little paths and by an old chariot-road that led to the city on the summit of the plateau. He said that to walk round the enclosing wall of the upper city took six hours, but it was too hot to put his statement to the test. We climbed into an immense number of the artificial caves, in many of which there were no loculi. They may have been intended for dwellings or storehouses rather than for tombs. At this time of the year they were all occupied by the silkworm breeders, who were now at their busiest moment, the larvae having just issued from the egg. The entrance of each cave was blocked by a screen of green boughs to keep out the sun, and the afternoon light filtered pleasantly through the budding leaves. At the southern end of the cliff there was a large necropolis, consisting of small caves set round with loculi, and of rock-hewn sarcophagi decorated, when they were decorated at all, with the garland motive that adorns the sarcophagi at Antioch. The most important group of tombs was at the northern end of the cliff. The entrance to it was by a pillared portico that led into a double cave. The larger chamber contained some thirty to forty loculi and a couple of canopied tombs, the canopies cut out of the living rock; the smaller held about half the number of loculi, the roof of it was supported by pillars and pilasters, and I noticed above the tombs a roughly cut design consisting of a scroll of ivy-shaped and of indented leaves.

The builders of Seleucia seem to have been much preoccupied with the distribution of the water-supply. Ibrahīm showed me along the face of the cliff a channel some two feet wide and five feet high, which was cut three or four feet behind the surface of the rock, and carried water from one end of the city to the other. We traced its course by occasional airholes or breaches in the outer wall of rock. The most difficult problem must have been the management of the torrent that flowed down a gorge to the north of the town. A great gallery had been hewn through the spur to the south of my camp to conduct the water to the sea and prevent it from swamping the houses at the foot of the cliff. The local name for this gallery is the Garīz. It began at the mouth of a narrow ravine and was tunnelled through a mass of rock for several hundred yards, after which it continued as a deep cutting open to the air till it reached the end of the spur. At the entrance of the tunnel there was an inscription in clear-cut letters, 'Divus Vespasianus,' it began, but the rest was buried in the rocky ground. There were several others along the further course of the Garīz, all of them in Latin: I imagine that the work was not Seleucid, but Roman.

To one more spectacle Ibrahīm tempted me. He declared that if I would follow him through the mulberry-gardens below the cliff he would show me 'a person made of stone'. My curiosity was somewhat jaded by the heat and the long walk; but I toiled back wearily over stones and other obstacles to find a god, bearded and robed, sitting under the mulberry trees. He was not a very magnificent god; his attitude was stiff, his robe roughly fashioned, and the top of his head was gone, but the low sun gilded his marble shoulder and the mulberry boughs whispered his ancient titles. We sat down beside him, and Ibrahīm remarked:

'There is another buried in this field, a woman, but she is deep deep under the earth.'

'Have you seen her?' said I.

'Yes,' said he. 'The owner of the field buried her, for he thought she might bring him ill luck. Perhaps if you gave him money he might dig her up.'

I did not rise to the suggestion; she was probably better left to the imagination.

Close to the statue I saw a long moulded cornice which was apparently *in situ*, though the wall it crowned was buried in a corn-field: so thickly does the earth cover the ruins of Seleucia. Some day there will be much to disclose here, but excavation will be exceedingly costly owing to the deep silt and to the demands of the proprietors of mulberry grove and cornfield. The site of the town is enormous, and will require years of digging if it is to be properly explored.

Near my tents a sluggish stream flowed through clumps of yellow iris and formed a pool in the sand. It provided water for our animals and tor the flocks of goats that Armenian shepherd boys herded morning and evening along the margin of the sea. The spot was so attractive and the weather so delightful that I spent an idle day there, the first really idle day since I had left Jerusalem, and as I could not hope to examine Seleucia exhaustively, I resolved to see no more of it than was visible from my tent door. This excellent decision gave me twenty-four hours, to which I look back with the keenest satisfaction, though there is nothing to be recorded of them except that I was not to escape so lightly from Armenian difficulties as I had hoped. I received in the morning a long visit from a woman who had walked down from Kabūseh, a village at the top of the gorge above the Garīz. She spoke English, a tongue she had acquired at the missionary schools of 'Aintāb, her home in the Kurdish mountains. Her name was Kymet. She had left 'Aintāb upon her marriage, a step she had never ceased to regret, for though her husband was a good man and an honest, he was so poor that she did not see how she was to bring up her two children. Besides, said she, the people round Kabūseh, Nosairis and Armenians alike, were all robbers, and she begged me to help her to escape to Cyprus. She told me a curious piece of family history, which showed how painful the position of the sect must be in the heart of a Mohammadan country, if it cannot be cited as an instance of official oppression. Her father had turned Muslim when she was a child, chiefly because he wished to take a second wife. Kymet's mother had left him and supported her children as best she might, rather than submit to the indignity that he had thrust upon her, and the bitter quarrel had darkened, said Kymet, all her own youth. She sent her husband down next morning with a hen and a copy of verses written by herself in English. I paid for the hen, but the verses were beyond price. They ran thus:

Welcome, welcome, my dearest dear, we are happy by
your coming!
For your coming welcome! Your arrival welcome!
Let us sing joyfully, joyfully,
Joyfully, my boys, joyfully!
The sun shines now with moon clearly, sweet light so
bright, my dear boys,
For your reaching welcome! By her smiling welcome!
The trees send us, my dear boys, with happiness the birds
rejoice;
Its nice smelling welcome! In their singing welcome!

> *I remain,*
> *Yours truly,*
> *GEORGE ABRAHAM.*

I hasten to add, lest the poem should be considered compromising, that its author was not George Abraham, who as I found in the negotiations over the hen had no word of English; Kymet had merely used her husband's name as forming a more impressive signature than her own. Moreover the boys she alludes to were a rhetorical figure. I can offer no suggestion as to what it was that the trees sent us; the text appears to be corrupt at this point. Perhaps 'us' should be taken as the accusative.

It was with real regret that I left Seleucia. Before dawn, when I went down to the sea to bathe, delicate bands of cloud were lying along the face of the hills, and as I swam out into the warm still water the first ray of the sun struck the snowy peak of Mount Cassius that closed so enchantingly the curve of the bay. We journeyed back to Antioch as we had come, and pitched tents outside the city by the high road. Two days later we set off at 6.30 for a long ride into Alexandretta. The road was abominable for the first few miles, broken by deep gulfs of mud, with here and there a scrap of pavement that afforded little better going than the mud itself. After three hours we reached the village of Kāramurt, and three quarters of an hour further we left the road and struck straight up the hills by a ruined khān that showed traces of fine Arab work. The path led up and down steep banks of earth between thickets of flowering shrubs, gorse and Judas trees, and an undergrowth of cistus. We saw to the left the picturesque castle of Baghrās, the ancient Pagrae, crowning a pointed hill: I do not believe that the complex of mountains north of Antioch has ever been explored systematically, and it may yet yield fragments of Seleucid or Roman fortifications that guarded the approach to the city. Presently we hit upon the old paved road that follows a steeper course than the present carriage road; it led us at one o'clock (we had stopped for three quarters of an hour to lunch under the shady bank of a stream) to the summit of the Pass of Bailān, where we joined the main road from Aleppo to Alexandretta. There was no trace of fortification, as far as I observed, at the Syrian Gates where Alexander turned and marched back to the Plain of Issus to meet Darius, but the pass is very narrow and must have been easy to defend against northern invaders. It is the only pass practicable for an army through the rugged Mount Amanus. The village of Bailān lay an hour further in a beautiful situation on the northern side of the mountains looking over the Bay of Alexandretta to the bold Cilician coast and the white chain of Taurus. From Bailān it is about four hours' ride to Alexandretta.

As we jogged down towards the shining sea by green and flowery slopes that were the last of Syria, Mikhāil and I fell into conversation. We reviewed, as fellow travellers will, the incidents of the way, and remembered the adventures that had befallen us by flood and field, and at the end I said:

'Oh Mikhāil, this is a pleasant world, though some have spoken ill of it, and for the most part the children of Adam are good not evil.'

'It is as God wills,' said Mikhāil.

'Without doubt,' said I. 'But consider, now, those whom we have met upon our journey, and think how all were glad to help us, and how well they used us. At the outset there was Najīb Fāris, who started us upon our way, and Namrūd and Gablān–'

'Māsha'llah!' interrupted Mikhāil. 'Gablān was an excellent man. Never have I seen an Arab so little grasping, for he would scarcely eat of the food that I prepared for him.'

'And Sheikh Muhammad en Nassār,' I pursued, 'and his nephew Fāiz, and the Kāimakām of Kal'at el Husn, who lodged us for two nights and fed us all, and the Kāimakām of Drekish, who made a great reception for us, and the zaptieh Mahmūd –' (Mikhāil gave a grunt here, for he had been at daggers drawn with Mahmūd.) 'And Sheikh Yūnis,' I went on hastily, 'and Mūsa the Kurd, who was the best of all.'

'He was an honest man,' observed Mikhāil, 'and served your Excellency well.'

'And even Reshīd Agha,' I continued, 'who was a rogue, treated us with hospitality.'

'Listen, oh lady,' said Mikhāil, 'and I will make it clear to you. Men are short of vision, and they see but that for which they look. Some look for evil and they find evil; some look for good and it is good that they find, and moreover some are fortunate and these find always what they want. Praise be to God! to that number you belong. And, please God! you shall journey in peace and return in safety to your own land, and there you shall meet his Excellency your father, and your mother and all your brothers and sisters in health and in happiness, and all your relations and friends,' added Mikhāil comprehensively, 'and again many times shall you travel in Syria with peace and safety and prosperity, please God!'

'Please God!' said I.

BIOGRAPHICAL NOTE

Gertrude Margaret Lowthian Bell was born in Durham on 14 July 1868. Following the death of her mother, she lived with her beloved father and brother, and later stepmother and step-siblings.

A woman far ahead of her time, Bell read modern history at Lady Margaret Hall, Oxford, in an era when very few subjects were open to women. She gained a first class honours degree and went on to take an active interest in politics before embarking on her one-woman travels across the Middle East.

A keen traveller and explorer, Bell's travels took her to Persia, Syria, Iraq and beyond. She documented her travels in books, letters and diaries, as well as doing archaeological and cartographical work alongside. Recruited to work for British Intelligence during the First World War, Bell later became an advisor to the King of Iraq. Meanwhile she campaigned tirelessly for women's right to an education, set up the Museum of Iraq and received a CBE for her diplomatic work.

Despite the many achievements of her career, her personal life was marred by losing the great love of her life, Major Charles Doughty-Wylie, who fell at the battle of Gallipoli in 1915. It said that Bell never truly recovered from the loss. She died in 1926 of an apparent overdose of sleeping pills.

HESPERUS PRESS

Under our three imprints, Hesperus Press publishes over 300 books by many of the greatest figures in worldwide literary history, as well as contemporary and debut authors well worth discovering.

Hesperus Classics handpicks the best of worldwide and translated literature, introducing forgotten and neglected books to new generations.

Hesperus Nova showcases quality contemporary fiction and non-fiction designed to entertain and inspire.

Hesperus Minor rediscovers well-loved children's books from the past – these are books which will bring back fond memories for adults, which they will want to share with their children and loved ones.

To find out more visit **www.hesperuspress.com**

@HesperusPress

SELECTED TITLES FROM HESPERUS PRESS

Author	Title	Foreword writer
Jane Austen	*Love and Friendship*	Fay Weldon
Charles Baudelaire	*On Wine and Hashish*	Margaret Drabble
Giovanni Boccaccio	*Life of Dante*	A.N. Wilson
Charlotte Brontë	*The Spell*	
Mikhail Bulgakov	*The Heart of a Dog*	A.S. Byatt
Giacomo Casanova	*The Duel*	Tim Parks
Anton Chekhov	*Three Years*	William Fiennes
Wilkie Collins	*The Frozen Deep*	
Joseph Conrad	*Heart of Darkness*	A.N. Wilson
Gabriele D'Annunzio	*The Book of the Virgins*	Tim Parks
Dante Alighieri	*New Life*	Louis de Bernières
Daniel Defoe	*The King of Pirates*	Peter Ackroyd
Charles Dickens	*The Haunted House*	Peter Ackroyd
Charles Dickens	*A House to Let*	
Alexandre Dumas	*One Thousand and One Ghosts*	
George Eliot	*Amos Barton*	Matthew Sweet
Henry Fielding	*Jonathan Wild the Great*	Peter Ackroyd
F. Scott Fitzgerald	*The Popular Girl*	Helen Dunmore
Ugo Foscolo	*Last Letters of Jacopo Ortis*	Valerio Massimo Manfredi
Théophile Gautier	*The Jinx*	Gilbert Adair
André Gide	*Theseus*	
Johann Wolfgang von Goethe	*The Man of Fifty*	A.S. Byatt
Nikolai Gogol	*The Squabble*	Patrick McCabe
E.T.A. Hoffmann	*Mademoiselle de Scudéri*	Gilbert Adair
Victor Hugo	*The Last Day of a Condemned Man*	Libby Purves

Joris-Karl Huysmans	*With the Flow*	Simon Callow
Henry James	*In the Cage*	Libby Purves
Franz Kafka	*Metamorphosis*	Martin Jarvis
Franz Kafka	*The Trial*	Zadie Smith
John Keats	*Fugitive Poems*	Andrew Motion
Heinrich von Kleist	*The Marquise of O–*	Andrew Miller
Nikolai Leskov	*Lady Macbeth of Mtsensk*	Gilbert Adair
Carlo Levi	*Words are Stones*	Anita Desai
Xavier de Maistre	*A Journey Around my Room*	Alain de Botton
André Malraux	*The Way of the Kings*	Rachel Seiffert
Sir Thomas More	*The History of King Richard III*	Sister Wendy Beckett
Luigi Pirandello	*Loveless Love*	
Edgar Allan Poe	*Eureka*	Sir Patrick Moore
Alexander Pope	*The Rape of the Lock* and *A Key to the Lock*	Peter Ackroyd
Antoine-François Prévost	*Manon Lescaut*	Germaine Greer
Marcel Proust	*Pleasures and Days*	A.N. Wilson
Alexander Pushkin	*Ruslan and Lyudmila*	Colm Tóibín
François Rabelais	*Pantagruel*	Paul Bailey
François Rabelais	*Gargantua*	Paul Bailey
Christina Rossetti	*Commonplace*	Andrew Motion
George Sand	*The Devil's Pool*	Victoria Glendinning
Jean-Paul Sartre	*The Wall*	Justin Cartwright
Friedrich von Schiller	*The Ghost-seer*	Martin Jarvis
Mary Shelley	*Transformation*	
Percy Bysshe Shelley	*Zastrozzi*	Germaine Greer
Stendhal	*Memoirs of an Egotist*	Doris Lessing
Robert Louis Stevenson	*Dr Jekyll and Mr Hyde*	Helen Dunmore
Theodor Storm	*The Lake of the Bees*	Alan Sillitoe
Leo Tolstoy	*Hadji Murat*	Colm Tóibín
Ivan Turgenev	*Faust*	Simon Callow